LETTERS FROM ROBBEN ISLAND

LETTERS
FROM
ROBBEN
ISLAND

A Selection of
Ahmed Kathrada's
Prison Correspondence,
1964–1989

Foreword by **Nelson Mandela**
Introduction by **Walter Sisulu**
Edited by **Robert D. Vassen**

Mayibuye Books in association with
the Robben Island Museum
Cape Town, South Africa

Michigan State University Press
East Lansing, USA

∞ The paper used in this publication meets the minimum requirements of ANSI/NISO Z39.48–1992 (R 1997) (Permanence of Paper).

Published simultaneously in South Africa by Mayibuye Books, Robben Island Museum and in the United States of America by Michigan State University Press.

Michigan State University Press
East Lansing, Michigan 48823–5202

The Mayibuye Centre for History and Culture in South Africa is based at the University of the Western Cape. Focusing on all aspects of apartheid, resistance, social life and culture in South Africa, it aims to help recover the rich heritage of all South Africans and to encourage cultural creativity and expression.

This publication was underwritten with support from the Office of the Provost, Michigan State University, The Office of the Vice Provost for Libraries, Computing, and Technology, Michigan State University; and College of Arts and Letters, Michigan State University.

04 03 02 01 00 99   1 2 3 4 5 6 7 8 9

Library of Congress Cataloging-in-Publication Data

Author: Kathrada, A. M. (Ahmed)
Title: Letters from Robben Island : A Selection of Ahmed Kathrada's prison
                 correspondence, 1964-1989 / Robert Vassen, editor.
Published: Cape Town, South Africa : Mayibuye Books ; East Lansing : Michigan State
                 University Press, c1999.
Description: p. cm.
LC Call No.:   DT1949.K38A4 1999
Dewey No.:   323/.092 B 21
ISBN: 1868084507 (Mayibuye Books : alk. paper)
                 0870135279 (Michigan State University Press : alk. paper)
Notes: Dedication and acknowledgments / Ahmed Kathrada—Foreword / Nelson
                 Mandela—Introduction / Walter Sisulu—Editor's introduction / Robert
                 Vassen—About Ahmed Kathrada—Sylvia Neame, February or March 1964 —
                 Sylvia Neame, February or March 1964—Sylvia Neame, May 1964—Sylvia
                 Neame, 9 June 1964—Sylvia Neame, 11 June 1964—Ahmed Kola, 30 August
                 1964—Kathrada family, 18 October 196 —Kathrada family, 24 December
                 1967—Essop Pahad, 3 April 1968—Goolam Hoosenbhai, 29 December
                 1968—Sylvia Neame, between 11-31 December 1970—Solly Kathrada,
                 March 26 1972—Zivia Shaban, 12 May 1973—Mrs. Neville Alexander, 16
                 February 1975—Sonia Bunting, 16 February 1975—Choti and Ismail, 28
                 March, 1975—Ruth and Ilse Fischer, 11 May 1975
Subjects: Kathrada, A. M. (Ahmed)—Correspondence. Political prisoners—South
                 Africa—Correspondence. South Africa—Politics and government—1948-1994.
Other authors: Vassen, Robert D., 1938-

Cover design by Ariana Grabec-Dingman
Book design by Michael J. Brooks

Printed and bound in the United States of America

Visit Michigan State University Press on the World-Wide Web at:
     www.msu.edu/unit/msupress

CONTENTS

The Letters

1964–1970

1971–1980

FOREWORD

Nelson Mandela

It is a delight to know that Kathy's letters from prison can at last be read by everyone. They will give people a new kind of insight into what it was like as a member of the liberation movement to live in an apartheid jail for year upon year.

I can think of no better person to do this than someone I have known as a comrade in arms for over fifty years. We spent over two decades in jail together, almost all the time on Robben Island. Much has been written about this experience in memoirs and other books that look back. Kathy's letters, despite the efforts of the prison censors, remind one of the texture of prison life on Robben Island as it felt at the time and how it developed month by month and year by year over a period of twenty-six years.

As I have often found to my cost he is a person of strong opinion and sharp insight. But he also has great humour and humanity. These qualities shine through the letters as they illuminate the ways in which we rose to the challenge facing every prisoner, especially political prisoners, how to survive prison intact, and to emerge from prison undiminished.

These letters provide an important record of a critical aspect of the struggle for freedom and justice in South Africa. I hope that many readers will seize the opportunity to benefit from their publication.

ACKNOWLEDGMENTS

It is not possible to mention the literally hundreds of family members, friends, comrades, and well-wishers in South Africa and abroad who contributed in one way or another towards my comfort and well-being before, and especially during, my prison years. This book, a selection of my prison letters, is dedicated to each and every one of them, many of whose names appear in the letters. The omission from the list of those mentioned does not in any way mean that I value my relationship with them less. The names singled out are by and large persons who were directly connected with my prison years.

I make special mention of my late mother, my sister, my brothers, and all their children and grandchildren for their loyalty, love, and care through all the years of my life, and especially during my twenty-six years in prison. In this regard, the name of my niece-in-law, Zohra, deserves to be singled out. For the greater part of my sentence she took upon herself the task on behalf of the family to look after my every need; she never failed to write to me regularly, and remained a pillar of strength. This did not escape the notice of the Security Police, who prohibited her from visiting me for fourteen years.

To Aminabhai Pahad, whom I regarded as my "second mother," and who in turn took me into her family as her sixth son. Her love and care from my late teen years right up to my arrest adequately compensated for the absence of my biological mother in distant Schweizer Reneke.

To Khatun Patel, to my late "Fordsburg Aunts," Aunty Rangee Vassen and Aunty Vengetty Pillay, and to Aunty Kissie Reddy, who is now back in South Africa, for their remarkable friendship, courage, and hospitality especially during the dark days, when some erstwhile "friends" sought to avoid any contact with me. This book would probably not have seen the light of day had it not been for the indefatigable work and enthusiasm of Ms. Verna Hunt. From the moment she was told of the letters she whole-heartedly threw herself into the arduous task of sorting, classifying, and typing them. For her it became a labour of love, so much so that after many months of hard work she could claim the unique distinction of knowing the contents of my letters better than anybody else, including myself. Through them she has even come to "know" scores of individuals and happenings I wrote about.

To my dear friend and "brother," Lalloo Chiba, who was closely associated with almost every part of our prison life—the legal and the illegal, including his role in literally stealing back these very letters that had been confiscated from me. His exemplary courage, hard work, and loyalty always remain a source of encouragement and inspiration to me.

To my dearest comrades, friends, and leaders whom I have known for over fifty years, our father Walter Sisulu and elder brother Nelson Mandela, who never wavered in the face of seemingly insurmountable odds. In the highs and lows of prison life they stood by me. Their courage, their foresight and political acumen, their warm and unshaking loyalty, care, friendship, and their principled positions on matters of policy as well as the mundane could always be relied upon to smooth the frequently bumpy road inside and outside prison.

To the late comrades Oliver Tambo, Chris Hani, Yusuf Dadoo, Joe Slovo, Ruth First, J. B. Marks, Moses Kotane, and others who have passed on; to comrade Thabo Mbeki, Alfred Nzo, and all the ANC leaders and members in exile, who under the brilliant and inspiring leadership of Comrade O. R. not only kept the ANC alive, but steered its growth and influence to all corners of the world.

To the leaders and members of affiliate organisations of the United Democratic Front and COSATU who courageously and at great risk and sacrifice successfully mobilised the masses in South Africa behind the African National Congress. It would be remiss of me if I did not pay tribute to the brilliant team of lawyers who defended us in the Rivonia Trial. No accused could have wished for a better team.

To the late Bram Fischer, who led the defence team, and to his wife Molly, both of whom we admired and loved as members of our family. It was Bram who smuggled out my letters to Sylvia while we were awaiting trial, and it was Molly who ensured that two-way communication between Sylvia and me continued throughout the trial.

To the rest of our brilliant defence team: the late Vernon Berrange, George Bizos, Arthur Chaskalson, and Joel Joffe. To Ismail Mohammed who was especially briefed to assist me in the preparation of my evidence.

Last but not least, to my dear friend, "Brother" Bob Vassen, Fred Bohm and his Michigan State University Press staff, and numerous academic and administrative staff members of Michigan State University; and to Barry Feinberg and staff members of Mayibuye Centre, for their hard work in bringing the project to fruition. Without their unceasing prodding and encouragement these letters may never have been published.

I want to remember twelve-year-old Michelle Brits, whose dying wish was to visit Robben Island and to see the President. Both those wishes were fulfilled a few months before she succumbed to leukemia. I had the privilege of meeting her on Robben Island, and from that moment on she moved me more deeply than anything else. Thank you, Michelle; in your dying days you enriched the lives of all of us connected with Robben Island. And thank you "Reach for a Dream" for making the little angel's visit possible.

A. M. Kathrada
21 August 1999

INTRODUCTION

Walter Sisulu

I first met Ahmed Kathrada, or Kathy as we have come to know him, when he was a dynamic youth leader in the mid-1940s. This was the beginning of a wonderful personal relationship between Kathy and me, and one that has endured to the present day—so much so, that over the years Kathy has come to be regarded by my folks as a member of the Sisulu family.

That meeting also was the beginning of a political association that has spanned a period of more than half a century. It is not possible for me to mention the many highlights of this association in so brief an introduction. Suffice to say, though, that Nelson, Kathy, and I participated in the important political campaigns of the day, as well as the major political trials of the 1950s and 1960s. Among these were the Trial of the Twenty, which followed the Defiance Campaign of 1952, the Treason Trial, which lasted for more than four years from 1957 to 1961, and, of course, the 1963–1964 Rivonia Trial.

It was during the Rivonia Trial that this book of his letters from prison had its humble beginnings. It was while he was on trial that several of Kathy's letters were smuggled out of prison by Bram Fischer, who was defending us; in turn, the letters were delivered to Sylvia Neame, a friend of Kathy's, by Bram's wife, Molly Fischer.

This was only the first instance where Kathy was able to smuggle correspondence out from prison. During our imprisonment on Robben Island and Pollsmoor he managed to smuggle out a number of letters—often with political prisoners who were being released after completing their sentences.

Writing letters from prison was a privilege which we cherished very dearly. During the early years of our imprisonment, we were only entitled to write and receive one letter every six months. But this was not the only restriction. We were not allowed to make any references to other prisoners, or to our prison conditions, nor to make comments which the prison authorities construed as "political." Failure to adhere to these restrictions invariably resulted either in the letters being heavily censored, or not being posted at all. It was therefore inevitable that through pseudonyms, oblique references, innuendoes etc., prisoners became adept at conveying more than what was actually stated in words. We were also not allowed to keep copies of letters we wrote.

Kathy had the enviable habit of making a copy of each and every letter he wrote and he managed to keep them. Copies of letters written between 1964 and 1971 were confiscated by our jailers. After his release, he managed to obtain many of these from the persons to whom they had been written. He continued to make copies after 1971; but these, too, were confiscated. On this occasion, his letters and the study material also taken from him, were stored under lock and key in one of the vacant cells in the same section where we were imprisoned.

One weekend, when the permanent guards were not on duty, Kathy and Laloo Chiba asked the replacement guards to open the cell so that it could be cleaned. This was done. As soon as they were left alone, Kathy and Chiba stole the letters and hid them elsewhere. Kathy managed to keep the correspondence until his release.

These letters make interesting reading. Despite the restriction imposed by prison authorities regarding the nature and contents of the letters, what clearly comes through is his engaging personality, his uncompromising views, and his sharp wit and humour.

Many things could be said about Kathy, but these need to be reserved for his own memoirs. Suffice it to say several things though. First, Kathy was a tower of strength and a source of inspiration to many prisoners, both young and old, and across the political spectrum. Second, it was at his initial suggestion and recommendation, not to mention his subsequent involvement and guidance, that Nelson Mandela's autobiography, *Long Walk to Freedom*, actually became a reality. Third, he pursued his academic studies with vigour on Robben Island and he acquired several degrees by the time he was released from prison. Finally, it is important to mention that Kathy was the recipient of the ANC's highest award for meritorious service to the liberation movement. The *Isithwalandwe* Award was, in fact, bestowed upon him while he was in prison, although it was not given to him physically until after his release.

For me, and I am sure for discerning readers everywhere who can "read in between the lines," this selection of correspondence presents a picture of Kathy as we all came to know and love him.

EDITOR'S NOTE

On 12 June 1964 Nelson Mandela, Walter Sisulu, Dennis Goldberg, Govan Mbeki, Ahmed Kathrada, Raymond Mhlaba, Elias Motsoaledi, and Andrew Mlangeni were found guilty of sabotage and sentenced to life in prison. The following day, all but Goldberg, who was transported to an all-white penitentiary, arrived on Robben Island to begin their sentences. In the beginning, each was permitted to write and to receive a single 500-word letter every six months; correspondence was permitted only with members of immediate families. As an option, prisoners could receive two letters, but then they were required to surrender their "right" to the single visitor they were permitted to see during that same period of time.

Censorship was thorough, arbitrary, and uncompromising during the early years. In addition to restrictions on correspondence with people outside their immediate families, the prisoners' letters could not mention or discuss prison conditions, politicians, political activity, prison colleagues, or former prisoners. At first, prison censors lined out "offending" passages. But when this practice proved embarrassing to authorities, censors took to underlining in red any offending sections. Letters would then be returned to prisoners who were instructed to re-write their correspondence leaving out the indicated portions. Prisoners were not allowed to keep the letters they received, nor were they were permitted to make copies of their correspondence with the outside world. Birthday cards were counted as letters, but there were few of them during the early years. There were also many occasions when censors simply chose not to send prisoners' letters; at other times, guards failed to pass along their incoming correspondence. In one instance, Kathrada's oldest brother wrote a letter in October 1964. In it, he mentioned that Harold Wilson, leader of the British Labour Party, had won in the general elections. Kathrada was given this letter eighteen years after it was sent. On rare occasions, prison authorities appeared lax and letters containing "sensitive information" slipped by them.

As the years dragged on, rules were changed. At one point, prisoners could, they were told, write one 500-word letter *or* a letter of one-and-a-half pages. Kathrada wrote as small as he could and this went unchallenged. Eventually, the Rivonia Trialists, as they were called, were permitted to write and receive forty letters and twelve cards per year. The authorities later allowed each of them to receive photographs, but only three per year. Images of "mixed" groups, that is, groups with whites and blacks in them, were prohibited. On one occasion, someone sent a photograph taken on a city street. All of the individuals in it, save one, were black. A censor spotted a white woman walking past in the background; the photograph was withheld. The apartheid regime's preoccupation with race and color can best be summed up by an incident that occurred on Robben Island in 1972. During a "raid" that year, numerous articles were removed from Kathrada's cell, among them a photograph of Sylvia Neame. Lieutenant Fourie, who was in charge of the raid declared that "Kathrada is an Indian and I can see no reason why he wants a photo of a European [white] woman. . . . He is not allowed to be in possession of a photo of a European woman in his cell. . . . He showed no mercy for Europeans while he was busy with his underground movement in Rivonia, thus he cannot expect mercy from me. . . ." He destroyed the photo in front of Kathrada. When more than three photographs were sent, only three were given to the intended recipients and the censors decided which three.

The Rivonia Trialists were classified as security, or political, prisoners. As such, they were not allowed to have "contact visits," that is, visits during which they might actually come into contact with their visitors; common criminals in South African prisons were permitted such visits. Throughout more than a quarter century of incarceration, the number and types of visits were meticulously recorded by prison authorities. In the beginning, a six-foot "no-man's land," with fences on either side, separated prisoners and visitors. The fences were imbedded in solid concrete bases that were waist high. Prisoner and visitor were forced to shout at each other above the din and hope that they might be heard.

Later, the fences were replaced by cubicles but the no-man's land remained. Telephones were tried for a time; later, loudspeakers were installed. Finally, in 1986, three years before their release, the Rivonia Trialists were permitted to have contact visits. Sometimes prison authorities stipulated that only "first-degree relatives" could see them, but here too, there were inconsistencies and, on occasion, others were allowed in.

Despite the fact they were prohibited from keeping the letters sent to them or retaining copies of the letters they sent, Kathrada managed to do both. Today, this original correspondence is housed at the Mayibuye Centre at the University of the Western Cape in South Africa; a duplicate set is maintained at Michigan State University in the United States. Kathrada bequeathed these collections to the Centre and the University for use by scholars and researchers. During Kathrada's incarceration, between 1964 and 1989, he wrote more than 900 letters; a small sampling is included here.

When the reader comes across the mention of a letter going "astray," or Kathrada stating that letters to him should be sent by way of his niece or through his lawyer, these are indications that the censors were making life difficult. To get out, or to receive, infomation not permitted by the censors, Kathrada and his correspondees adopted various, ingenious codes for naming people, organizations, places, and events; these are indicated where known. Every attempt has been made to identify these codes, especially in Kathrada's letters to Sylvia Neame. Unfortunately, time's passing has contributed to these once-memorized, ever-changing ciphers being forgotten. But even without the specific details, without precise knowledge of who a particular indivudual might be, Kathrada's letters and his words bear eloquent testimony to the Rivonia Trialists and to their struggle for all South Africans to be free.

The Rivonia Trialists were gradually released from prison over a period of five years. Dennis Goldberg was set free in 1985, Govan Mbeki in 1988; Walter Sisulu, Ahmed Kathrada, Raymond Mhlaba, Elias Motsoaledi, and Andrew Mlangeni were released in 1989; Nelson Mandela was freed in February 1990.

I take full responsibility for the choice of letters made in this present volume and for the commentary preceding each of them. If my interpretation is inaccurate or inappropriate, I assure the reader it was unintentional and I offer my apologies. As pointed out above, this volume contains only a small sampling of the much larger collection of Kathrada's letters. Michigan State University Press and the Mayibuye

Centre hope to publish a complete set of these important documents in the near future.

I wish to acknowledge several individuals for their contributions to this present volume: Verna Hunt and Laloo Chiba (in his own special way) who made this all possible in the first instance; André Odendaal, Barry Feinberg, and the staff at Mayibuye Centre, University of the Western Cape; Provost Lou Anna Kimsey Simon, Vice Provost for Libraries, Computing, and Technology Paul Hunt, Dean of the College of Arts and Letters, Wendy Wilkins, Associate Dean Patrick McConeghy, as well as John Eadie, Peter Berg, Lori Hudson, Annette Tanner, Michael Rip, and Elizabeth Eldrege, all at Michigan State University; and Karen Bouwer and Tumi Thiba, who assisted me with the translation of Afrikaans poetry; Myra Ford for all the typing; Sharon Gelman from "Artists for a New South Africa"; Susan Bohm for her keen editorial eye; and Ursula, my wife, whose love, support, and encouragement sustained me throughout this project.

ABOUT AHMED KATHRADA

Ahmed Mohamed Kathrada, or "Kathy" as he popularly became known, was born on 21 August 1929 in Schweizer Reneke, South Africa. He grew up in an environment in which his deeply religious father instilled in him the principles of justice and the equality of all people. As a boy, Kathy was puzzled by the curfew placed on African people. What was equally puzzling to him was the fact that, as an Indian child, he was not allowed to attend a school for white children, nor could he attend a school for black children. Consequently, his parents sent him to Johannesburg to be educated.

During the time when Kathy was growing up, politics had split South Africa's Indian community into two factions. The first, the reactionaries, were opposed to active resistance to government repression and racial discrimination; they were equally opposed to participation in the United Front, an umbrella organization that included groups made up of individuals determined to defend their rights. The reactionaries controlled the Transvaal Indian Congress. The second faction, the progressives under the leadership of Dr. Yusuf Dadoo, favored a campaign of resistance to injustice and oppression; the progressives also favored cooperation with organizations that represented other oppressed people.

Violence erupted between the two factions at a mass meeting hosted by the progressive forces in June 1939. Several passive resistance volunteers were seriously injured and one, Dayabhai Govindjee, was fatally wounded. This incident marked the beginning of Kathy's life as a political activist. As a ten-year-old schoolboy, he distributed leaflets and chalked freedom slogans on walls. Two years later, in 1941, he joined the

Young Communist League and later the Communist Party of South Africa. During World War II he also became involved in the anti-war campaign of the Non-European United Front.

In 1946 Kathrada left school to work full time in the offices of the Passive Resistance Council. At the time, the Transvaal Indian Congress and the Natal Indian Congress were making preparations for the Passive Resistance Campaign to protest the "Ghetto Act," legislation that defined the areas where people of Indian origin could live, trade, and own land. Kathy was among the 2,000 who defied the law; he was sentenced to a month's imprisonment in December 1946. It was at this time that he came into contact with Nelson Mandela, Walter Sisulu, and others involved in the campaign against white supremacy in South Africa. In the whites-only election of 1948, the Nationalist Party, the architects of apartheid, came to power. In light of their virulent racist agenda, and following South Africa's anti-Indian riots of 1949, Kathrada became convinced that the only way to elevate the struggle for freedom to a higher plane was the formation of a united front of oppressed people.

In 1951, Kathrada was nominated to represent the Transvaal Indian Youth Congress at the World Youth Festival in Berlin. After the festival, he traveled to Warsaw, Poland, where he attended a congress of the International Union of Students. It was during this trip that he visited the concentration camp at Auschwitz. The Auschwitz visit impressed upon him, once again, the immoral nature of racism and racialism. He became more convinced than ever of the urgent need to eradicate the poison from South Africa. Finally, he traveled from Poland to Budapest, Hungary, where he worked for the World Federation of Democratic Youth for nine months.

In 1952 he returned to South Africa to participate in what became known as the Defiance Campaign, which targeted six unjust apartheid laws. The Defiance Campaign was jointly sponsored by the African National Congress and the South African Indian Congress. More than 8,000 volunteers defied the new apartheid legislation. Many were arrested, tried, convicted, and sentenced to various terms of imprisonment as a result. Kathrada was among a group of twenty officials from the African National Congress and the South African Indian Congress who were charged with violating the Suppression of Communism Act and organizing the Defiance Campaign. They were found guilty and given nine-month suspended sentences. Amongst Kathrada's co-accused were Nelson Mandela, Walter Sisulu, Yusuf Dadoo, and Moses Kotane.

The Defiance Campaign laid the foundation for the Congress Alliance, which was made up of the African National Congress, the South African Indian Congress, the South African Coloured People's Organisation, and the South African Congress of Democrats. In 1954 the Congress alliance embarked on a series of campaigns culminating in the drafting of the Freedom Charter in 1955. In turn, the Freedom Charter became a policy document for all member organizations of the Alliance. Kathrada was involved in this campaign and served on the Alliance's General Purposes Committee.

In October 1954 the South African government served Kathrada with a "banning order," declaring that he must resign from 39 specified organizations and prohibiting him from attending public gatherings for two years. Paying no heed to the order, Kathrada went about his work; he was arrested and charged on several occasions.

In December 1956, security police conducted a nationwide sweep in which 144 leaders, including Nelson Mandela, were arrested. Subsequently, Kathrada played an important role on the "Stand by our Leaders" committee; within a week, he, too, was arrested for addressing a solidarity meeting. Additional arrests, including those of Walter Sisulu and ten others brought the total number of detainees to 156; all were charged with high treason. By the end of 1957 many were acquitted, and ultimately 30 of the original group, including Kathrada, were left to stand trial. Known as the "Treason Trial," the case lasted for more than four years; eventually all were found not guilty.

Following the Sharpeville Massacre in 1960, the South African government declared a State of Emergency during which "the 30," including Kathrada, were detained. Immediately after their release, Nelson Mandela went "underground"; Kathrada served on a committee that attended to his needs. But, in 1961, Kathrada also was arrested, this time for serving on a strike committee that opposed Prime Minister Henrik Verwoerd's plans to declare South Africa a republic.

On 16 December 1961, *Umkonto we Sizwe* (*MK*), the military wing of the African National Congress was launched. Here, too, Kathrada played an active role. When Nelson Mandela was arrested in August 1962, Kathrada served as secretary for the "Free Mandela Campaign." Four months later he was served with several additional banning orders and was placed under house arrest. All attempts to persuade Kathy to leave the country and go into exile failed. He did, however, agree to go underground. During this period of hiding, he attended secret meetings at

Rivonia—the underground headquarters for the African National Congress. It was there that he was arrested along with Walter Sisulu, Govan Mbeki, and Raymond Mhlaba in July 1963.

The Rivonia Trial, as it has become known, followed this arrest and began in October 1963; it ended on 11 June 1964. Ahmed Kathrada, along with Nelson Mandela, Walter Sisulu, Govan Mbeki, Dennis Goldberg, Raymond Mhlaba, Elias Motsoaledi, and Andrew Mlangeni, was found guilty of committing specified acts of sabotage and sentenced to life in prison.

After serving 26 years, mainly on Robben Island and at Pollsmoor Prison, Kathrada was released on October 15, 1989. After the unbanning of the African National Congress in February 1990, Kathrada became Acting Head of the ANC's Department of Information and Publicity; subsequently he became Head of Public Relations. He was elected to the National Executive Committee of the African National Congress in 1991 and again in 1994; he declined re-nomination in 1997.

In 1994, Ahmed Kathrada was elected as a Member of Parliament in South Africa's first general election in which *all* South Africans were eligible to participate. He also served as Parliamentary Counsellor in the Office of the President. Kathrada was nominated for a second parliamentary term, but took leave of parliamentary politics in June 1999.

Kathy remains active in politics. At the time of this publication, he serves as Chairperson of the Robben Island Museum Council and of the Ex-Political Prisoner's Committee. He pursues these jobs with the same vigor and passion with which he embraced his political responsibilities over a period of six decades.

1964—1970

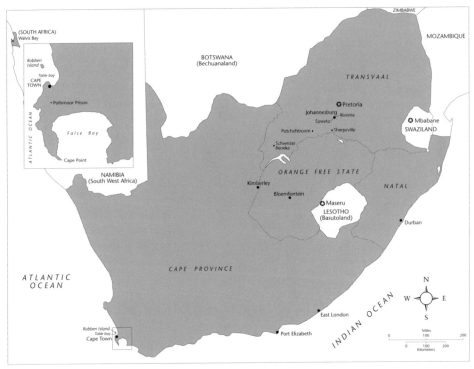

Republic of South Africa

~ ~ ~

Sylvia Neame—*February or March 1964*

On the night of 10 July 1963, Ahmed Kathrada, age 34, disguised as "Pedro Pereira," a Portugese national, left his "safe house" in Mountain View to attend a meeting in Rivonia. The following day, he and several African National Congress leaders were arrested by South African police. Initially he and the others were detained under the so-called "90-Day Detention Act" and held in solitary confinement in Pretoria Prison. In October, their trial, the famous Rivonia Trial, began. It was during the latter stages of this proceeding that Kathrada wrote to his girlfriend, Sylvia Neame. Like Kathrada and the others, she was a committed South African political activist. As these letters were smuggled out of prison by Kathrada's lawyer, the advocate Bram Fischer, he did not have to worry about censorship. Nevertheless, he took every precaution to protect people mentioned, referring to them by code names or using initials. The first part of this letter is about overcoming racial barriers. Kathrada is a South African of Indian origin; Sylvia Neame is a South African of white origin. Their relationship, illegal according to South African law, would have raised a few eyebrows considering the exaggerated prominence given to color and race in South Africa at that time. We learn in this letter of mean-spirited government authorities who, after Kathrada's brother and sister had traveled 250 miles, would not allow them to see him. Kathrada writes about the trial, its outcome, and his confidence about the inevitability of change, about the innocence of a young prison guard (warder) who could not understand why Kathrada became "involved" in politics. How, Kathrada asks, can one explain to this type of person that "a life of humiliation and without dignity is not worth living?" Kathrada knows he will be sentenced and he is prepared for it.

1

~

I do hope by now the little storm in your mind about the discovery by my folks has completely blown away and will not recur. Your view that the exaggerated report could be due to some sort of jealousy on the part of old man's wife[1] has got some merit. I agree it is very sweet of her to take such a kind interest. Of course it will be good for you to remember that the origin of this business must have been as a result of small-town gossip or even mischief on the part of some ill-disposed person. But whatever it was, it certainly wasn't serious and deserved to be ignored. If ever there is a similar business in the future, please just don't allow yourself to be disturbed by it. And in the unlikely event of it being raised with you by anybody from home, the same applies. I can well understand how this must have shaken you. It's a great pity that I never related to you some of the things that were said about me over the years to the family. By now both they and I are immune to its effects. As for the old lady, well you know how old people are. As I said, I'm sure she must have made some adverse comment in passing and forgotten about it again. I hope old man's wife is not unduly disturbed by the allegation that she was responsible for our affair. Please apologise to her for me. Incidentally, since your message, I saw two lots of people from home and they did not mention a word. If there was anything in it at all, my sister-in-law (the one you know) would have raised it with me. She brought messages from my mother but nothing about this. I did not raise it with her but did tell her to get my sister to collect the photo from old man's wife. I hope this was done. I would suggest that you leave one there if you haven't done so yet. I wish they had allowed my sister to see me last Thursday. The poor folks came all the way, 250 miles, to see me and the authorities only allowed 2 of them in. So, because my sister and brother had seen me previously, my brother-in-law and a sister-in-law saw me. The others just waited outside and went all the way back. My sister must have felt terrible—I too was quite upset by the meanness of the authorities. Anyway, I hope to see her one of these days. Now that the case is drawing to a close, the folks from home will come more often—as you know, there are so many of them and they all want to come up. I can confidently assure you that you need have no fear of this "backing" falling away. If anything, I have the feeling it will come closer and stronger. Would you mind if I told my folks a bit more about your attitude, viz. that you have adjusted yourself to waiting, etc.

---

[1] Ayesha and Amien Cajee, longtime friends.

Please give some thought to it and let me know. It will be a great help if they are told this is not merely a casual affair—then, in spite of difficulties and all that, you will be regarded as a member of the family. This being a serious proposition, I don't expect you to rush into it. Please think about it very carefully from all angles and only when you are absolutely convinced of the wisdom, you can let me know.

Before leaving the question of the photo, I wish you'd give a good one of yours to uncle.[2] The one they had the last time was simply horrible. The one who is making a weekly contribution, is he the uncle or grandpa? How much does he know about us, and, if so, what is the attitude like? I am very glad that you are on good terms with uncle and his family. As long as they don't have an adverse influence on your outlook and our relationship.

By now your arrangements to go away on the 21st must be well advanced. I hope everything goes smoothly and they don't mess you around unnecessarily. I'm sure a break will do you the world of good. You will of course let me know as soon as things are finalised. I take it, after visiting your brother's place, you will be going on to Camilla's mother's.[3] I like the company you will be travelling with. Will they be with you throughout? You will of course be going by car? I wish you have a most wonderful trip. Please look after yourself very carefully. You will make some arrangements to keep in touch with me. This is most important.

From my point of view, this is not the best time for you to be away. But I fully realise that from other and perhaps equally important points of view it cannot be otherwise. I therefore want you to go ahead with arrangements with my fullest approval. You see the position is we just don't know how long the defence case will last, and I certainly want you to be around when it reaches its very final stages. Fortunately, you must have heard we will only be starting on the 20th now. So I think if you are away for 3 weeks (the most), the case will most probably be still on when you return. You will almost certainly be far away when I give evidence, but that doesn't really matter. I will let you have a copy of my statement afterwards. Otherwise I can't think of anything that will necessitate your sticking around.

This brings me again to a suggestion I made last time about keeping in touch with me through the personal column and which you, for some

---

[2] Sylvia's uncle, a Mr. Neame, was the editor of the *Rand Daily Mail*.

[3] Caroline de Crepigny, a friend of Sylvia's.

reason, failed to comment on. It is efficient, easy and cheap, and now, especially while you will be away, you could and should use it effectively and frequently. All you have to do is to keep in touch with your local best friend and ask her to have a few words inserted once or twice a week. Signing yourself Y . . . n.[4] You must let me know what you think. Of course, in addition to this, it will be good to have one or two longer messages of the usual type if this can be arranged. There might be a possibility of using this other method in the future too but will let you know about it later.

I have only recently discovered how my messages reach you and must say I am filled with deep gratitude. I wish I could do something to express it. If you have some time in the coming few days, I will be very grateful if you would get a nice gift for the young gentleman[5] from both of us. I know it is not fair to throw all these assignments onto your shoulders, but I'm afraid this is one necessary burden you'll have to bear. Once again I must insist that you use my money. Otherwise don't go ahead with the suggestion. By the way, how are you off with cash to finance your trip? Please let me, even at the cost of being a terrible bore, suggest once again that you collect my money if you need it. Same applies, I think I've already told you, to gifts for Savi's baby and other presents you make every now and then on our behalf. Oh yes, I believe our friend Charles's brother[6] will soon have to be given something. I don't have to tell you how terribly decent he has been to both of us. Perhaps a good book or something will be nice. Or you could bring back something from home. Nothing elaborate.

I should have said at the outset that your last message was most encouraging and boosted up my morale a great deal. It is always so nice to receive such a message, especially when it's so frank and uninhibited. I thought at first it might have been immediately after a discussion with Mr. Lucas and hence the extra warmth and affection, but then found it was in a similar strain throughout. I am sorry that you find it difficult about m? or rather lack of it but am so happy and relieved that you have oriented yourself to it remaining this way. I shall always hope that there will be no distractions or deviations along this long and difficult path. Do you at all times feel as strong on the question as you mention?

---

[4] Yasmin: a code name for Sylvia.

[5] The late Paul Fischer, son of the late Bram Fischer, senior counsel in the Rivonia trial.

[6] Dr. Essop Jassat, a friend and a leading activist throughout the struggle. He went on to become a member of Parliament.

A great change must have come over you if you have lost your shyness with kids, and I see the enthusiasm with which you seem to be pursuing this new-found hobby. Tell me more about the 2 kids staying with you. Re the advice of your friends, in this regard I will certainly have no objection–you know very well my feelings about it. When the occasion arises, you can depend on me for my most enthusiastic co-operation. Your assurances about A. are most welcome. But I remember of course on the last occasion, Dec. 1962, Sakina was unwilling but the task was nevertheless completed. Oh yes, I always meant to ask—you remember the occasion when Sakina visited my place with a friend late one night; it was only a few days after I met you. Do you think she will tell you whether there wasn't really a bit more in that affair than we know. I don't know why this keeps gnawing at my brain, but for some reason it does. I just hope Sakina does not mind my curiosity. I don't want to annoy or embarrass her in any way.

I am very happy that you generally feel relaxed and in good health. By what I gather from your message, you must have really been in a bad way after I went away, what with your being in a state of shock for 5 or 6 months. Yes, everything did happen rather suddenly and with all the mental preparation, the shock of our arrest must have been enough to upset it. You are very brave when you say you have adjusted yourself to waiting for me. If you continue with your present plans, of course, this wait might be easier. I am sure you must have arrived at this decision after careful thought and consideration. As I have pointed out already, to me this remains a source of great encouragement and inspiration. It is difficult to state how long this wait will be, but I feel confident as ever that things won't remain this way for long in this country. A change is inevitable and I feel it is almost imminent. Of course I'm by no means a dreamer who believes that freedom is around the corner, but I say a change is imminent. We won't have the Nats [Nationalist Party][7] for much longer. International pressure cannot be ignored by them. I think one of the most heartening things is the significant changes in United States policy, even more so than Britain. Then internally too they are not going to remain so homogenous as they appear. Of course there is no doubt that they have the emotional backing of the majority of whites. But this is not something they can bank on for all time. There are bound to be cracks in the granite.

---

[7] The Nationalist Party, in power in South Africa from 1948 to 1994.

I don't know what the outcome of our case is going to be eventually. I am prepared mentally for a heavy sentence. As long as they don't hang us, we are confident we won't have to remain in jail for a very long time. It is almost a year since I broke my house arrest. Strange what laws I actually and wittingly broke and what I get charged with. The fact remains that I expected to be arrested sooner or later, so what difference does it really make if I am serving under the Suppression of Communism Act, the Group Areas Act or the Sabotage Act. In the end we will be saboteurs or communists or both, and in the South African context it is nothing to be ashamed of. There are lots of things concerning the period of my underground days which I am tempted to write about but which it is inadvisable to broach at this stage. They are things best left for history. That is one of the reasons why I ask you again to give serious thought to the diary, collection of material, etc. The problem about keeping them safely can be overcome by sending everything out to England to be kept there. I am getting more and more keen that one day these must be written up and feel that, with my assistance, you will be the best person to write it. The great advantage is that we already see eye to eye on a number of important questions, and it will be from this point of view that I want to see something tackled. (I don't know if you will still remember one night in the car when you observed that you had never seen me so unhappy. I didn't attempt to answer you save for some flippant remark which only made you angry. I wish I knew what went on in your mind at the time, whether you had an inkling of why I was in that state.) My one big regret is that having held certain attitudes in the past, I did not do enough to make them felt. This must all sound Greek to you. I best discontinue. In the years to come there will be different versions of the history of the past 20 to 30 years—and I just must see at least one version influenced by the way I have lived through these years and the way I look at them. My underground days confirmed and considerably solidified my attitudes. On reflection, I am glad that I resisted suggestions to go overseas when political work became so difficult.

I was a bit hesitant to ask you more about your treatment, but now having had some details, I feel very happy that I did. He seems to be saying a lot of nice things–and reassuring too. Your description sounds almost as if the views were given in answer to my enquiries for a good reference. It is good to hear him thinking that our relationship is healthy and that you don't want anyone to come between us. I hope all these visits will do you a lot of good and remove completely any semblance of ill-effects as result of your childhood experiences. I am not surprised at his shock on discovering more about me—does he know exactly now who I am, my doings, etc.? I just hope and pray he doesn't disapprove to the extent of trying to influence you away. Please continue with the treatment until you feel completely better. The thought has crossed my mind that this course might end up by your looking upon me as a father, which wouldn't be too nice would it? Be careful there.

Did you see in the press the results of a survey among white schools by Henry Lever (p. 3, mid-page) on race attitudes wherein he said that the Indians were the most hated of 9 population groups in South Africa? He did it for his M.A. I knew the chap and would have loved to have seen more of it and discuss the thing. He does not investigate the reasons for the attitudes, but I think they are quite obvious and should not dishearten any of our people. I was just saying to someone here that not only am I most surprised but I feel complimented. In almost every field of endeavour in South Africa, the Indian has proved himself as an undisputed equal. Isn't this enough to evoke such attitudes among whites who are so steeped in inferiority complex.

I was interested to notice your anger about the doings of some people, but unfortunately [you] don't say enough to give me an idea as to who and why and what. Perhaps you feel it unnecessary or indiscreet. But I can venture a guess, and if I'm correct, I don't blame you at all. I only wish that if and when you allow your patience to give way to anger, the results will be all to the good. The best thing of course would be to ignore these things altogether if it were at all possible.

Thanks for clearing the misunderstanding re your attitude if you are mentioned. Let's just hope it never arises. As I have said, the other side won't hesitate to use any opportunity to sling mud so it's best to be prepared for it.

I am most distressed to hear about the trouble Camilla's mother has been having, particularly the loss of the manuscripts. Although I haven't had the good fortune of meeting her, I feel as if this has happened to one of my good friends. Through our indirect contact I suppose I can regard her as such. When next you see her or write, you will convey my feelings and best wishes. Tell her not to be disheartened. I have just seen burnt blanket[8] and friends and am glad they are as cheerful as ever. Only for

---

[8] "Burnt blanket" is a code name for Jack Tarshish, a detainee under the 90-Day Detention Act. The friends are Ben Turok and Harold Strachan.

your information, I was most disturbed to hear ten days ago that he tried
to do an Oosie.[9] I saw him the day after and was relieved to see no out-
ward signs of it. So it couldn't have been serious. But please keep this to
yourself; it might have undesirable results if spread further as you will
imagine.

You can tell Oosie's pal that her clarification is well taken and I shall
divorce the idea from my mind completely. It is unfortunate that these little doings of Mr. W. have to linger on. In fact I am sad because I always
have been and still am very fond of Mr. W. Perhaps the complete change of
environment will be a great help. Please convey my best wishes to her and
tell her how very grateful I am to her for being so good to you. I am pleasantly surprised at the number of old and new friends you are meeting up
with and your observations about some of them are interesting and encouraging. I notice you go out of your way to stress that they are either women
or married couples. I hope this is not a subconscious manifestation of guilt.
This is not meant seriously—please go ahead. But prepare them so that
when I come out of here I will also have a whole host of new friends.

No you did not tell me that you had met the "whiter than white man."
In fact I am surprised, considering his circumstances. Anyway you
decided wisely not to encourage a "*toenadering*;"[10] just keep it that way
until I'm able to supply more news.

The Easter weekend was rather long and I can't say I didn't feel a bit
off colour now and then. Mostly it was the wish and desire to be with
you. I thought of the last time when you made an effort to cook supper
for us and produced, *inter alia*, potato crisps. How guilty you felt and
how the slightest observation on my part made you uncontrollably angry.
And the best part of it, the special sessions to pacify you. Fortunately I
did have books to compensate and we were allowed to have two consultations. These lessened the boredom considerably. I would very much
like to get the other Bonds, etc., thank you.

My throat hasn't been troubling me much again. Maybe it is just psychological as you say. But you remember it all started in Aug. 1962, and
I can't remember if I had any cause for anxiety then. The doctors at
Bara[gwanath Hospital] seem to have put an idea into my mind of a
growth, and this is a bit disturbing. Every now and then I get the feeling

---

[9] "To do an Oosie," in this context means to commit suicide. Kathrada is making reference to "Oosie" Oosthuizen, a friend who committed suicide.

[10] *Toenadering*: an Afrikaans word meaning "closeness."

there is something there. What I propose doing is to get the case history from Bara and making an application thereafter to see a specialist. I know after we are sentenced it will be most difficult, if not impossible.

I am disappointed that you have such a hatred for italics. I just don't know how else I can improve my writing. I shall see to it that mine will be free and not stiff and correct which is what you dislike.

I hope by now you have been around to my aunts and cousins and conveyed my greetings, etc. You should drum it into my cousin's little daughter's head that she is anticipating a supreme court judgement by referring to me in those terms. Maybe the courts might yet find against her. Good to see you are more discreet than ever. Every now and then, when I see a new cop, it makes me shudder. Some are good looking playboy types, well dressed and, what is worst, some of them even have a little bit of sense. I won't be surprised if a number are recruited from the university. I can just imagine how easily these types could mislead people outside, especially when we are so used to expecting all of them to look like Dirker[11] with their low intelligence and all. Pass this on in case you folks are not aware.

Well it's time to end again and get down to the papers. Hope you are having a nice weekend. Think of me when you are with "Mr. Lucas." Remember me to all friends. And please look after yourself carefully. You have a difficult wait ahead of you, but bear in mind we will be together again–and we will then really make up in a big way for this temporary hardship and separation. All my love to you and please don't delay in sending me your message.

You know there is a bit of a smallpox epidemic in P[ort] E[lizabeth]. originating from the jail there. A few weeks ago there was an item in the press that there is nothing to fear as far as our jail is concerned as there have been no transfers from P.E. to here recently. But I notice on Saturday they started vaccinating the whites here. Just hope they do us as well. I think the last time I had smallpox injections was when I went overseas in 1951, so I can be a good candidate for the disease. You notice how my health has assumed such importance since I am in jail. The slightest aches and pains and pimples do not go unnoticed. I suppose it is really for want of something better to do.

A few days ago one of the nicer warders got talking to me and said he wondered why I got "mixed up" in all this business, meaning politics generally. How does one explain to a chap like him that to live a life of

---

[11] Sergeant Dirker of the Special Branch, a particularly aggressive and hostile policeman.

humiliation and without dignity is not worth living. He seems to have gathered over the months from supervising the visits that I was not down-and-out and poor and was having a comfortable life outside. To him that is enough. He is so sincere in his interest. The tragedy is there must be thousands and thousands of whites who think like him. When will they ever emerge from the mental *backveld* in which they are living? In spite of its simplicity, it is an honest belief. Of course in the end it is going to be easier to come to terms with this type of a person who I still believe constitutes a large portion of the Afrikaans people. To me this increases the guilt of the white supremacists and Nationalist politicians tremendously. When the tide turns, it will unfortunately be the simple, honest types who will bear the brunt of the hardship that will follow.

It's Monday night—thank God the holidays are over. Am out of books—but spent a few pleasant hours with Shakespeare and a little bit of Afrikaans poetry. Am going to start a little Penguin called *The Great Invasion*, dealing I believe with archaeology. Am told it's simple and good. Bye bye and all my love.

≈ ≈ ≈

Sylvia Neame—*February or March 1964*

Kathrada is concerned for Sylvia's health. He expresses his great sadness at the betrayal by former comrades who testify against them. What he finds even more hurtful are the lies they tell. He writes about the prospect of prison and how Sylvia should start thinking of getting his clothing and keeping it safely for him when he gets out. He expresses concern that his mother should not see him behind bars, as this would be too much for her to bear. He feels relieved and grateful that she will be spared this. Later, he reflects how easy it would be for blacks and whites to live together in harmony if only contact were possible. He implores Sylvia to remain strong and firm of resolve as he is certain that "we will win."

≈

I was beginning to get terribly worried, not having heard from you or about you for the last three weeks. But thank God, this anxiety has now been relieved by the news this morning (Sat.) that you are keeping well. I am so pleased to hear that you are actually putting on weight. I hope you are no longer suffering from the periodic bouts of illness and anxiety which you mentioned in your last message. You did say you had seen a specialist but omitted to let me know what his opinion was. Please, you must let me know what he said.

I am also glad to hear you are working hard. It is interesting to hear that the Sakina[1] business is a contributory factor towards your feeling unwell. I don't think I laughed at your feelings at the time, as you allege. It is just that I wrongly placed greater emphasis on other factors. Do you really believe there will be another opportunity? And do you think Sakina will be able to wait? With the same keenness? I wouldn't wish for anything more if this were still possible. It's wonderful how you've been able to give up smoking altogether. Touch wood. Just hope you'll be able to keep it up. I never could understand why people smoke, and especially women. You can put that down to my oriental conservatism. Though I am not nearly as conservative in the matter of the occasional sundowner, as you well know. That reminds me. At one interrogation during the 90 days,[2] the cops wanted to know if I was fond of Bols brandy. A very strange question I thought. But now it is clear. This interrogation took place a day after they discovered the cottage in Mountainview; they found two bottles of the same brand there with fingerprints of Wolpe and Goldreich.[3] Who would have ever thought that the simple booze bottle was going to play

---

[1] Sakina, Yasmin, Yasmina, Y, Khala are Sylvia's code names.

[2] "90 Days" refers to the 90-Day Detention Act (the General Law Amendment Act of 1963) passed to give the police the authority to interrogate and to extract information. Under this law, the police had the power to arrest anyone they suspected of being engaged or involved in any act against the State and to hold them *incommunicado* for 90 days at a time. If no charges were to be laid, they had to release the individual after this 90-day period. In practice they would release the person and as soon as she or he stepped into the street, they would be re-arrested for a further 90 days. The government soon found this too cumbersome and introduced the 180 Day Detention Act. Later, this too would be scrapped and be replaced by a law that could hold people indefinitely. Once arrested the detainees literally disappeared. The authorities did not have to inform the next of kin of their whereabouts. While under detention many were brutally tortured and a number were killed. When death occurred as a result of torture, the authorities would invariably release a press report stating that the detainee had committed suicide or had slipped on a bar of soap and had subsequently died from the fall.

[3] Harold Wolpe and Arthur Goldreich, close friends and both active in the liberation movement, were arrested more or less at the same time as Kathrada and expected to be involved in the Rivonia Trial had they not made a dramatic escape from Johannesburg's Marshall Square, together with Moosa Moolla and Abdulhay Jassat. They were never caught. Wolpe went to London, Goldreich to Israel, Jassat first to Tanzania and then to London, and Moolla to various countries representing the African National Congress (ANC). Today, Moolla is the South African Ambassador to Iran, Jassat is in South Africa, and Harold Wolpe died in South Africa.

an important part in a sabotage trial. There has also been evidence, for instance, that in the Eastern Cape this liquid container was used to make petrol bombs. Only there, in accordance with Cape habits, it was wine bottles. Then there appears an item in a diary of Mandela's where a certain "K" failed to turn up to see him because he was reported to be boozing. The prosecutor said this "K" is Kathrada. How they come to such a conclusion remains to be seen. Another incident which provided some humour to the proceedings was when the notorious "Mr. X" was in the box. When under cross examination about his stay at Rivonia, he admitted having wet his bed as a result of having drinks the previous night. Incidentally, coming back to the Mountainview cottage, I hope you were not unduly disturbed by a newspaper report that when Williams[4] left the cottage, two men and a woman stayed on.

It seems the case is not going to last much longer. About a hundred witnesses have given evidence already. I doubt very much if they will still call the 200 they originally spoke about. Our policy has been not to waste time by lengthy cross-examination of all witnesses. Of course, where witnesses have deliberately fabricated evidence and told blatant lies, they have been dealt with, mostly very effectively. It is really sad to see former comrades whom one loved and respected coming one by one into the witness box to give evidence. And what hurts is when these people tell lies, some of them quite unashamedly. Can you imagine what it is like when a place like P[ort] E[lizabeth] sends 4 delegates to the Lobatsi conference[5] and 2 of the 4 come into the box as state witnesses. And they both tell the same lies and stick religiously to their stories. Then there is the old lady of the ANC, almost 70 years old, who is brought to tell just about 2 or 3 sentences of lies about Sisulu. The poor woman was uncomfortable and wept, but she told her lies. For she knew it would be 90 days again. Needless to say, like all similar witnesses she too was detained. Only, she was detained twice, and also had a type of house arrest imposed against her before giving evidence. The 90-day detention has succeeded in breaking many people. Of course the physical torture has played no small part, no matter what the authorities say about it.

---

[4] This could have been a code name for Dennis Goldberg.

[5] The town, Lobatse, in the former British protectorate of Bechuanaland (now Botswana), was the site of an important ANC conference in October 1962. It was at this meeting that the ANC established its formal link with *Umkonto we Sizwe*.

Thanks for your assurance about m. b . . . r. It is most encouraging to know. It must be awfully hard and really very cruel of me to insist on this. How does Sakina feel about it? Or are there "mild deviations" now and then? Every time one opens the papers nowadays there are reports of new restrictions. Life must be becoming impossible outside. I can just imagine the constant tension and anxiety. If it were not for the enforced separation from you, and similar matters I am almost tempted to say it is better to be in jail than outside.

I was upset to hear about the strange attitude of my "mother" but I think I can understand the cause. I'm sure it is influenced by other people. You can guess who I'm particularly referring to. I just hope you don't take it too badly. It was so good to hear about the kindness shown towards you by people generally, particularly your former student mates. I hope this will go some way towards making up for the loss of other friends—I should really say, for the enforced breaking of contact with other friends. This is a matter which is a constant source of worry for me. Since I'm writing this over the weekend, you are more in my thoughts than ever. A little while ago I could have been sure that you would be lunching and spending some pleasant hours at my aunts'. Now this I suppose is also impossible. Have you been able to adjust this and find suitable alternatives? Have you been able at least to see the old ladies recently and my cousins? You know I haven't heard about that part of my family for many months now. In fact since the old man[6] had to stop visiting me I haven't heard a thing about them. Please don't go out of your way, but if it is possible, I would very much like to know about the goings-on there. There was mention of some K. L. and his wife visiting you but I'm afraid I just could not make out who this referred to. The other, whose initials are G. A., etc., who is supposed to be leaving soon, I don't know at all. But that is not important. What I'm most concerned about is, I don't want to hear that you are spending long hours in loneliness and brooding. I'll be most happy to hear that you are still able to spend some time enjoyably in pleasant social circumstances. Of course with the usual proviso. Glad you felt nice after reading the Shakespeare passages I referred you to. I might have told you before, I know them off by heart and recite them daily. I was touched at the manner in which you are using my gift, with the engraving and all. I hope it has taken the place of the other, you know the expensive one you got on your birthday in

---

[6] Amien Cajee.

1962. You seem to be in some doubt as to my attitude when you say you are using it this way without my permission. I thought we had between us agreed on this over and over again. It was just the formality that was lacking. The lovely blue tie has been noticed by many people and caused favourable comment. I'm very proud of it and shall be wearing it again this week. On this question, should you see the old man's wife tell them to please stop sending the white sports shirts and vests. Excepting for the weekends, I don't get a chance to wear the sports shirts at all. In fact tell them I'm quite happy with the two check shirts and of course the brown one of yours. I'm sure it suits you beautifully too. What I will do is I'll send it back to you just before we are sentenced, for safe keeping. You can wear it every time you feel nostalgic. But on condition that it will be still there if and when I'm released. Is that a deal?

The attitude and advice of Savi's husband[7] to you to stick here is both surprising and interesting. What do you think is the reason? Is it they're fed up with conditions there or is it a bit of patriotic advice? By the way, how did he react to your ordeal? I promised him faithfully I'd look after you, so I hope he is not too fed up with me for causing you all the trouble. We will discuss again the question of your joining them, at the end of the trial. Should you be writing to them soon, please convey my fondest wishes to both, though I haven't had an opportunity of meeting Savi yet. But I'm sure she is well aware of things. By the way did the old chap deliver the gift you sent along for their baby?

I have been able to trace the five books you sent. In fact I'm through with two of them and shall be returning them soon. It would be you to go and buy such expensive books. I thought a few Penguins would have been adequate. I must say I found Camus very morbid and uninspiring and I've been advised by one of the lawyers not the read the Dostoevsky. But I'm going to have a go at it. The Sayers holiday book is really the type of light stuff one wants in jail. You know what you can do if you have the time, is to collect a few James Bonds, if they are available in Penguins. I'm sure we will have a long break at the end of the State case when these could be handy. If and when you have these, the best will be to hand them to Mr. Joffe, our attorney.[8] But please do not hurry about this. The State case will be another few weeks still.

---

[7] "Savi's husband" is Dr. Peter Neame, Sylvia's brother; they live in Canada.

[8] Joel Joffe was the instructing attorney who represented the accused. On the eve of his emigration to Australia with his family, he cancelled his trip to represent the accused. Mandela, writing on behalf of all the accused had this to say of Joel Joffe: "As the general

As far as my studies go, they will only allow us to make applications after sentence. I haven't seen the syllabus yet so have not given any thought to the subjects. The quiet prison atmosphere seems most conducive to studying I think. That is if we are kept here, which I doubt. It seems they'll bundle us off to Robben Island to join the rest of the politicals. The Captain and Lieut. from there are now in Pretoria—Col. Aucamp is now with head office. The Capt. is an understanding chap and hasn't made things difficult. In fact on the question of the books he has been quite easy. You know an Afrikaans poetry book was brought in for me by Amien in Oct. 1963. The authorities refused to give it to me because it contained notes on the poems and some translations. I made several attempts to get it but was unsuccessful. Last week I took a chance and raised the question with the Capt. and he allowed me to have it without any trouble. You didn't know I was fond of Afrikaans poetry did you? Well I am. In fact I recited one verse to Lieut. Swanepoel[9] and his friend during an interrogation, when they were trying to persuade me to answer questions. *"Ek hou van 'n man wat sy man kan staan"*[10] you know that one. This incident was mentioned in court last week, much to the amusement of the judge, etc.

Soon it will be the end of the fasting month and the Eid celebrations. You remember last year we had lunch together at my mother's, and Savi's hubby was with us. The year has sure gone very fast, hasn't it? I believe

---

behind the scenes of our defence, he has managed and marshalled this most complex case with understanding and skill." Later, Mandela goes on to say, "We have come to admire and respect this quiet and courageous man, whose devotion to the cause of justice has been shown to be in the very highest tradition of his calling." From the 1995 book, *The Rivonia Story,* by Joel Joffe.

[9] Lt. Swanepoel, a member of the Special Branch, known for his hatred of the ANC and communism.

[10] Translation: "I appreciate or respect a man who can hold his ground." This is the first line from a poem by the noted Afrikaaner poet, Jan F. E. Cilliers:

Ek hou van 'n man wat sy man kan staan (I like a man who stands as a man)
Ek hou van 'n arm wat 'n slag kan slaan (I like an arm that can strike a blow)
'n Oog wat nie wyk, wat 'n bars kan kyk (An eye that never shies away, that can pierce a crack)
En 'n wil wat so vas soos n' klipsteen staan. (And a will that stands steadfast as a rock.)

When Swanepoel, an Afrikaner himself, began interrogating Kathrada to extract information from him using coercion and force, Kathrada recited this verse in fluent Afrikaans, Swanepoel's mother tongue. This poem is in praise of a person who in the face of adversity can hold his own. An embarrassed Swanepoel backed off immediately and left Kathrada alone.

the folks from home will be coming up to see me on Eid. I'm looking forward to this. I have seen all my brothers and sister. Only I haven't seen my mom. But I have advised against her coming here. It will be too much for her. I remember the occasion when I was being transferred to Christiana jail and the friendly police escort took me to see her. She collapsed and had to be in bed for a week. Seeing me through the grille will be much worse. I'm surprised how well my sister took it when she came along with a sister-in-law a few weeks ago. There is one person I'm longing to see and speak to and that is you. Will this be ever possible I wonder. Yet, one never can tell, with things moving so fast. I'll just have to remain patient and hope for the best.

What do you mean you still owe me money? I hope this was a misprint. Actually I owe you and it must be quite a bit. I don't want to hear any argument on this because I know I'm right. I used to keep notes you will remember. So don't be shy to ask me—after all some of it is your own. By the looks of things you will not be able to last till June. Please let me know. I'm referring to your financial position.

You surprise me when you say you were at one time regarded as a beat. Anything further than that I could not imagine. Unless of course this is an aspect of your life of which I'm still in the dark. Or unless the "mac" was an indication of beat clothing, in which case I know it very well. Where is poor Oosie now to advise you to give it away to a jumble sale?

Thinking of Oosie, among the many dreams I have, are some of dead people. This is most worrying. You know for instance I dreamt one night of you and Oosie and all of us. Then there are two other dead people I saw and spoke to. Any significance?

You say in some ways you feel "aged." What do you mean? I hope it's been just a temporary feeling. Since my last message to you I have completely stopped ordering chocolates from the canteen. Of course it hasn't made any difference to my weight yet. If anything I feel I'm putting on. I suppose one of these days I'll just have to start exercising again, in desperation. It certainly does not seem to be the food which is responsible, although this is 90% starch. But I have very little of it. One advantage of going to court is the two European accused and I get the same lunch as the warders and police. It is quite nice. The poor Africans get the usual porridge.

You know it is such a pity that people of different race groups are not allowed to come into contact with each other in South Africa. Because it is so easy to get along together. Perhaps that is the reason why the Nats[11] won't allow it. This is not a sudden realisation for us. But every time we find ourselves in jail, in court, etc., this is brought home so forcefully. The attitude of jail warders, the police and other officials must and does change after a few weeks of contact. Just the other day we were quite surprised when a member of the prosecution team came up to us while we were waiting on the steps of the courtroom, to say goodbye to Nelson. He has resigned to take on another job. This is Mr. Naude, former Senior Prosecutor of Pretoria. There are always such incidents. If only the men of the Nat hierarchy can be made to see the utter futility of their theories and beliefs. Of course everybody must have been quite shocked by the news that the Mountain View cottage was given away by Bob Hepple. I must say I wasn't. From the first day when we were released from 90-day detention, I suspected him of telling the police more than he admitted. In fact I should say I started suspecting him even before this, when during interrogation I was told that some of my friends were talking. At the time I thought this was to induce me to talk, though there were little things they said here and there which made one suspect. What can one do? I suppose these things happen in any struggle. I feel very sorry for his poor wife. She is such a nice girl and must be taking this very badly. I managed to have another glimpse yesterday of our burnt-blanket friend and his 2 companions. They all looked well to me.

Must be ending now. Hope this finds you in good health. Also hope your morale is and remains as high as ever. I would love to hear from you as soon as possible, so please do not delay. Am particularly anxious to hear about your health and the specialist's opinion. The brief message on Sat. that you are well and putting on weight is not enough. I will be satisfied only if I hear from you in more detail. My health is fine and my morale as high as before. I'm confident this will remain, no matter what happens. The thought and constant knowledge of you standing loyally and sincerely by me is a source of great strength and encouragement. There must be moments for you when things look gloomy and hopeless. But I am sure you will not allow this feeling to dominate. In spite of everything, with my reservations are criticisms of certain things, my confidence is stronger than ever. I know we will win. If only this will be soon, so that we could be together again to partake of the fruits in peace and happiness. I have no doubt whatsoever that we will. Missing you more

---

[11] The Nationalist Party.

and more each day I shall be eagerly waiting to hear from you. All my love to you. My fondest wishes to all friends should you see any of them. Let me hear from you regularly and as frequently as possible. Also verbally, but this is not satisfactory at all, as you can imagine.

I've had several messages from the old ladies of K. H.[Kholvad House][12] who want to visit me. I'd love to see them but the difficulty is the jail authorities insist on English or Afrikaans, both of which they don't speak. So I really don't know what to do. I heard that Herb and Fati were visited by the S.B.[13] recently. Any idea what they wanted to know. Don't go out of your way to find out if you don't know. It isn't important. I think sometime ago I sent you a message to try and keep a diary of important happenings, both personal and otherwise. Hope you've started. It will be quite interesting and important one day. Isn't the weather terrible these days. Hope you haven't suffered from the hail damage. I get quite scared at times. Oh for a kingsize hangover and for a few cups of Aunty's russo on a Sunday morning. Wouldn't it be lovely. I'm sure there will be many opportunities yet. Lots of love. Look after yourself.

$\approx$ $\approx$ $\approx$

Sylvia Neame—*May 1964*

This is, in fact, a continuation and was sent to Sylvia at the same time as the previous letter.

$\approx$

Monday evening. We have had another good day in court. The tall, dignified figure and intellect of Mbeki still dominates the court. It is in many ways a tragedy that a man of this calibre has been forced into politics when he should be giving his all to fields where he would make an undoubted mark. Yet I suppose I shouldn't be complaining. It must be precisely the frustrations that the non-white intellectual comes up against which forced him into politics. And, his life and achievements so effectively mirror the lives of hundreds and thousands of thinking non-whites.

---

[12] Kathrada lived in Flat 13, Kholvad House, an apartment block in Johannesburg.

[13] The Special Branch, a section of the South African police force, that dedicated itself to fighting political opponents of the government and to crushing the liberation movement.

As I have often said before, I remain as optimistic as ever about our struggle. In fact, I feel more confident than I did a year ago. I am happy that I have been able to make some contribution. When I look back at the years gone by, perhaps my one regret would be that I was not able to do more. I wish I could transplant my feelings to your heart and to the hearts of all my dear colleagues and friends. There is no such thing as defeat in our struggle. And this is certainly not the time to even think of it. No matter what happens to us who are on trial at present, no matter how many of our former comrades have fallen by the wayside, and no matter how many will still leave us before we achieve our goal, the invincibility of the cause is becoming clearer by the day. It cannot possibly be otherwise. I want you to remember this, for I am certain it will help to lighten the burdens of waiting.

One thing more. If I feel so optimistic today, it is to no small measure due to the absolutely wonderful, unselfish, unfailing loyalty and attachment shown by you—by my political colleagues and by personal friends. Above all of course has been the great inspiration from the masses of oppressed people, in whose service we, without the slightest regret, are about to enter the next phase of our lives.

I want to come back to you. If only you know how much you have come to mean to me. How much I value your closeness and courage and loyalty. I really can't imagine what more you could have done for me even if you tried. I know you will not want to be thanked for all this. But you have been so marvellous—I can only wish time flies so fast so that we can be united once again and make up for the hardships of this enforced separation.

A word for the old lady and old man.[1] In my last message I did indicate how grateful I am to these two for doing all that they have done. Because of them—and with you forming the trio—I did not for one moment feel that my own family was so far away. My sister and brothers couldn't have done more for me. For my cousins and aunts and the whole family centered there,[2] I have the greatest affection. Together with

---

[1] Ayesha and Amien Cajee.

[2] Three sisters, Rangee Vassen, Vengetamah Pillay, and Kissie Reddy, were all from Fordsburg. Their homes were always open to Kathrada and he was regarded as one of the family. Rangee always made sure to cook his favorite dishes when he came to visit. Even when Kathrada was "underground," she managed to get his favorite foods to him. Her two sons, Tom and Bob, are the "cousin" and "little cousin" referred to in Sylvia's letters. Herby (H) is the son of Vengetamah Pillay. His sister, Harlene, is married to Abdulhay Jassat.

my Jo'burg mother,[3] these people have really provided a home for me. Away from the tension, the anxiety and humdrum of political life, in these homes I have always found relaxation, and warm friendship so necessary to keep one's balance and sanity. Never have I met anything but generosity and kindness.

Then of course there are the scores of other friends who have been so good over the years. I would like to thank each and every one of them, and will certainly think of them all in the months and years ahead of us. Though I do not single out any of them, you will know who all I am thinking of. And—my babies.[4] Someday they must know how important they became to my life, during the months of house-arrest.[5] How I came to look forward to their little knocks, how they lifted my spirit. And how, even now they nag their mothers to send things to me. There is much comfort in the thought that at least they will grow up in a different South Africa. Tonight I feel very close to you. I wish I can express my feelings somehow. You have entered my life when I needed you most. How beautifully things were working out—then I went "underground," and then the arrests. Never mind, there will be compensation yet. The bell has gone. I still have an hour, but I'm going to leave off to finish my book. Will continue tomorrow. Hope I haven't been too sentimental. Goodnight my darling.

Sylvia Neame—*9 June 1964*

A moving and poignant letter—the last before sentence is passed. It shows us Kathrada's vision, when he insists that newspaper clippings of this trial be

---

[3] Mrs. Amina Pahad, whose home was Kathrada's home too. She was his "Joburg Ma."

[4] The babies are the neighbors' children, who would often take food and other delicacies to him, especially when he was under house arrest. The food was brought by children because adults would have been regarded as "visitors." House arrest orders prohibited visitors.

[5] As the name suggests, the individual's home became a prison. A person under house arrest was required to remain at home from 6:00 p.m. to 7:00 a.m., Monday to Friday, and then confined over the entire weekend. They could not speak to a fellow banned person; they could not be part of a gathering at which more than two people were present; and they could not enter specified business or social premises. They had to remain within the area proscribed by the statutes of the banning order. In Kathrada's case, he was confined to the magisterial district of Johannesburg. This meant he could not even visit his mother as she was outside this area. He had to report to the police station daily. In practice, he could not receive visitors.

preserved as artifacts of an historically important moment in South Africa's history. "Since the very first day of our arrest, I had made up my mind that I'd be convicted although I had no doubt about my innocence. . . ." This is the first and only time he writes of his being innocent but, given the atmosphere of the times, he is also aware that an acquittal might not be the final verdict. He believes he is innocent for two reasons: (1) there was little evidence linking him with Umkonto we Sizwe, *although he was one of its earliest members (he withdrew from "MK" in 1962) and (2) he was on the* Regional Command *but never on the* High Command *as alleged in the indictment. He analyses the trial at this point and feels the case against them is weak. He is, however, in a quandary: if released, he might be re-arrested and tried on other charges. He would then be alone and cut off from his comrades—a thought he does not relish. Later he indulges in something that he is so good at: teasing. "His cousin," really no relation but a very close friend, found himself in a matrimonial tangle and facing a divorce. He had been discovered in a compromising situation with a female fellow-teacher in a classroom close to a table. Using the news article in the Sunday paper about a Willem Smit choosing to live under a table, Kathrada has a dig at his friend, Tom Vassen, the "impatient pedagogue" and the table. The friend did get divorced but then remarried his first wife after about three years. Today they are living happily in London with their children and their grandchildren. All his earlier letters end with the customary "goodnight"; this one ends with "goodbye sweetheart" and words of advice. At one point he writes about his possible release, at other times he discusses being sentenced. He writes about one visit every six months and one letter every six months. He seems to be in a turmoil but deep down he seems to be expecting to be imprisoned. The last part of this letter was written on the 10ᵗʰ June, 1964. Two days later, on 12 June, he was sentenced to life in prison.*

～

It is about 9 o'clock, Monday morning. I just couldn't get myself to start writing. Yesterday, though I had finished with the papers fairly early, I couldn't get myself to touch the history book either and spent many hours loafing about the cell—and thinking. The case seems to have taken quite an unprecedented turn for me as you most probably must have gathered from the newspapers. If the remarks and general attitude of the judge during the defence argument are an indication of his state of mind, then [Rusty] Bernstein and I should expect to be acquitted. And perhaps Mhlaba as well. Since the very first day of our arrest, I had made up my mind that I'd be convicted, although I had no doubts at all about my innocence. With the circumstances of the arrest, the blatantly false evidence of at least one witness against me and the general atmosphere, I could see no chance of establishing my innocence. So I prepared myself mentally and otherwise for the inevitable. The judge made a few remarks during Yutar's "argument" which finally confirmed my belief. I was furious as hell of course because Yutar so unashamedly misled the court, and the only ostensible reaction of the judge seemed to be one of agreement. It was not until the defence case started, when with authoritative and painstaking references to the law, to decided cases and to the record of evidence in our case itself, that a new picture began to emerge. Yutar of course was so cocksure of his case that he did neither of the above and preferred to spend his 3 or 4 days in mudslinging and a harangue, which most of the time had no relation to the evidence in the case. In the first few hours of our argument the judge conceded important defence submissions which knocked out the hysterical prophecies of Yutar in connection with the document "Operation Mayibuye" and guerrilla warfare. You will remember how Yutar ended his "argument" by thanking the police for saving the country from civil war and bloodshed. Now it turns out that the self-established "saviour" of white supremacy, the Jew, Dr. Percy Yutar, had miscalculated, and I won't be at all surprised if he has earned for himself the displeasure of the police and the Nats. There was in fact no agreed plan which would have plunged the country into strife and a bloodbath. All that then remains of the case is that the Umkonto-we-Sizwe carried out acts of sabotage since Dec. 1961, that it sent out men for military training, that it gave consideration to guerrilla warfare and carried out investigations in this regard. All of which is a far cry from what the country was led to expect from the rantings and ravings of the prosecution/prosecutor. And if the judge upholds certain legal submissions made by the defence, he will have to find that the State has failed to prove the 190 acts of sabotage alleged—but merely succeeded in proving 19. So, all in all, the whole perspective seems to have changed for all of us. Another important allegation which too has been knocked out is that this was a "sinister Communist conspiracy"; that the ANC, Umkonto and the entire national liberation movement were parties to this plot.

Forgive me, I've allowed myself to run away with my feelings. I find this happens to me whenever I think about the conduct of Dr. Yutar. It will not be long before I change my attitude, when I'll shed any feeling of hatred and bitterness and place the man in his correct category, which is that he is sick man, a paranoiac with a burning ambition. Then, I suppose

I will pity him, which is what he needs. Fortunately my nature will not allow me to harbour hatred for anybody, no matter how deeply he may have wounded my feelings. This is, I suppose, the Gandhian influence on my life.

To get back to what I originally set out to tell you. This turn in the case has put me in a quandary, and I don't know whether to be happy or sad. If there were not the definite prospect of an immediate re-arrest and further charges, of course I would have been the happiest man to be out and be with you. But knowing the police as I do, I am certain I will not even be allowed to leave the court building. Which means further cases and months of delay before sentences. And, worst of all, I will be alone. It is this which makes me unhappy. That is why I've always said that if I have to be in jail in any case, it doesn't really matter if I'm sentenced under the Sabotage Act or Communism Act or any other. Now I face the prospect of separation and have no idea whether I will eventually meet up with the others again. And, think of how this will prolong the anxiety and inconvenience for you and so many others, particularly if they keep me here and have the trial here. The thought of this makes me most unhappy. I have some feelings about the eventuality and will let you know when we are a bit more definite about things.

I will be so pleased if they give me a few weeks' break so that I can spend a few days with my mother and the folks at home and of course be with you again. But such nice things just don't happen to me so I shall not indulge in wishful thinking.

I am certain this business will also cause perhaps even more anxiety and tension for you. How I wish I can find some way to help relieve you of it. I feel so helpless and frustrated when I think of you. Why should you bear the cruel brunt of these uncertainties? I can only find some release in the sure knowledge that it will not be too long before things change, when we will be together again and double make up for everything. I hope—in fact, I am sure you will continue to bear the rigours of the time ahead with the same patience, love and devotion which you have so wonderfully shown.

I was so happy to see Ayesha[1] on Saturday. She told me you were in good health and working hard. This gives me no end of pleasure. Once having accepted the reality of what is facing us, time will pass fairly quickly. And uppermost in our minds will be the thought that the end of

---

[1] Ayesha Cajee.

this difficult road will see us together again, to partake of the fruit of what we have been striving for.

Ayesha told me that the printer is messing around with my commission. Apparently he says he knows nothing about it. How people can stoop. This type of thing just hurts. I have told her to tell Amien to contact the person whose catalogue I had printed and on which this commission is owed. If this approach does not help, I suppose we'll just have to leave the matter alone. I am sure this friend of mine will be disturbed as well. He had already obtained cheaper quotations from other printers and only gave this job to Golden Era because I was to get commission on it. He often asked me whether I had collected my money, but I told him I'd leave it until I need it. I had trust in the printers. I suppose one has to get used to this type of thing.

She also said Amien has been refused permission to see me. I wonder why they are messing around. First of all, Lieut. Van Wyk told me two weeks ago that they were not aware of any application by Amien. And now the refusal. He did indicate that permission would be granted. On his advice I sent in an application to the Minister. We will just wait and see.

In the meantime I will make out a detailed list and description of the articles and ask Mr. Joffe to give it to Amien, together with a power of attorney in his favour authorising him to collect these on my behalf. It will be a pity to lose it all. I believe the Kreel case should end sometime this month. After that I will have to claim some of my belongings taken by the police from the cottage which I occupied.

I don't know if the papers carried a bit of cross examination about Amien directed at me. Anyway it was suggested to me that he was a member of the Youth League. I was forced to divulge his age to the court, much to the surprise of my co-accused and of course the laughter. I put his age at a rather conservative figure of 50. Wonder what he would feel about it. Incidentally, I think in the next few weeks I might be able to let you have the official transcript of my evidence and cross examination. This will give you a good idea of how things went.

Reading the *Sunday Times* yesterday, I came across an article about one Oom Willem Smit, a recluse somewhere in the Cape, who prefers to live his life under a table. I thought this rather funny but by no means unique insofar as the manifold uses that man in his ingenuity has made of this humble piece of furniture. Of course I was thinking of my dear cousin, whose harnessing of the table was made known to the people when the news broke through the columns of the press via the Supreme

Court, some two or three items, but one dare not sink into complacency. For who knows how and when this seemingly innocuous four-legged friend of mankind will once again burst into our lives, to provide new and fascinating problems and solutions for the mathematician, the homeless human, the roofless recluse and the impatient pedagogue. We must always be prepared and fortify ourselves for this event. All this may sound nonsense to you. In which case I suggest you copy it out and refer it to my cousin for clarification. Perhaps you should refer it to him in any case with my compliments and tons of apologies.

While conveying this, you might also thank aunty for the lovely fish curry which as usual I thoroughly enjoyed.

Wasn't there something in my Stars in the Express last week about a bit of luck at the end of the week? You think it could possibly have had something to do with the developments in our case? It does fit somehow. And when final judgement is given, I might strengthen my belief in the signs of the Zodiac. By the way, judgement will definitely be given during the week beginning on the 9th June, and I suppose sentence will be almost immediately thereafter. Certainly in the same week I think. This brings me to the question of contact. This might very well be my last for the time being. There is a slight chance that there will be one more, but don't bank on it. We will just have to wait for developments thereafter. In the meantime I will expect old lady to keep me informed. Just hope they don't stick me back into 90 days.

I suppose there will be one more chance of a message from you, but I don't know. I have told you all I wanted to. Excepting that I love you more and more each day. Please my darling, look after yourself while you are waiting for me and love me always. This is my daily wish.

They did, after all, allow me to have "Claudia" and "Death in the Stocks." I sent back 11 and hope you got them. I will most probably be allowed to have the 4 which were brought on Saturday. That should see me through till the end of this case.

In case it might become important in the future, please remember that I do not get the *Daily Mail*. I've been borrowing it from my colleagues. The *Star* I get, as well as the Sunday papers. I think the *Star* is the best. Might add more later, or tomorrow.

It is still Monday. They have just brought our supper, which means it must be about 3 p.m. They've also given me a chicken, fruit, etc., which I'm told was brought for me sometime today. Obviously the persons who brought it must have tried to get a visit but were unsuccessful. I wonder who it was. Perhaps it was my cousin Kola from the farm. I'm sorry I could not see him. Holidays and Sundays are impossible in prison. They are generally short-staffed and just will not allow visitors. I hope somebody manages to come on Thursday or Saturday so that I can send some more of my clothing back. I want to have the minimum of stuff by the day judgement is given. Ayesha wasn't too sure whether my folks will be coming on that day. You never know, they might even be able to give me a lift back. That is, if the judge doesn't change his mind and if the police decide to be kind to me for a change. This is a very big if.

There are two things I want you to do if after judgement I'm re-arrested and put back into awaiting trial. Firstly, in addition to verbal messages via old lady, you must try and write in her letters. Secondly, try and borrow a copy of the book, *Sewe dae by die Silbersteins*[2] by Etienne Le Roux. This promises to be entertaining reading. I just hope it will pass our prison censor.

Quite a few times this morning the wish crossed my mind that somebody will be kind enough to bring some food. How wonderful that the wish has materialised. I did justice to the chicken and once again have that satisfying feeling of a full stomach. Wonder where and what you had for lunch.

The last few days have been quite cold, but it's not too bad once I'm under the blankets with warm underwear. Been doing a fantastic amount of dreaming since Friday night. With the judge's remarks fresh in our minds, I had a terribly restless night. When I did sleep, I just dreamt and dreamt. But, fortunately, the dreams were all nice. The following nights were okay. I slept very well, the dreams continued. Naturally the main content of my dreams was that I was free and going to parties and meeting all sorts of people. In one of them I attended a court case where you were one of the accused. And I proudly saw you putting up quite a fight. You've been figuring in most of them.

Let me stop dreaming and get back to some reading.

Tuesday morning. Had a sleepless night again and got up with a bit of a cold, which is a bore. Otherwise I'm feeling fine. Just wishing this business is over one way or the other. Imagine if they had charged me after arrest for my banning orders. I would have by now completed almost a year of my sentence. Which means a whole year nearer to you. But I suppose it's all in the game and we'll just have to take it as it comes.

---

[2] The Afrikaans novel, *Seven Days with the Silbersteins*.

Tuesday evening. Your message is lovely and I have the satisfying feeling that you have given attention to all my points. I will return to this just now.

The defence case ended late this afternoon and Yutar too finished his reply. For one uncomfortable moment, I got the feeling that he managed to catch our lawyer/s off-guard with legal points, some concerning Bernstein and me. But at the [end] the judge pointed out to him that it was unfair to raise new legal points at a time when the defence could not reply; whereupon he withdrew them again. To me the attitude of the judge seems to be consistent with the attitude he has taken since the defence argument began, and, on the face of it sounds favourable to the two of us. Just keep your fingers crossed, though as I've said earlier, I still don't know whether I am happy or sad about it all. The thought of facing the new charges on my own is not attractive at all. At present the position seems to be that he will give judgement on the 11th and pass sentences on the 12th, i.e. of this month.

If I gave you the impression that I haven't been feeling well lately, let me immediately set your mind at ease. There is no such thing. My health is still as always, apart from a slight cold which started today. What I really meant to convey was that during this last lap, there will be heightened anxiety, tension and restlessness. This is only natural and inevitable as you say and certainly nothing to worry about. This feeling doesn't remain the same all the time—in fact most of the time I feel perfect. I don't know how Ayesha got the impression that I was tense on Saturday. I think the main trouble is, without practice in the past year, I am finding it a bit difficult to express myself in Gujarati.[3] At the best of times I wasn't too fluent. Now it's much worse. I am even more surprised at her observation about my weight. My clothes indicate that I am almost back to my original weight, which is terrible. This, despite the fact that I've cut down on sweets. It must be all the lovely food you folk have been sending. Just to take old lady up on her promise about joining in a drinking celebration, I am prepared to be discharged. How would you like that. My wonderful plans about studying are once again up in the air at present. They'll have to remain this way until I am sentenced.

I don't know if your desire of late to be alone is good. There is always the chance that you'd spend your time brooding, particularly on a Saturday night. And I will be unhappy if this is so. I must repeat, I want

---

[3] A language from Central India.

you to enjoy yourself in every way, provided of course you bear in mind always that you are mine. This limitation I don't have to stress, for I am confident you are fully conscious of it. And I don't doubt your loyalty and devotion to me. The last thing I want to see when I come out one day is a picture of a haggard woman, face lined with worry and troubles. I want you to mix and make friends (with usual discretion), play tennis and work hard. I don't expect a complete severance with Mr. L particularly in view of the assurance you give. Your explanation about the night at my place makes my heart feel good, and I shall try and stop troubling my mind over it again.

I'm afraid your explanation about my recent young visitor and someone with the same initial on the Rand, does not make sense yet. But don't bother, I'll figure it out one of these days. I did indicate that he struck me as a nice chap. I'm sorry to hear about the two brothers and your views about their father. Unfortunately he does have a knack of doing things which easily give rise to all sorts of speculation. But he is essentially a good man with certain outstanding characteristics. I've always been and still am very attached to the whole family, particularly my "ma." I just hope there are no grounds for the disturbing rumours about him which I've heard. This would aggravate my ma's health a great deal. While on this, I think I like your suggestion to give her a photo, but please choose a nice one. And try and avoid the one like W Herbst.

Yes, I noticed my cousin from the farm, in court this morning. I take it he must have been here yesterday. Did anyone mention to him my request re books in the future. I'm sure this will be easy once I know what the position will be.

I am very worried about the newspapers. They are absolutely invaluable, and I will consider it a great tragedy if they are lost through negligence. I wonder if old man, etc., appreciate their value. Please deary, sit on him until you have the assurance they've been safely entrusted. By the way, what happened to the tall visitor? How is his wife? Do you ever see them nowadays? I used to enjoy seeing him.

Re: my application to see Amien, I spoke to Lieut. Van Wyk this morning, and he has assured me that he will give it his attention now that he won't be coming to Pretoria any more. There seems to be some hope still.

Your observations about M. are interesting. Perhaps you are right not to push them. I notice you want to work by corrupting the children first, then the parents. It's a nice coincidence that M. is at the same place as

Hano's young namesake. I certainly am glad that you've made enough progress to feel that they will be friendly towards me. That is something at least. There would have been no danger in them attending as the place is always full of their types most of the time. Anyway it's too late now.

I hope I didn't annoy you by calling you a square. I was merely teasing you. You have told me something of your "unsquare" days, and I am sure I will be most unhappy if there is the slightest chance of your going back to those days. No, I prefer you as you are, and I wand to find you as I left you. The information about your past interest in poetry, music, literature and drama comes as no surprise to me. You will be able to teach me a lot on these subjects, of which my knowledge is very limited.

I can imagine my dreams making you nostalgic, etc. Wish you can have similar dreams too. Then it won't be too hard.

About your treatment, as I've mentioned before, it seems to be doing you a lot of good. It will be most unfortunate if you have to discontinue due to lack of money. I'm sure I can make some arrangements for this—provided I still have the opportunity. On no account should this be interrupted if the doctor feels you should continue. And, provided, of course, that you feel it beneficial. You will be the best judge in the end I suppose. Your description of the treatment sounds interesting, but I just don't know enough to make an intelligent comment. On this subject too you'll have to bring me up to date one day.

I am sure the picture of Savi[4] and the kids must have made you feel jealous. Just be patient darling, your desires will be fulfilled. Thanks for their regards and best wishes. When writing to them again, please remember me.

Ayesha told me about the wedding. I will always regret the fact that he[5] and I were not able to spend a holiday together in Cape Town and Durban, a thing the poor bloke had been looking forward to. I would have loved to show him around. We missed, or rather he missed, the chance when I spent about 5 weeks in Cape Town at the beginning of 1962. Apparently he made plane reservations and all, and because of wrong information that I had left for P.E., he cancelled everything. Anyway, we'll make up for it one day. As to his bride crying a great deal, this is normal at Indian weddings. And the non-sobriety of my cousins,

---

[4] Sylvia's sister-in-law.

[5] Dr. Essop Jassat, a prominent political activist. Now a member of parliament in the present government.

I should say, was also normal. Perhaps when you convey to him the message about the table, you might be able to get his reactions to my views on the slander action. Of course if it is embarrassing for either of you to discuss it, just forget about it.

I'm glad about F. Were it not for the obstinacy of the father, this should've happened ages ago. I tried to help in this direction but unfortunately didn't succeed. And I agree with old man that it will also have a good effect on H. As for the "eloping partner," this comes to me as a surprise, but shall not comment as I have no background information.

Incidentally, I'm writing this on Wednesday. I didn't realise what the time was last night, and by the time I finished the first few lines of this page, it was already 8 p.m. We no longer have lights till 9—but they've been kind enough to leave the table and stool. I will arrange for a few words from my brother[6] to facilitate your business with the man from Anna's place.

I'm glad that our feelings were conveyed to uncle's colleague. In fact after I sent this message, the same suggestion came from others here. Your comments re my brother are interesting and I shall try to convey them to him. Also your best wishes to him and the other friend.

I took it for granted that whatever you get for my aunts, mother, the kids, etc., will be from both of us. I have ceased thinking in terms of myself as one individual. This goes for everything you do on my behalf in future as well.

It is very nice of your brother to give you so much for winter clothing, and I'm also happy that you have taken some of the other. It's all yours deary, so don't be shy. I'll expect you to be an expert in my favourite dishes and others as well. And you will have plenty of time to learn. You are well aware of the masses of people who pop in and have a bite, etc. You didn't seem to have any objections to this, and I'll expect you will gladly agree to this continuing in the future. Of course there'll be minor adjustments, but basically I will always want my place to remain an "open house" for friends, political colleagues, etc., etc. I should say our place, though on this question I seem to be actually dictating terms.

I don't know if you are quite right when you say you noticed me stroking Margaret's back. And if I did, I certainly wasn't conscious of anything irregular. I might as well have been massaging a statue for all the feelings I have for her as a woman. After all, I stayed with her for so

---

[6] Nelson Mandela.

many weeks and the thought didn't even cross my mind. As for the pro., you will remember we've just known each other on the phone. I've met her only once, and I'm sure I will not be able to recognise her today. And besides, I respect the institution of marriage. I will have to find out about *Huisgenoot*[7] and let you know.

After sentence, they will, I think [allow] one visit from relatives before sending us away. I think I should be allowed to see my lawyer once or twice to help me wind up my affairs, etc. After that, unless I'm involved in other cases, either as an accused or as a witness, no lawyers will be allowed either. Thereafter our only contact with the outside world will be through the 6-monthly visits and letters, also 6-monthly.

Thanks for the assurance about your health, meals, etc. It is a great help. Your partiality towards the Rockers we shall discuss some day. But I suppose by that time, they will no longer be in vogue and will have been replaced. Anyway, there are sure to be similar matters on which we can air our disagreement.

No, I don't notice tension in your last message. I did think that it was a temporary thing in the previous one. This one makes me feel on top of the world. I would like to know what impression you get from mine since you say you've been studying assiduously. I will be happy if you meet up with the lawyer friend and his wife.

There is no doubt that in the long run the left wing forces will definitely move faster now that Nehru is no longer on the scene. But what is worrying me is the immediate possible effect on the internal and international scene, more particularly on the Indo-Pakistan conflict. The diehard communal forces in India could not make much headway while Nehru was there. He was very strong and ruthlessly intolerant of racialism and communalism. I don't know how the new leaders will fare.

It seems to be such a pity that you have a cold relationship with your sister. While I don't know anything about the reasons, I do find it a bit difficult to understand. But, you know best I suppose, and we shall not quarrel over it.

I will end now. In case you don't hear from me again, you will appreciate the reasons. And the same applies to a message from you. Let me wish you the best of luck and success in everything you do. Please be very, very careful, work hard, don't be distracted unnecessarily, think of me and love me always while you are waiting for me. I love you very

---

[7] An Afrikaans language magazine.

much and will long for you no matter where I am and what I do. Goodbye sweetheart. I know that in the time ahead, many occasions will arise which might be controversial or over which you may be provoked to lose your temper. Whenever this happens, please try and think of me if it will help you to control yourself, and try your very best to keep away from this sort of unpleasantness. It will always make me happy to know that you have not allowed yourself to be weakened or distracted in any way by matters caused by petty jealousies, gossip, and small-mindedness. This is not to say that I'm in favour of your complete withdrawal from everything. Remain firm and resolute in your fundamental purpose, as always. On matters of principle, there can be no compromise or weakening. I'm sure you understand what I'm trying to convey. Bye bye my love and keep well. One thing more. Please always remember that, should you ever feel that it might be best for you to join Savi,[8] that you will have my fullest understanding, sympathy and support. Don't for one moment allow other considerations to influence you, especially if they concern me. I have made this clear to you before. It will in no way diminish my love and affection for you.

I must once again ask you to convey my fondest wishes and gratitude to my aunts, their children, etc., to my Joburg mother and children and most important to old lady and old man.[9] Also to everybody else, friends of mine and others who have been so wonderful all these months. I shall always be looking forward to being with them all again.

∼ ∼ ∼

Letter to Sylvia Neame—*11 June 1964*

This letter was written on 11 June, the day that Kathrada and his compatriots were found guilty and were waiting to hear what sentence they would serve. At this point, the death sentence was still a possibility. Kathrada realizes that soon he will have "to change into convict clothes." He describes the uprooting of families in his hometown of Schweizer Reneke and how his home, where his father had settled in 1919, was to be demolished, not because it was old or because a road was to be built. It was to be destroyed because it was next door to a white church. "The apartheid juggernaut moves on." He wonders how white South

---

8 "Join Savi," that is, to go to Canada.

9 Amien and Ayesha Cajee.

*Africans can be so smug about such a thing and about those who might dis-
agree and say nothing. This type of upheaval and uprooting of families was a
regular humiliation and indignity that non-white groups had to suffer; in
"apartheid speak" it was the removal of "black spots." Again he gets asked,
probably by a guard, why he had chosen this life when he could have been living comfortably. How, he asks, can this inquirer understand "life without dignity"? He describes the clothing he will wear on the day of judgment, the tie
and jersey Sylvia had given to him. The Rivonia Trialists were sentenced to life
in prison on 12 June 1964. Only Rusty Bernstein was released. Shortly after
midnight, under the tightest security and secrecy, shackled and in leg irons,
Kathrada and his colleagues were flown to Robben Island to begin their sentences. For political prisoners in 1964, "life in prison" meant no possibility of
parole.*

∽

By this time next week our fate will have been decided, and we will be
already facing what is in store for us in the next phase. The tension and
anxiety which I expected would be my constant companion these last
days just has not come. Perhaps it is because of the long process of mental preparation to expect the worst. Or perhaps there is a certain amount
of suppressed tension. I just don't know. Today (Sunday) I feel more or
less the same as I did at the beginning of the trial. But I am sure the
blood pressure will go up in the next few days. The best way is not to
think too much of what is coming. When it comes, whatever it is, I find
that one manages to adapt oneself. That is so true of the past year. First
there was the relative suddenness with which I went underground, to live
a type of life which I never imagined I'd be able to. Then, just as sudden,
came the arrests. This was followed by the 90-day detention and all that
goes with it. Then the trial and the quashing of the indictment—and the
immediate re-arrest and the new trial. The ending of this trial almost certainly to be followed by another, and then . . . who knows? But so it goes
on. And what about all that has happened to you in this period, so closely
interwoven with my life—and what of the experiences of so many other
near and dear ones. How many hundreds of times this story can be
repeated in the South Africa of the sixties. And with so much more
drama. Yes, whatever else can be said about it, we are living in interesting times.

The question was again put to me by someone this week. Is all this
suffering really necessary when you can easily live a comfortable life
outside? And the usual jazz about how well off we are in South Africa

compared to the conditions in the rest of Africa and Asia. Simple as all that—in SA all can be well clothed, fed and roofs over their heads, and schools and sports, etc., etc. But how could I explain my feelings to him, for he just won't understand. Of what good are these things to me when I haven't got dignity? And what is life without dignity. On that very morning I read in the papers about a move to uproot settled communities in Schweizer-Reneke, Ottosdal and other places in the Western Transvaal. In Schweizer-Reneke, the house where I was born and where my father settled in 1919 has to be moved. Not because of any road or town development project, not for hygienic reasons or slum clearance, but simply because we are Indians and because our house happens to be next to the Dutch Reformed Church. The fact that my father and other Indians settled there before the Church was built, indeed when the town was almost barren, seems to be of no consequence. The apartheid juggernaut must move on, trampling mercilessly on life and livelihood, oblivious to any injury to human feelings and desires. And on more or less the same day, the so-called Minister of Indian Affairs, with cruel callousness, can say that the Indian people are happy under the Group Areas Act and speaks of its so-called advantages. What is worse is white South Africa believes him, and those who don't are acquiescing by their silence. Can it be that they feel so snug and secure within the laager that they can comfortably close their eyes to all this and not expect to be disturbed in their way of life? Altogether it presents a frightening picture. Not that the march to freedom can be stopped by this apathy. But just think of the colossal problems of adjustment after freedom.

Anyway, why am I unburdening myself onto you? Let me get on to other things. I have given my general power of attorney in favour of Amien. He must collect it from Mr. Joffe. This is together with a description of everything he has to claim from the police. With this he will also be able to attend to the business of transferring the car to my sister, etc. Also, I still have about 80 [pounds sterling] in my account at the jail here. For the present, this must be left alone. If and when, after sentence, I think it necessary to transfer this, I will let him know. The stuff taken from the Mountainview cottage[1] I suppose can only be

---

[1] Mountainview was the "safe house" where Kathrada went to live when he went underground. He had gone to Lilliesleaf Farm in Rivonia to attend a meeting, with the intention of returning to Mountainview afterwards.

claimed at the end of the Kreel case. I think his best bet will be to nego-tiate through Lieut. Van Wyk whom I have spoken to in this regard.

I have made arrangements with Mr. Joffe to let you have the transcript of my evidence and cross-examination. Also a photo of mine in disguise, which is an exhibit in our case. I thought you might like to have it. He has agreed to give you these when he is through with it. You will have to make arrangements with him. Actually I don't think I specifically men-tioned that you will be calling, but that shouldn't present any difficulties.

I have also sent back the brown shirt, which you will collect from Ayesha. I still have the blue tie and red jersey. These I will wear with my blue shirt on the day of judgement and send back after sentence.

We have been told we will be allowed one visit after sentence, i.e. on Saturday morning when we can send our things back. Also, while we are waiting to be classified, we will be allowed one visit a month. But this is really academic as we don't know where they will keep us immediately after sentence and how long the classification business takes.

Just in case I don't get sentenced with this mob and have to face new charges, I'm afraid I am going to continue to be a burden on you and all the other good people. Washing, food, visits, etc. I'm feeling terribly guilty about it all, but unfortunately there isn't much I can do. And of course I mustn't forget books. Depending on how long the other cases take, I would like to get the Shakespeare, the Oxford poetry and the History books back. These, in addition to other reading matter. But there is no hurry. We will know soon.

I have finished 2 of the last 4 books and have just started on Chesterton's autobiography, which promises to be interesting. This should see me through until Thursday I think. Then I've also got the English version of the Koran. I'm afraid I have been very slow with it, only managing about a chapter a day. But I'll be able to keep it after sentence and therefore did not send it back. I hope to be able to study it a bit more carefully then.

Other than this, the only things I have still with me are the blue suit, a couple of shirts, 2 pairs of shoes, a pair of fawn trousers and a few items of underwear. I'm so happy I have cleared away so much in the last 2 vis-its. Now I'm all ready to change into convict clothes. Incidentally, I asked the authorities to hand over my wrist watch to my cousin from the farm; I hope they didn't forget to. I was very glad to see him, especially since he was able to tell me that he had seen Sakina, who looked very well and cheerful, which makes me feel fine.

It was also nice to see my brothers yesterday. They agreed with me when I expressed the hope that I am sentenced with this group so that we can be together, instead of all the inconveniences of new trial, etc. They are becoming more and more realistic as time goes on. It is good that the story of ill-treatment at Robben Island appeared in the *Express* today. Nice timing by the *Observer*.

I'm going to interrupt this and continue tomorrow. You are so much in my thoughts and [I] look forward more and more to the time when we are re-united. Hope you keep well lovey and look after yourself. Goodnight my love.

What a bitterly cold Monday morning; I think it is the worst we've had this year. Let's hope it improves by the end of the week when we will no longer have long pants and warm underwear, etc. Since early this morning, I've been thinking of my cousin and what a terrible Monday morning he must be having. For today, in addition to his usual Monday morning troubles, he has to brave the hazards of the weather. For me it is so wonderful to be able to get up fresh and alert, with no A. R.? In some ways I must be the envy of many suffering friends. I hope you've had a good weekend and ready for hard work again. Did I hear correctly that your schedule has been changed once again and you now have to be ready only by early next year. Is this good or bad, and what are the reasons for it? I hope nothing has gone wrong.

I was informed by my cousin from the farm that there isn't much remaining from the £100 I had. Apparently quite a bit of it has been used for providing food, etc., for me. Just as well the matter came up, for here I was insisting that you draw on it, and it might have placed you in an embarrassing position to find it all used up. Anyway, please make use of whatever is left. I have also made a suggestion to him which will see you through the next months. Please do not in any way feel embarrassed by this, and give whatever information you can about your requirements when you are asked. You did mention before that, while you will hesitate to seek assistance from your sister, the same does not apply to me. So I will consider the matter as closed and expect no arguments from you. In case he didn't see you again, I will send a message to remind him. Rest assured that there is absolutely nothing to be embarrassed about; I wouldn't have raised it if I had the slightest doubt. I suppose it will take a bit of time for you to get accustomed to it, but you are one of the family now.

I had hoped to receive a message from you and then send this off. But since there is nothing, I'll get this off today. It is now definite that this will be the last for the time being. Won't say any more—only repeat my love for you. I'll be expecting you to wait for me with the same patience, courage and devotion you have shown so far. Thumbs up always my darling and all the very best to you.

I was going to write individually to a lot of friends but have decided not to. You will convey my greetings and thanks to all, particularly old man and old lady, my aunts, cousins and the folks there, and all other friends. All the best to you.

Have just heard that you've collected the notebooks. I'm sending one more, which will be the last. After Thursday, when I'm re-arrested and charged, our attorney will be able to keep you informed about me.

~ ~ ~

Ahmed Kola—30 August 1964

This is in all likelihood Kathrada's first letter from Robben Island; it is to his cousin, Kola. He mentions his concern for friends who had been arrested under the 90-Day Detention Law and held incommunicado. Immediately after the sentencing of the Rivonia Trialists, the government set out to eliminate all remaining resistance. The letter provides a glimpse into life on the island and the work of prisoners. When sentenced, seven Rivonia Trialists were sent to Robben Island. Dennis Goldberg, being white, was incarcerated in Pretoria Central Prison, which was for whites only. The seven were all classified as "D" prisoners, the lowest ranking prisoners, which meant, among other things, they were permitted one, 500-word letter every six months. Hence Kathrada's reference to special letters for studies.

~

To Ahmed Kola, Ottosdal. 30.8.64
Robben Island
30th August 1964

Dear Kola,

Being used to the practice in Pretoria jail where delivery time either way was about a week, even for overseas letters, assumed it would be the same here; but I've since been told that it would take a month or longer.

I wonder what happened to the Afrikaans poetry book *Uit ons Digkuns*. Please check when you are at the flat[1] next time. You will also find the Oxford Atlas which I would like to have. Talking about the flat, I hope Amien and the other friends of mine are out again. I spend many hours thinking of possible reasons why some of these chaps got into difficulties but am still at a loss. I suppose it's "guilt by association." Tell Amien that I was most distressed to hear of my Khala's[2] indisposition again—I fervently hope and pray she is up and about again and in perfect health. This causes me constant anxiety and worry. Please also ask him to convey my dearest love and fondness. I still recite the passages from Shakespeare daily, which brings back a host of pleasant and cherished memories. She is uppermost in my mind.

My health is fine and my morale and confidence is even higher. Assure the family not to worry on that score. We're thankful that winter is over. We started working a few days ago, mending clothes and sewing buttons; don't know for how long.

I am allowed to receive and write "special letters" for studies. So if you confine yourself to this question, I think I'll be able to get it sooner. I am told that a battery shaver is unheard of in the Cape jails, so I hope Solly[3] has not bought a new one for me.

≈   ≈   ≈

Kathrada Family—*18 October 1964*

This is the first letter Kathrada wrote to his mother, brothers, and sisters. He informs them that he and the other prisoners are breaking stones, a form of hard labor. He goes on to discuss his future and regrets that he had ignored his formal education. Always concerned about others, he remarks that his mother should think of him "not in jail but at university." Kathrada would become the first prisoner on Robben Island to receive a university degree.

≈

[1] Kathrada's apartment, Flat 13, was a legend in itself. Mandela ran his legal practice from here at one of the difficult periods in the struggle.

[2] A reference to Sylvia Neame.

[3] Kathrada's eldest brother.

To Kathrada Family, Schweizer Reneke. 18.10.64
Robben Island
18.10.64

Dear folks,

The nights are still fairly cold—can you imagine it's the middle of October and here I'm sitting with my jersey and jacket still on. I made a mistake when I told Kola in August that summer was already here. Although it has been quite warm in the stone yard where we work, in fact I'm quite black from the sun. My health has been perfect so far; I've lost a number of pounds, but it was excess weight in any case. You all will remember how much extra weight I had put on while awaiting trial. Only I can't get used to the water yet; it's a bit salty and I don't think I've had more than 6 mugs so far. But I'll get used to it. So you can assure Ma there is nothing to worry about as far as my health goes.

Unfortunately I haven't really started with studies yet; there has been a delay but things are being smoothed out. Also I'm still awaiting some literature from Unisa[1] and the University of London before I finally decide what I'm going to do. I know you all have for many years been keen that I do law. I might still do it. So when Ma or anyone at home starts worrying about me, they must just imagine that I'm not in jail but at university. Only now I really appreciate how hasty and unwise I was to give up my studies 18 years ago. And if I wasn't in jail, I wouldn't have had an inclination to go back to it. So please be very firm with all our kids who are neglecting their studies. Do not let them give up. . . .

[6 lines blacked out by censors]

≈ ≈ ≈

Kathrada Family—*24 December 1967*

Maintaining the right to study proved to be an ongoing battle between the political prisoners and prison authorities; it would last until Kathrada's release in 1989. It was no secret that the authorities wanted to break the spirit of the political prisoners and render them weak and submissive. The political prisoners, on

---

[1] The University of South Africa which made it possible for people to study by correspondence. Most of the political prisoners on the Island studied through UNISA.

the other hand, refused to bow to these pressures and indeed became more resolute as time passed.

~

To Family Kathrada, Schweizer Reneke. 24.12.67
Robben Island
24.12.67

My Dear folks,

I got through History and Xhosa, but failed Criminology. This means I have to spend the whole year doing it again. I'm ashamed because it is such a simple subject and the standard is unbelievably low. In fact I long ago lost interest in it. . . . I'm glad however that I've got Xhosa out of the way. I was very worried about it—it's a very difficult language. Now I shall just carry on talking it and hope after some years to be able to have a reasonable command of it. . . . Last week we were given some information about the new attitude of the prison authorities towards studies. It appears that, after completing one degree, we will not be allowed to continue studying. Looking at it from this point of view, therefore, it's just as well that I ploughed.[1] In the meantime I'm going to cost you a bit of money again. I shall be needing R50[2] to see me through 1968.

~ ~ ~

Essop Pahad—*3 April 1968*

This letter is addressed to a whole group of South Africans, all of whom are in exile in London. Essop and Aziz Pahad are brothers and it was their mother to whom Kathrada refers as his "Joburg Ma." They were neighbors, living about a block from Kathrada. Tommy Vassen, who Kathrada refers to as his "cousin" in "Letters to Sylvia" and Bobby, "the young cousin" are brothers; Herby Pillay, referred to as "H," is their cousin. Harry Naidoo went to London in 1962. Billy Nannan arrived in London in 1965 after being detained under the 90-Day Detention Laws, where he was tortured and placed in solitary confinement. All continued to be active in ANC politics and political structures.

---

[1] A popular term in that period meaning *failed.*

[2] The Rand was valued at about $1.00 in U.S. currency at that time.

Billy Nannan, one of the shining lights in the ANC, died in London in 1993, robbing the movement of one of its true intellectuals. Abdulhay Jassat and Mosy (Moosa Moolla), together with Wolpe and Goldreich, made a daring 1963 escape from Marshall Square, a jail in Johannesburg. In the reference to Abdulhay being unwell, Kathrada wants to know if the torture Abdulhay had suffered while in detention is still affecting him. In fact, to this day Abdulhay still has occasional blackouts as a result of the torture in 1963. The Pahad brothers are both in the present South African government; Tommy, Herby, and Harry are still living in London, and Bobby Vassen is at Michigan State University in the United States. Kathrada, now coming up to four years in jail, is still the same indomitable spirit. While he admits that life in jail "is no bed of roses," he is finding a lot for which to be thankful: time for reflection, time to study, and even perhaps time to take up the guitar. We learn that for three years they had no access to reading matter. The magazines he quotes are certainly not ones to inspire, but for political prisoners, getting permission to subscribe to them was a "breakthrough." It was little battles like these that kept their spirits up. After almost four years Kathrada was still a "D" prisoner—the lowest category possible. It took him thirteen years to be reclassified "A." In the interim, he became a "B," and on two occasions while a "B," he was demoted. He was the last of his group to get to the "A" category, probably for his uncompromising stand. The other names Kathrada mentions in this letter are South Africans in exile, most of whom are active in ANC politics.

〜

To Essop Pahad, London, United Kingdom. 3.4.68
Robben Island
3.4.68

My Dear Essop, Aziz, Tommy, Harry, Herby, Bobby, Billy and the boys—and Ursula, Dela, Theresa, Fati,[1] and the girls; and of course all the children, my aunties, etc.

It was really wonderful to receive your letter on 29th March. Needless to say it brought back heaps of memories of the many years we spent together. It is not without a tinge of anguish that I think of you all who are so far away from home. Therefore your letter was like a happy reunion; only, instead of the conventional beverages that go with such occasions, we

---

[1] Ursula, Dela, and Theresa are the wives of Bob and Tommy Vassen and Billy Nannan, respectively. Fati Dollie, a friend.

satisfy our thirst and hunger with the good news about all our near and dear ones. From this point of view the last weekend for me has been a veritable orgy. Your letter arrived on Friday, my brother Solly visited me on Saturday, and the authorities were kind enough to allow an additional visit on Sunday from my nephew. So you can imagine what a feast I've been having. I was happy to hear that Mummy & Daddy are presently in South Africa and that they are well. I expect Hassim will write again one of these days and tell me more about them. You can't imagine how happy and proud I am of your academic achievements. What pleased me even more is the subject of Essop's thesis.[2] How often have I not wished, outside and inside jail, that some of our younger graduates should get stuck into research on different aspects of our history. Bobby & Billy will remember our discussing it. I hope there are other South Africans pursuing similar themes & should like to hear some details. Last year I read an MA thesis by some chap called Pachhai on the "History of Indian Opinion up to 1916." It wasn't up to much—in fact parts of it positively offended one's nostrils. I hope a group of you could do something to replace Joshi's book![3] And, if you'll allow me to indulge my fancies, perhaps one day even Walker's book will be suitably replaced. What has made Sylvia invade the "all man's-world" of Oxford to do her doctorate? What is her topic? What about her research on the ICU?[4] I'm surprised when you say that "she looks much better" as I was not aware of her being unwell. I'm anxious to know about her health & hope she is looking after herself. Give her my love. I should like to know about you all, your studies, social activities, etc. And also about people like Ismail, Dasoo, Vella, Barney, M.P., Issy, Paul, Abe, etc., and their families and kids. Has Abdulhay also been unwell? Has Juby joined Mosy? We heard some terrible gossip some time ago about Mosy's "second marriage" and about Issy following suit and were happy to hear it was untrue. Also heard some rumours about a squabble in Moosabhai's family and hope it is likewise untrue. Thab[5] has been very naughty in not keeping in touch with his family. Give him my regards. Is he also doing a doctorate? There are so many other friends about whom I

---

[2] The subject of the thesis was the South African Indians.

[3] *The Tyranny of Colour: A Study of the Indian Problem in South Africa* written by P. S. Joshi, in 1942.

[4] In his letters to Sylvia Neame Kathrada often refers to this research on Trades Unions.

[5] Very likely Thabo Mbeki, who was a fellow-student with Essop Pahad at this time at Sussex University.

should like to know; but as a lot of them are political, I'll have to resist the temptation to enquire after them. It may just rub the authorities the wrong way and may prejudice our communications. Incidentally I am not allowed to write or receive any messages as relating to my fellow prisoners. Give my regards to Joel and the colony of South Africans working with him. What ever happened to the book he wrote? When I see some of the local asthmatics suffer in the English-type climate on Robben Island, I often wonder what happens to Oliver[6] in London. Or has he succeeded in curing himself? Is his wife a doctor already? If you ever happen to see them, please convey my fondest regards and wishes to them. I can rely on you chaps to set up a little bit of Fordsburg[7] wherever you go. I suppose the pub on the corner has taken the place of "aunty's shebeen" in Terrace Road,[8] which you used to frequent. I hope Tommy is taking it easy. Now I suppose you'd like to hear a bit about life here. Healthwise, I'm fine, i.e. besides the bit of arthritis and other little aches and pains that go with prison life. Spiritwise, I couldn't be better. I suppose a very important factor here is that, long before my arrest, I had conditioned myself to the prospect of spending a long time in jail. And, as you will probably imagine, almost everything depends on one's mental attitude. So I don't for a moment regret my refusal to accept the suggestion in 1963 that I should take refuge in Swaziland or overseas. Having said this, I don't of course mean that I'm finding prison life to be a bed of roses, or that I shouldn't like to be with my loved ones. But at the same time, looking back over the past few years, I must say that my being in prison has not been without its advantages. It has been a real boon to have been able to devote time to reflection and thought and also to be able to acquire a bit of education. Almost everyday that passes reveals to me how really ignorant I've been, educationwise; and I cannot but be thankful that I've had a bit of opportunity to make up a little in this direction. As you most probably know, I've been trying to do a B.A. since ±May 1965, with majors in History and Criminology. I should have completed at the end of last year, but unfortunately flopped Criminology. So I'm doing it again this year. My original intention was to do History Honours, but unfortunately the new prison

---

[6] The late Oliver Tambo, president of the African National Congress in exile.

[7] Fordsburg, an area set aside for Indians under The Group Areas Act of 1950. Most of the people addressed in this letter were from Fordsburg.

[8] The equivalent of a speakeasy. The entire non-white population was prohibited from purchasing or consuming alcohol. Shebeens, illegal drinking houses, flourished and many were run by women, hence the reference to "aunty's shebeen."

regulations won't allow me to. So, as things stand at present, it seems as if I shall be tackling another B.A., i.e. if the prisons and university agree. I'm toying with the idea of 3 majors—Anthropology, Sociology, "Native" Administration. I've also managed to do a bit of general reading. I suppose you are aware of the games we are allowed to play since August last—Table Tennis, Scrabble, Chess, Monopoly, Bridge, Klaberjas, etc. And, believe it or not, I'm contemplating learning to play the guitar; Alec's influence of course. Esu[9] is already doing fine with the Melodica, though his tunes are rather Indianized. And we are also allowed monthly visits & letters. We may subscribe to Huisgenoot, Panorama, Farmers Weekly, Lantern, Landbon Weekblod & Reader's Digest; not exactly an inspiring list but nevertheless a welcome breakthrough. And the smokers are allowed to buy cigarettes. Not doing too badly, are we? I am still a "D" group prisoner. That's all about myself. I suppose both Mummy and Daddy speak English well nowadays. Have you folks a lot of English friends? Do you also find them cold & reserved? I hope you don't get influenced by some of the unfortunate English habits and customs—you know, "special invitations" for tea, the insipid food, and the surfeit of manners, etc. I couldn't stick England at all & ran away as quickly as I could to the Continent. Is Mota[10] back from India? Give him my love. You must write again. It is so much better if you can, or get Tommy to, type your letters. No reflection on your writing, but it will be easier for my old eyes. And please write <u>directly</u> to me at the Island. You can just inform Nassim when you do write. Keep well. I wonder if our Yasmin still remembers me. She was small when I was arrested. My very best wishes and love to all of you.

Goolam Hoosenbhai—*29 December 1968*

An interesting letter setting out Kathrada's philosophy for dealing with enforced and indefinite incarceration. This philosophy and the discipline of the Rivonia group were to remain their hallmarks throughout the 26-plus years that they would spend in jail. A thread that runs throughout these letters is the importance of studying, both to keep the mind active and the quest for knowledge.

---

[9] A fellow prisoner who was serving an 18-year sentence on the Island.

[10] Dr. Y. M. Dadoo.

∽

To Goolam Hoosenbhai c/o Kathradas, Schweizer Reneke. 29.12.68
Robben Island
29th December 1968

My Dear Goolam Hoosenbhai,

Soon it will be 6 years since our arrest. How many more years of imprisonment, no one can tell. There is no fixed period for a life sentence. Besides, there is no remission for political prisoners. So I am under no illusion as to the time I still have to serve. Fortunately, long before my arrest I had mentally conditioned myself to a lengthy stay in prison so that adaptation to this environment has not been too taxing or difficult. So much depends on one's mental attitude. I found quite early on already the wisdom of trying not to be unduly affected by the hundred and one pinpricks and hazards that are part and parcel of prison life. I found that if one allows oneself to be excited and carried away by every triviality, life can really become miserable. Misery and unhappiness are so contagious, particularly in an institution where people live so close to one another. I have therefore found it to our advantage to adopt a broad outlook to things and to try to occupy ourselves in such a way as to leave little time for pettiness and idle thought. This has proved to be a boon for our mental and physical well being and happiness.

The authorities, in gradually making concessions, must have foreseen the wisdom of a policy which would have the effect of leaving less and less room for disgruntlement. To fill the time when we are not working, we have our studies, library books, games, musical instruments, magazines. You must of course not get the idea that all is rosy and that we have no complaints. There is plenty of room for improvement. There are still unfortunately too many aspects of penology which are outdated and unnecessarily retributive and burdensome.

Perhaps the most important concession, in my opinion, has been to allow us to study. More than anything else, over the years, our books have helped to keep our minds fully occupied. I have therefore been most surprised and disappointed that the authorities have now seen fit to drastically curtail this privilege. Sollymota[1] must have told you that I have

---

[1] Kathrada's eldest brother: "*mota*" affixed to the name denotes elder/eldest as a form of respect, just as the affix "*bhai*" in his opening salutation denotes "brother."

been refused permission for all the subjects which I had applied to do next year. He seemed quite confident that all will be well; that is after his interview with a high prison official. I hope he is right.

~ ~ ~

Sylvia Neame—*sometime between 11 December 1970 and 9 January 1971*

This letter, written to Sylvia Neame, was smuggled out of Robben Island. In it Kathrada describes prison life and conditions on the island. Wide in scope, it covers relationships between prisoners and guards, prisoners and fellow-prisoners, the "educating" of the guards, work in the quarry, food, censorship, recreation, the reign of terror when new guards set about to instill discipline, and the hunger strikes.

~

I want to try to give you a picture of some aspects of our life here though I'm sure you're well up with quite a bit already. I must emphasise that I can only speak authoritatively of life in the single cells section, for that is where I've lived ever since our arrival. There are over 80 single cells, but our permanent population remains about 30. Except for the occasional new arrival, we live with the same persons all the years. In this way they have effectively isolated us from the rest of the population which totals ±800. I believe, of these, under 400 are politicals. You will be surprised to learn that in all these years I have only managed to have an occasional glimpse of chaps like Shirish, Reg, Indres,[1] etc. The authorities claim there are 5 kept apart: (a) General cells—political prisoners ±300; (b) Single cells ±30; (c) SWA guerrillas[2] ±40; (d) ANC guerrillas[3] ±12; (e) Non politicals ±400. Since their arrival 3 years ago, we've only managed to have one accidental glimpse of the Namibians. The ANC guerrillas are confined to their yard even for work, so we don't see them at all. At the present we are 32 in single cells, 23

---

[1] Shirish, Reg, and Indres: Three ANC *Umkonto We Sizwe* members sentenced to 10 years in prison for sabotage.

[2] SWA: South West Africa, now Namibia.

[3] ANC: African National Congress, the organization to which Kathrada, Mandela, Sisulu, and others belonged.

Congressites, 4 PAC,[4] 4 YCC [NEUM[5] offshoot] and 1 ARM.[6] In the rest of the jail the ANC–PAC proportion could be more or less equal. The single cells inmates range from Nelson, Walter, etc., to ordinary rank and filers. We are taken to and from work in a closed lorry, are taken separately to visits, have separate church services, write exams separately—film shows, games, everything is separate. A conscientious warder would even clear the road when our lorry approaches. So you see the extent of our isolation. My cell is about 8 x 8 feet—the only items of furniture are a table and bench. We sleep on two mats on the cement floor. It can be terribly cold. Living with the same faces day in and day out must be having adverse psychological effects on us. We do get on one another's nerves and we have long exhausted all conversation relating to our experiences outside. All the jokes have been told; even gossip has become repetitive. There are inevitable tensions arising from such a situation. But, on the whole, we have coped remarkably well. The studies are a great help. Wish they'd allow us newspapers. We sometimes look forward to new arrivals, especially if they are lively and talkative, like our mutual friends, the "Capies."[7]

Our (i.e. single cells) relationship with warders has been quite cordial and with some decidedly warm. There is considerable exchange of small talk, which is not without benefit. Most warders are very young, some barely 17. Generally they are decent, and, if they spend their impressionable years working with political prisoners, I am sure it will have a healthy impact on their outlook. Unfortunately they stay a very short time with us and are once again exposed to the unwholesome and brutalising influences of prison life. Then I suppose they become the ordinary white South Africans with all their prejudices, hates, fears and irrationality. Isn't it tragic? Because, ironically, it is in jail that we have closest fraternisation between the opponents and supporters of apartheid; we have eaten of their food, and they ours; they have blown the same musical instruments that have been "soiled" by black lips; they

---

[4] PAC: Pan African Congress, a breakaway group from the ANC. PAC was more nationalistic with their cry of "Africa for the Africans."

[5] NEUM: the Non European Unity Movement.

[6] ARM: African Resistance Movement. A group which believed that armed struggle and not symbolic attacks on government installations was the solution.

[7] Capies: the people from Cape Town.

have discussed most intimate matters and sought advice; a blind man listening in to a tête-à-tête will find it hard to believe it is between prisoner and warder. One of them once related to me an argument among them which centred on the visit to S. A. of a black dignitary and the lavish entertainments meted out. His stand was that, if Vorster could eat and drink with a neighbouring African, why couldn't he do so with Mandela and for this he received much support.

But of course there are the *verkramptes*[8] and rabid racialists as well. What a job we will have to rehabilitate them. Then we can realise how formidable our problems are. In the meantime we will continue to do all we can to make the rehabilitation of some as easy as possible. The relationship among the different political groups of prisoners is on the whole cordial, though it fluctuates at times. The PAC chaps in our section over the years have been generally colourless, bigoted, narrow and racialistic. Invariably most suffer from massive inferiority complexes. Nevertheless even among them one can occasionally discern some changes for the better. The poor YCC chaps (all 6 of them) first woke to the reality of politics with the shock of their arrest and imprisonment. On the whole their approach still remains very naive and idealistic. In their lively imagination they still seem to see themselves as the indispensable leaders of what they frequently call the SA revolution. But all their personal plans after their release take them as far away as possible from the revolutionary path and into comfortable chairs of academic life. Leslie v.d. Heyden (now in UK) and Neville Alexander are of course brilliant chaps—Les on English and Neville all round, but especially in History and German. What a marvelous brain. What a great thing for himself and for our people generally if he decides to quit the political arena—where he will meet only frustration and disappointment—and devote himself to academic work. Given proper guidance he certainly can make a great contribution here. Fiks[9] you may know. He was a great friend of the "Black White man," and was really a playboy who got caught in the rush. He knows you.

To get back to jail life. Work. Our official work still remains the lime quarry and pick and shovels. But for the past few years we have not really worked. We have demanded creative work. They say they are unable to. So we just go to the quarry and do nothing. We are not on strike, only

---

[8] *Verkarmptes*: conservative and rigid followers of apartheid.

[9] Fiks: Fikile Bam a member of NEUM.

bored and frustrated with this type of work. They of course don't like our not working. But there is a stalemate. I don't know how long this farce will last. Incidentally the Congress chaps addressed a letter to the Minister of Justice last year, demanding that we be treated as political prisoners, which inter alia means we do only the essential work.

Food. They've been promising improvements. But there has been little change. On 14 Nov. they surprised us by giving chicken instead of beef. Since then we've been getting chicken every Saturday. Since then we are also being given one egg three times a week. But there had to be a catch somewhere. The timing of this innovation coincided with the visit to the Island of members of the International Red Cross. Secondly they've made it clear that chicken and eggs will be given as long as the glut continues. Finally, in their cockeyed way of reasoning, they believe that non-white prisoners do not need as much protein as whites. Therefore when they introduced chicken and eggs they officially cut down the already meagre ration of beef, pork and fish. Saturday, Sunday and Tuesday still remain meat days, and Thursday, Fish day. But now the meat ration is as little as 5 cubes of 3/4" each. On 10th Dec.—Human Rights Day—we got another surprise. Together with fish we got mince and mashed potatoes. But we were told this was just an experiment. Otherwise prison food still remains the same.

Censorship. In our studies and general reading we suffer from narrow verkrampte censorship. They have to keep away from us every scrap of paper containing political news, outside of government publications—*Fiat Lux, Alpha, Bantu,* etc. Scantily dressed women must also be torn out of *Panorama* and other magazines to which we subscribe. I once raised this indiscriminate mutilation of our magazines with a senior officer, in fact with the officer in charge of studies. I was doing anthropology and pointed out to him that in my textbooks there were pictures of entirely naked women, let alone the bikini-clad ones. To this he observed, *"Hulle is seker bantu vrouens"*![10] Need I say more! Then, from the next year we will no longer be allowed to do politics, history, economic history, and any other subject which necessitates books considered objectionable. So much for the *verligte*[11] winds of change.

Visits. For me 1970 has been a bad year for visits. My brother Solly continued his efforts to see me but has been unsuccessful. They are

---

[10] In translation, this Afrikaans term means: "They are obviously African women."

[11] *Verligte*: Enlightened group of government supporters who believed that a more progressive approach was desirable.

refusing to grant him a visiting permit for the Cape so that rules out Robben Island. The local Nat. MP[12] even took up the matter with the Minister, but it was in vain. In July Fatima Meer [13] from Durban applied to see me but was refused. No reasons given. Moms, who had visited me in previous years was told by the special branch that she will not get a passport if she continues. So that put paid to her visits. Poor woman. She feels terrible about it. This story naturally got around, with the result that a number of C[ape]T[own] friends are now afraid. Helen Suzman[14] promised to do something about the visits. But I haven't heard. I wish a row is kicked up. The S[pecial] B[ranch] has also interfered with people with whom I correspond.

Recreation. Apart from the games we ourselves purchase—Scrabble, cards, chess, etc.—about the only recreation provided by the authorities is the monthly film show. Again, they can only show us what is good for us, so most of the really good films are out. Occasionally a decent film slips in. On the whole this is a welcome diversion. Then there is a radio rediffusion service, which has virtually ceased functioning for about a year. All because the news slipped in once or twice. Now we've been told that this whole system was donated by the DRC[15] for the purpose of rendering church services and nothing else. So as far as we are concerned, its only purpose is to show the impressive equipment to visitors. Earlier in the year they started building a special recreation hall for our section, but the work has been at a standstill.

Assaults. Here again there is differential treatment. In our section there have been virtually no assaults ever since our arrival. And among the rest of the political prisoners, assaults have almost ceased, though there are occasional incidents. But this cannot be said for our non-political fellows. For them jail is still what it has always been for non-whites— a veritable hell. And this includes Robben Island. Even we are surprised to learn of the horrible conditions prevailing in that section. On 14, 15 and 16 November, for instance, a series of organized brutal assaults were conducted on them which resulted in broken arms, heads and huge weals all over the body. The matter was reported to the Red Cross chaps,

---

[12] The Nationalist Party, the party in power from 1947 to 1994.

[13] Fatima Meer, a renowned academic, author, and an active member of the liberation struggle.

[14] Helen Suzman: the sole member of the Progressive Party in the South African Parliament and often the lone voice of opposition to the government.

[15] The Dutch Reformed Church.

but they said they could do nothing about it as their mission was restricted to political prisoners. Suddenly there are political prisoners in S.A.

General. They've started installing a warm water system. This will be most welcome, though over the years I became quite used to cold water on the coldest of days. There are all sorts of rumours of other improvements. Now that the 10th anniversary of the Republic is approaching, there are fresh rumours of remissions. What does remission of a life sentence mean? I suppose you know of the large number of appeals which have resulted in substantial reduction of sentences for several prisoners. Thus far the lawyers have only dealt with sentences under unlawful organisations. Now they've started working on some sabotage cases. Isu's group[16] are also attempting to apply for condonation for late appeal. I don't know if anyone ever explained to you why I did not appeal in 1964 when the lawyers were so confident that at least Mhlaba and I stood good chances of acquittal? No serious thought has since been given to reconsidering the matter, though a number of people have made casual suggestions. I myself remain undecided, though I can't say I've given it full consideration. My inclination would be to leave the question for decision by the folks outside, that is if there are people who give thought to this kind of business. In the meantime we might as well wait for developments in the other cases. Though there is nothing I'd like more than being with Yasmin[17] as soon as possible, I must say the idea of being in England does not appeal to me. Neither any other place for that matter that is so far away from S.A. On the other hand, remaining in S.A. has certain insurmountable problems which you'll appreciate. All this must make you think that it's all hopeless. I shall let you know if something tangible arises. Until then, we'll sit and wait—or pray! Incidentally I've become a great church goer. Rev. Hughes of the Anglicans and his assistant, Rev. Dixie [ex-Grahamstown] conduct fine services and so does Presbyterian Rev. Craig. What a delightful man Rev. Hughes is and what sense of humour. Have just heard there is a departmental committee presently reviewing all long sentences especially of 1963, 1964 period. But then this is the time for all sorts of rumours.

I am writing this on 9th January. Beginning from about Christmas time there have been vast changes in our way of life. A new officer commanding

---

[16] Isu/Lalloo Chiba, who served an 18-year sentence for sabotage.

[17] A pseudonym for Sylvia Neame.

has been installed and a host of new head warders have been brought over. We are told they have come to "clear up" this jail and to impose discipline, which they maintain has completely broken down. In pursuance of this aim they have launched a sort of a reign of terror, i.e. short of physical violence, although we know of at least one prisoner who was actually beaten up. Just to give you a picture you must bear in mind—I shall refer to the single cells as our section; the bulk of the political prisoners are in the "Big" section or general cells. Then there is "our quarry," i.e. the lime quarry where we work; and the "big quarry," i.e. the stone quarry where the big section's chaps work. It is clear that the whole onslaught has been well planned with the fullest connivance of Pretoria. The kick off was about three weeks ago. When the chaps arrived at work at the big quarry, they found that all their improvised seats (for which they had received permission from the previous administration) had been taken and burnt. The chaps sought an immediate interview with the higher ups. In the meantime they stopped working. To the best of my knowledge they are still not working though they are taken out to work daily. The 5-man delegation appointed to see the authorities were summarily taken and locked up in our section, which is the isolation section. Of course, though in our section, they are in their own wing and are isolated from us as well. When the authorities refused to see them, they, together with 5 others who had already been previously isolated, went on a hunger strike, which lasted for 4 1/2 days. The authorities just did not budge. When they eventually resumed eating, each of them was seen by the Colonel, who arbitrarily downgraded them one group, and five of the ten were sent back to the big section. This more or less ended this episode.

In the big section tension continued to rise as the prisoners faced one provocation after another. On Monday, while on their way to work, the authorities felt they were walking too slowly and they set the dogs upon them. Four prisoners were bitten, one of whom I believe has been hospitalised. This naturally incensed the population and, since Wednesday, all the prisoners in the big section have been on hunger strike. Today is Saturday and I believe they are still on. For various reasons our section has not joined in yet. But by the looks of things we will not be able to keep out of action much longer. Incidentally, the first big hunger strike of the Island took place in 1966 when the whole jail, including us, came out. Again last July all of us took part in a similar strike which lasted 3 days.

It seems we have entered a period of intensive provocation and repression which will require tremendous patience, careful planning and bold action. They have brought the most backward group of officials to "discipline" us, men of the old school who have not the slightest ideas of their own reputedly "progressive" thought on penology. The younger lot, just graduating from warders training college, at least talk of rehabilitation and many of them seem sincere. But, as for this lot, they only know one thing and that is revenge and constant punishment. Every moment the prisoner must be made to feel that he is in jail. For this they use all sorts of pinpricks. In our section, for instance, since 1967, we've been allowed to spend the whole day in the court yard over weekends. Now this has been cut, and we are locked in our individual cells for lunch, which is 3 hours. Then they are now restricting our letters to 500 words. Such petty little things. The Colonel also turned up to our quarry and, finding no work going on, demoted the chaps one group. Luckily, I was not at work that day, so I am still "C." He has made known that he does not believe in charging us. He will use other methods, like taking away our privileges. For instance, we are no longer allowed to play games during lunch at work. They have also taken away the long trousers and jerseys from the chaps in the big section, even from the old and sickly. This is terrible; especially the last winter has been severe. In fact, we still have cold days.

So, you see, we have a tremendous task ahead of us. It has been relatively easy to educate and even rehabilitate the younger warders. But it is not going to be so smooth for this lot. However, we are in good spirits and prepared for the attacks. We've been through worse days, and I am confident we will weather the storm.

The worst attack so far has been on our studies. They have now forced us to surrender for storage all books relating to subjects we have already finished. For instance, I've had to give up all my history, anthropology, politics, and other books. We are not even allowed to keep Shakespeare, or poetry or even our Xhosa or German books. We are told if anything is found in our cells which is not pertinent to our present studies, we are liable to lose the privilege.

. . . the portions . . . which deal with life here may be of interest to other friends. But as long as no part of it is given to the press.

1971—1980

~ ~ ~

Solly Kathrada—*26 March 1972*

This is one of Ahmed Kathrada's most moving, touching, and eloquent letters. In it, he describes learning of his mother's death. He hopes that somehow "this spectre (of death) will be kept away from one's near and dear ones. . . . Yet when the blow strikes the faculties are numbed and one reacts with all the emotions that are normal to human beings. . . ." He reminisces about his childhood when, at the age of eight, he had to leave home to attend school 200 miles away. In Schweizer Reneke, there was a school for African children and one for white children but none for "Indian" children. The laws demanded strict segregation, even for the young, so the only school he could attend was the one in Fordsburg, Johannesburg. The teachers finding him to be academically well above the other children moved him from Grade I to Grade II. Instead of the usual one year per class, he completed Grade II in three months. In 1939 he completed two grades in one year. By this time, at the age of 11, when most of his peers were playing soccer and cricket, he was already active in politics, handing out leaflets. In 1946 he was in his final year in high school. In June of that year, Kathrada left school to work full-time in the offices of the Passive Resistance Council. In December 1946, Kathrada was jailed for one month for taking part in the Passive Resistance Campaign. One of his teachers and a role model, Mervyth Thandray, himself a stalwart in the struggle, was among those arrested, so pupil and teacher walked triumphantly into prison. As Kathrada points out, visits home after this were few and far between. (The translation of the Afrikaans note written by a prison authority reads: "A letter to his brother in connection with the death of his mother.")

~

To Solly Kathrada. 26.3.72
26th March 1972
[Marked at top: "DEATH, *S/Brief aan Broer i[n] v[erband met] afsterwe van sy moeder.*"]

My Dear folks,
On Friday 24th March at about 4:30 p.m. I was called to the office and informed that Ma had passed away. Unfortunately the telegram has not yet arrived so I do not know any details, but I assume she never recovered from the illness with which she was afflicted earlier this year. In her letter of 1st Feb. Zohra mentioned that Ma was in hospital and that her condition was causing anxiety. I wrote back to her on 7th Feb. and to Behn's Farouk (via Nassim) on 10th March and asked them to keep me informed. Although I had not heard again from anyone, I was already mentally prepared for the worst. Thanks to Zohra, the shock of the news was not so great.

Nevertheless it is not possible to condition oneself fully for death. Deep in the recesses of the mind there always flickers a hope that somehow this spectre will be kept away from one's near and dear ones. One has reasoned and convinced oneself that one day it has to come; yet when the blow strikes, the faculties are numbed and one reacts with all the emotion that is normal to human beings.

Of all our family I have spent the least time with Ma. In 1938, when I was just a little over 8 years old, I left home to attend school in Johannesburg. Until about 1946 I used to spend the school holidays at home. Some of you will recall the earlier years how unsuccessfully I tried to hide my feelings each time I had to return to JHB[1] after the holidays. Mine must have been the normal reaction of a child who is wrenched away from its parents at so tender an age in order to attend school over 200 miles away. From 1946 my visits became shorter and less frequent. Then came my accident,[2] the overseas trip, the return, the arrests, court cases, police raids, bannings, house arrest. I'm sure each of these must

---

[1] Johannesburg.

[2] In 1947, on the eve of his departure to Prague to attend the World Federation of Democratic Youth, he was knocked down by a motor cyclist, suffered a broken leg, and was in a plaster cast for 14 months. The motor cycle was the kind used only by the police force—the type with a side car attached.

have caused Ma tremendous anxiety and sorrow. I'll never forget how she collapsed that day in June 1961 when I was brought home under escort on my way to Christiana[3] jail. How happy she was for the few months in 1962 when I was free from bans and came home a good few times. But alas, the respite was too short. In Oct. came the house arrest; a few months later I disappeared from home, and then came the Rivonia arrests, which ended in the life sentences. I last saw her about 10 years ago. In jail I have often reflected over the fact that I have been a constant source of worry and trouble to Ma and to all of you. I have lived with a slight feeling of guilt and have thought of ways and means of making good. But now Ma has been removed from us and I've been deprived of the opportunity. I do, however, find some consolation from the fact that all of you, more particularly her many grandchildren, and now the great-grandchildren, more than made up for my absence.

We have always been a close-knit family, and our attachment to one another and to Ma has therefore been greater. Consequently, we will all feel her loss a lot more. Yet we realise that the procession of life moves on. While we honour, remember and always commemorate the dead, we have to think of the present and the future—of the living, especially the young ones. We must continue to behave to one another and to remain as a whole in a manner which would have made Ma happy. That would be the best way of honouring her memory.

All my colleagues here, especially Mr. Mandela and Mr. Sisulu, have asked to convey their deepest sympathy.

Love to all of you, from,

AMK

≈ ≈ ≈

Zivia Shaban—12 May 1973

Cut off from the world and not allowed newspapers, it was not easy to keep abreast of what was happening beyond the shores of Robben Island. Kathrada, always keenly interested in social changes, writes to this young lady, the daughter of his good friends, Rose and Barney Desai. He reminisces about the "good old days" in Cape Town with Barney and all his friends. It is interesting to note that the censors let slip his mentioning by name Nelson (Mandela), Walter

---

[3] A town near to where his mother lived.

(Sisulu), Esu (Chiba), Billy (Nair)—all political prisoners on the Island. He is on his second Bachelors degree but has given up trying to play the melodica, a venture that for him ended "ignominiously." Kathrada realized that his talents lay elsewhere. Barney being an activist, Kathrada was not permitted to write directly to him. By writing to Zivia, he knows, however, that Barney will be given an opportunity to read the letter.

~

To Zivia Shaban. 12.5.73
Robben Island Prison
12th May 1973

My Dear Zivia,

I'm sure this is going to be a big surprise. A letter from Robben Island and from someone you'd never remember. I last saw you—and your mom and dad for that matter—on 19th August 1962. (I remember it because it was Mom's birthday and two days before mine). Isn't that a good reason to remember? Besides, mine is on the same day as Princess Margaret's. Which fills me with "pride"! Anyway, that Sunday 19th was a very rainy day, and my late friend "Oosie" and I were due to leave back for home. So Daddy suggested we should have our farewell lunch at home. (This lunch started about elevenish and ended about 4). Mummy and Daddy will remember I was accompanied by Oosie, a lady friend Selma, and of course Uncle Ebrahim was there and I think Uncle Aggie. I'll never forget because we just kept on eating, and I'm sure cleaned out the pantry.

Now you could hardly have been six then, could you? So all I have in my mind is a picture of a sweet and shy little lady. Now for the life of me, I just cannot remember your little brother's name. And since then, I believe the family has increased a bit. Wait a bit. I think I've remembered. Is it not Rashan? or something pretty like it?

I have long been promising myself to write to you folks. At the same time I've harboured a slight hope that I'd hear a word or two from Daddy—even if only on a Xmas card. About a year and a half ago, I wrote to Uncle Abe but did not receive an acknowledgement. I assumed the two of them were still closely in touch and I'd hear a bit about you all. Incidentally, I understand Daddy has also followed Abe's footsteps—professionwise?[1] I'm sure he'll be most successful. Remind him of the night he visited me in Bloemfontein police cells. He was most impressive and

---

[1] The legal profession. Abe Gani was a lawyer and friend.

"spirited." The authorities he quoted were not eventually upheld, but I got off nevertheless–on other grounds.

Now why have I chosen to write to you–and not to Daddy or Mommy? I'm sure you'll be anxious to know. It is simple. You know on 11th July it will be 10 years since our arrest. And that means I'm ten years older, which takes me well into the mid-forties. At this age one not only starts feeling age creeping up, but one tends to lose so much of the trends, the developments, the thoughts, and hopes and desires of young people. And how much more so in jail! We keep on hearing of youth problems, youth unrest, youth movements, youth breaking with tradition and losing their roots. We hear of hippies, flower children, "long hair"— a seemingly general rebellion against custom and the "good old ways." We hear of the "generation gap" and of attempts to come to grips with the consequent problems. Now all this makes one feel older and also not altogether guiltless of the issues. I'm merely trying to establish some rapport with teenagers, to come to know them better, to try to see the world through their eyes. I'd like to know more about you, your studies, your interests, your friends and teachers, etc.

Of course I also wish to know more about Daddy and Mummy. You just can't believe how very cut off one is in jail no matter how near the mainland we are. At odd times I've heard about Daddy—but very little. About two years ago I heard he was thinking of settling in Canada. I do know also of the estrangement—which hurt me very much. For some years I just did not believe it and still try to dismiss it as a passing phase. I wonder if he still remembers the "sundowners" the two of us had one evening at the Tafelberg? He opened his heart to me as seldom before, made speculations, sought assurances. I'm sure for both of us it was an eventful evening. What went wrong thereafter? To some extent I can guess. As much as I know his ability, his erudition, his indomitable ties, his sense of humour, so too I can imagine some of his frustrations, disillusionment and disappointment. But did it warrant such a major casus belli? as to cause dissonance and divorce? Of course from the little information at my disposal, I cannot pass judgement. After all, it is a delicate, personal matter, and my interference would be out of place. Anyhow, I can just hope all will be patched up again; and when I see you one day, it will be all as before.

I have to end now. I wonder if Daddy still remembers a trip to Signal Hill in 1962 together with a writer from U.K.? He pointed to the Island and said to our companion, "There's Kathy's future home." How prophetic! I also remember the Friday night "bull sessions" in the coombies.[2] Where is Uncle Ebrahim? I hear nothing of Aggie either. And the old gentleman with the other coombie? I forget his name. In retrospect I thought those sessions to be somewhat strange—what with so many facilities—but they were enjoyable. Is Housein still in U.K. I hear he is married and announced the birth of a baby in the *Times*. How very English but very Houseinlike. As some garment workers once told Abe & Housein—"*Julle misters het te veel dignity*."[3] It was in Jo'burg.

Just yesterday we were talking about the real "Passionaria,"[4] who inspired your name, or at least part of it. Is she still in good health?

I'm keeping well—in fact all of us are—some of whom Daddy might know or might have met at my flat—Nelson, Walter, Esu, Billy, etc. Also in top spirits. I suppose Daddy knows I managed to complete B.A. in 1968 and am now busy with B. Bibliography. I've 4 courses to go. Also managed to do a bit of German & Xhosa—but very little. Dabbled a bit with the melodica, but the venture ended ignominiously. Just haven't the right genes.

Goodbye, keep well. My love to you and to all others we know. Write soon. All the best from—AMK.

P.S. I'm writing this through Tommy because I haven't your address. All I know is: Miss Zivia Shaban, Rissik St., London.

Mrs. Neville Alexander—*16 February 1975*

A thank you note to Dr. Neville Alexander's mother for her card and kind thoughts. Kathrada cannot mention Neville by name as he was a former political prisoner on Robben Island.

---

[2] A coombie is similar to a mini van. It could seat between 6 and 8 people and was very popular in this period.

[3] Translation: "You gentlemen suffer from too much dignity."

[4] La Passionaria, the Spanish revolutionary who settled in the Soviet Union in the early 1900s.

A. M. Kathrada,
Robben Island Prison
16th February 1975

Dear Mrs. Alexander,

This is to thank you for your Christmas card and the kind thoughts expressed therein. We had our usual end-of-the-year festivities and our thoughts went out to all of you.

I hope you and the children are all keeping well. I am getting along fine. I have just finished writing the last course for the B. Bibliography and am awaiting results.

Thank you very much once more for your wishes.

All the best to you and the family.

From

AM Kathrada

≈   ≈   ≈

Sonia Bunting—*16 February 1975*

Kathrada was obliged, at times, to send letters to family members via his niece, Zohra Kathrada. This letter to Sonia Bunting is one example. Sonia was co-accused with Kathrada in a 1956 treason trial; like so many others, she was forced into exile. Now in London, with her husband, Brian, she was a part of an exile community that continued to carry on the Struggle. She lives in London and in this letter Kathrada writes about the music he likes and has come to like and he regales her with a description of their garden and the gardeners.

≈

A. M. Kathrada,
Robben Island Prison
16th February 1975

My Dear Sonia,

You can't imagine what a lovely surprise it was for me to receive your letter (which arrived on 25th January). As I'm writing this the daily music program is going on (5 pm–8 pm). We started off the afternoon with Nat King Cole, who is still quite a hit with many of us. Then a few minutes ago we had Miriam Makeba and Harry Belafonte. Just now he is singing "There's a Hole in the Bucket." In a while he will be singing "Hava nagila" (I hope the spelling's right) and then "Silvie," who brought him "a little coffee and a little tea. She brought me nearly every damned thing but she didn't bring the jailhouse key." What a treat. And Miriam still sends us. We had been cut off from music for some years. And when it started we were met with a barrage of pop stuff and for sometime we didn't know what hit us. It all sounded like one hell of a big noise, and I was imprudent enough to say so. But alas I had to retract for after a little while this noise—or at least some of it—managed to insinuate itself into my system. And I quite unashamedly started looking forward to Mardi Gras, Johnny and others, much to the annoyance of our culture vultures. Let me leave this. I can already hear some dainty English ladies shocked by such talk. By the way, the prisoners have about 250 L.Ps—some very good. We have to wait for weeks & weeks to listen to Robeson or the Cossack Choir or a good Indian record.

I don't know what I can tell you that will be new to you. Oh heavens! We have just descended to the ridiculous—Ge Korsten has just come over the rediffusion. What a bore. Never mind, it will be 1 pm just now, and silence.

We're so advanced into the new year already and it's useless my writing about our annual games competition. For the past couple of years, however, there has been a new feature, viz. a play reading. This year the chaps did Jean Anouilh's *Antigone*. It was very enjoyable. I don't think you'd know the participants, except for Nelson, who was Creon. He more than made up for his dethronement as the domino champion of 1973.

Let me tell you about our little garden. It is about a year old. Come into the courtyard any morning and you're sure to witness the daily inspection, mostly by our little Indian community. (They're the chief gardeners). They'd walk along the patch, give a glance in the direction of the dozen or so flowers, make a few appropriate remarks about the effect of the south easter on tomatoes—then the next time you look, they'd be clustered around a modest little plant and be engaged in animated discussion. Out comes the ruler, crepe bandage, string, sticks, label and ballpoint. The innocent onlooker surveying the scene and the actors would easily conclude that it's just Chiba and his economics class. But you go nearer and find no economics or any other class. It is the orientals gauging the maturation (or otherwise) of the chili plant. This explains the ungardenlike tools. For they'd measure every millimeter of its growth and make some record on a yellow label suspended from the neck of the chili. Some weeks ago it reached the size of a marble—then it just stopped growing. After numerous confabs our friends announced that it's a variety that does not grow any bigger. So they plucked half a dozen and cut them up into the salad. The community sighed a sigh of relief that only half a dozen were available. Otherwise the only consumers of the salad would have been the half a dozen Indians. The chilies were mighty powerful.

It's wonderful to read of Arnold's progress and that of his brothers. This was the first and only letter received from you, so everything contained therein was news to us. I didn't even know that Peter was married. Congrats to him and Audrey and to you on being grandma. Hope you've had a nice trip to Canada. What you say about the position of education in UK, France, etc., gives me a lot to think about. How is this general waywardness to be characterised?

I have to end now. I'm keeping very well and in good spirits. And so are the others. I was writing exams till Friday, hence the delay in replying. It was my last subject, and if I get through, I complete the B. Bibliography. Thereafter I shall take it easy. I am sending this via my niece in Jo'burg and suggest you do likewise. Pity I could only get these three points from your letter. Lots of love to you and everybody else from.

AMK

~ ~ ~

Choti and Ismail—*28 March 1975*

A letter to a South African couple living in Canada. Kathrada had lived outside South Africa for a year and got terribly homesick and returned only to be jailed a short time afterwards. He had the choice to go into exile but he refused. Jail for him is preferable to exile and he believes that one day he and his colleagues will play a role again in South Africa. Canada became home to a large number of South African Indians, most of whom settled in Ontario. He inquires about life in Canada and asks about various friends. Aggie Patel, the father of his godchild, Shireen, is also in Canada, and Kathrada wishes to be

remembered to him. He has successfully completed his second degree and hopes
to start another.

⁓

A. M. Kathrada
Robben Island Prison
28th March 1975

My Dear Choti and Ismail,

I should really say, "Hi," shouldn't I? I was very pleased to receive
your 5-page letter in February. You really gave a good picture of your life
in Canada, and it was really worth waiting for the reply. I was surprised
to see that you actually received my letter in 1968 for the reports from
home indicated that it had been misplaced and never posted.

I can imagine how homesick you must be. Long ago I was away from
South Africa for only a year, and I felt so nostalgic and longed for home
so I rushed back. And I landed in jail within a few months of my return,
but I wasn't sorry. Even before the Rivonia arrest in 1963 some folks
insisted that I leave the country. But I was stubborn and refused. And
here am I doing a life sentence. Am I sorry now that I did not go away?
No, I am not one bit sorry. It is not nice to be in jail, and already we
have been inside for almost 12 years. But I had to choose between the
life of an exile and going underground. I knew I could be caught one
day. I have read a little about the life of exiles and have also heard from
friends. I think in some ways I'm better off here. The poet Milton wrote,
"They also serve who stand and wait." That is in some ways applicable
to us.

Is it impossible to get South African citizenship for Yusuf? Alternatively,
can you bring him on a visit? I'm sure your father and mother would love
to see him. Does he speak any Gujerati at all? He seems to be a proper little Canadian. Incidentally, he and I share the same birthday month—only
40 years and a few days difference! How lovely it must be to see him play
ice hockey and to watch his reactions to the T.V. programs.

With the cost of living so high, I'm surprised you can still afford to
have T.V. Do you have money left over for clothing and food? Can you
go for holidays? Have you been to America? Choti, can you still cook
Indian dishes or have you switched over to Western food?

Yes, it is lovely in the snow. I saw snow for the first time in my life
when I was in Hungary. It was fascinating, and I just stood and looked

at it for hours. In fact I was with a Canadian friend, Ben Shek. He used to live in Toronto. I introduced Bibi [Miriam's niece] to him when she first went over in 1961 or 1962. By the way, where is she?

Thanks for telling me about the local friends who have settled there. Do the South Africans ever get together at social functions as they do in England? When you meet any of them, please pass my fondest regards. Tell Aggie I had a lovely letter from his daughter, Shireen. She said she and her mother were planning to visit me. I often think of him and Bapuji, especially when it is sundown. I'd love to hear about Bis and Joan. Has Bis specialized? You know he stayed at the flat until he qualified? Yes, I do remember Dr. Miriam Vania. She once scolded us terribly at some function; thereafter I was always a bit scared of her. Is Hamid in business? Have you met a new arrival, Dr. Raman Mavjee? If you do see him, please thank him and Lilian for the gift subscription to "Ring." And Fatima Dollie? I believe she too has settled there. Please remember me to Behn & Dawood, Ahmed Bhabha, Miriam & Ebrahim, Hafsa & Ahmed, Bree Bulbulia, Don Mooljee, Solly Boorani and his wife, and all other friends. Also to Boetie's sister-in-law, Farida, and her hubby. It would be nice one day to visit Canada and be among so many friends and relatives.

I had a nice visit from Ismailmota and Unus a little while ago. They said all the folks at home were well. I especially asked about your father and mother. I was happy to hear he is free to move about again. I also had a lovely Eid card last year from Sarah and Fowzia. Uncle Amien was trying to visit me this weekend but didn't pitch up.

My health is fine. About a month ago I broke my little finger while playing volleyball. It's a small injury but a nuisance. I'll have to wait until it heals before I can play again. I'm actually a learner but am quite fond of the game.

I received my final results last week. I managed to get through. So now I've completed the Bachelor of Bibliography. I'm not going to tackle another degree. This year I've registered for only one course, Ancient History, just to help while away the time. There are so many books I still want to read.

We're having a spell of lovely weather—Cape Town will have a glorious Easter weekend. As for us, our Easter is like any other day in jail.

I'm going to end now. Keep well, and do write once in a while. Lots of love to Choti, Yusuf and yourself from

AMK

~ ~ ~

Ruth and Ilse Fischer—*11 May 1975*

This is a letter of sympathy to Ruth and Ilse Fischer on the death of their father, Advocate Bram Fischer. It is a moving tribute to the great person he was. His wife, Molly, who was also a wonderful human being, had died tragically in 1964 when their car plunged into a river. Of the countless people who sacrificed their lives for a better South Africa, Bram Fischer has to rank as one of the country's heroes. For Kathrada, he was "my fellow countryman, my mentor, my comrade, my lawyer, my co-prisoner, my friend." After Kathrada was sentenced to life imprisonment, Bram Fischer went underground to continue the struggle but was captured and sentenced to life imprisonment for conspiracy to commit sabotage. On humanitarian grounds, Bram, suffering from cancer, was released to his brother's house where he died in 1975. "In many ways, Bram Fischer, the grandson of the Prime Minister of the Orange River Colony, had made the greatest sacrifice of all. No matter what I suffered in my pursuit of freedom, I always took strength from the fact that I was fighting with and for my own people. Bram was a free man who fought against his own people to ensure the freedom of others." Long Walk to Freedom, Nelson Mandela.

~

A. M. Kathrada
Robben Island Prison
11th May 1975

My Dear Ruth and Ilse,

For the third time in the last decade death has struck and removed a beloved member of your family. We had only been on the Island about a fortnight in 1964 when we received the shocking news of your mother's death. A few years ago Paul breathed his last. And now, your dad. You have been cruelly singled out for tragedy to strike its harsh and relentless blows—almost as if to test your power of endurance. I am well aware that words can do little to lessen the impact of such irreparable loss. But I'm writing, nevertheless, in the hope that knowledge of shared grief will somehow help to bring a little bit of comfort at this dark hour.

To you Bram was father, the kindest and very best that any child could wish for. But he also meant so much for so many people throughout our country and, indeed, all over the world. Literally millions will, therefore, grieve at his passing.

South Africa could ill afford to lose him for he was a great patriot and statesman, rich in wisdom, selfless, fearless and determined in leadership. To the legal fraternity he brought brilliance, lustre and distinction. To his political colleagues he showed the path of courage, clarity and undying hope. To the prisoner he reenacted the well-established maxim that the road to light and progress traverses through the darkness of prison walls. To humanity at large he gave of his abundant love, his charm, his unequalled modesty, quiet dignity and disinterestedness. Bram possessed in profusion all the elements that go to make a perfect human being.

In all these capacities I lovingly remember and honour him—my fellow countryman, my mentor, my comrade, my lawyer, my co-prisoner, my friend. It is above all as a human being that he will forever stand out in my memory. His stature and eminence in all other fields stem essentially from his greatness as a human being. For this he enjoyed the love and respect, devotion and admiration of everyone.

Innumerable are the incidents and events that spring to mind relating to Molly and Bram since I first met them way back, I think, in 1944. I was fifteen and enthusiastic with almost four years of "political involvement" behind me. It was at an age when one sought and attached oneself to one's own brand of heroes. Already looming large in my horizon was Yusuf Dadoo. He was soon joined, among others, by Bram and Molly! They made a big impression in my little mind, and my childish heart responded with a love that only children know how to give. I went with Bram to Pietersburg in 1946, and in 1947 I went with Molly to Potchefstroom. Every minute that I was in their company I was bursting with pride. This was the beginning of a personal relationship which grew with the passage of years. And with it grew my love and respect and admiration. How I looked forward to being with them again after this incarceration is over. But, alas, death has snatched them both away. It has caused me deep hurt and left a huge void in my life.

Yet I dare not allow myself to give way to despair, dejection or disillusionment. That would be disobedient to the wishes of Bram and Molly. Sorrow I cannot help, but mingled with it is the overpowering feeling of richness, pride and gratitude at having been privileged to be so closely associated with them. If I could but emulate, to the slightest degree, their exemplary lives, their goodness, warmth and love of humanity, their generosity, their confidence and tireless contribution towards the attainment of our common ideals, I shall have paid my tribute to two of the most wonderful people I have known.

Lots of love and good wishes to you, Ruth and Ilse, and to all relatives and friends from

AMK

≈ ≈ ≈

Raman Chiba—*20 September 1975*

Raman was the younger brother of Isu Chiba, who was serving an 18-year sentence on the Island. Raman was part of the circle of friends who would meet regularly when Isu and Kathrada were still free. In this letter Kathrada reminds Raman of the time when, while at Mrs. Chalmers' shebeen, in a moment of devilment Raman removed the front gate as a joke. The gate was later returned, but remained an in-joke for many years. This is one of the few occasions where Kathrada sounds a low note about being behind bars. "The years roll by very quickly—it's the minutes and hours that go rather slowly. After 12 years they can now have hot showers and Isu has been promoted to Group 'A,' with the privileges that that brings." Kathrada was the last to get to Group "A," and that would be after thirteen years. We learn, too, of Kathrada's tastes in music and sport and his likes and dislikes, usually motivated by his political beliefs, so that people like Mohammed Ali, Harry Belafonte, Joan Baez, etc., would be held in high esteem. Canada was a popular destination for people who chose to leave South Africa and Kathrada inquires about some who settled there.

≈

A. M. Kathrada
Robben Island Prison
20th September 1975

My Dear Lilian and Raman,

This morning I read your letters to Isu and was pleased to see that you and the kids have settled down nicely in your new environment. South Africans seem to find it easy to adapt to the Canadian way of life. Of course kids should have little difficulty, save perhaps for the weather. Lovely how Ramesh and Maya are progressing at school. I must say right now I wouldn't mind a loan of a couple of coupons from Ramesh in order to savour a morsel of hamburger, with fried onions and sauce. And wouldn't it enhance the Saturday if there were suitable provisions from the Gaza Strip, or Mrs. Chalmers![1] Provided of course some of us could leave the good lady's gate alone.

I read somewhere that the years roll by very quickly in jail—it's the minutes and the hours that go rather slowly. There is much truth in this statement. I could hardly believe it when I checked and realised that you've been away over a year already. Yet reckoned in terms of the thousands of minutes and hour upon hour of monotonous dull routine that go to make jail life, what a colossal age it seems! From a distance the mere thought of such a life seems prohibitive. But once in it one finds that adaptation, both physical and mental, comes quite easily. Of course, with the passage of years there has been the steady improvement of conditions, in certain respects that have helped make life less difficult. Just to take a few things at random. This year, for the first time in 12 years, we've been provided with hot showers; twice we have eaten guavas; Isu has been promoted to "A" group, which enables him to buy some chocolates, coffee, sugar, cocoa, etc., each month; small things all, but they make a big difference. Then we've seen some good films: *The Godfather, The Great Escape, Lion in Winter*, etc.; we've been thrilled to be able to get a glimpse of Mohammed Ali trouncing "that flag-waving nigger," albeit only through the columns of the disgracefully anti-Ali "Ring." Then we have our studies, sports, music, etc. But best of all are the letters, the visits, the cards from our folks. This afternoon we had a couple of rubbers of bridge with Isu. Just now we've been listening to Nat King Cole, only to be spoilt by Sinatra. We also have about a dozen Indian records. Let's hope tomorrow we'll have some Belafonte, Joan Baez, Nancy Ames, etc. Some of what I have mentioned above will make you realise how much you have contributed towards making things easier for us. You have the thanks of all of us.

It is so good to hear about Behn and other friends. Do you come across Miriam & Ebe, Fati, Aggi, Hamid, Bis, and other friends? Did you manage to contact Ben Shek? When you see any of them, please pass my fondest regards.

---

[1] The Gaza Strip and Mrs. Chalmers, two shebeens, or illegal drinking houses. It was only in 1962 that legislation was passed making the consumption of alcohol legal for non-whites in the Transvaal. Prior to this time, shebeens flourished and functioned as social meeting places. Kathrada has long since given up drinking. In fact, has not taken a drink since 1963.

I should like you to please send me some information and advice about medical studies in Canada. A young relative of mine interrupted his medical studies on the eve of his third year final exams and is interested in continuing in a couple of years' time. He was at Wits. Please send information about admission, recognition of degree in S.A., will he have to start all over again?, costs, possibilities of scholarship, etc.

This will be all for today. We're getting along fine. You know of course of Isu's ulcers, pyorrhea and arthritis. But all of these seem to be under control, except for the gum trouble. He'll most probably be sent to a specialist soon. We're both taking it a bit easy with studies. I managed to complete the B. Bibliography. I'm only doing Ancient History this year. Next year I'll do Archaeology and Communication. All for non-degree purposes.

Keep well. Lots of love to you, Ramesh and Maya, and to all friends.

From

AMK

≈ ≈ ≈

George Peake—22 November 1975

"Tajoo" is the code name for George Peake, former prisoner and one of the 156 in the Treason Trial. The references to "sport" are really inquiries about the different political groups of the day. "Your team" is a reference to the African National Congress and the "Endstreeters" is the generic term for all congresses. End Street is where Dr. Dadoo lived. The Trotters are the Trotskyites. Kathrada cannot mention former prisoners, banned people, or people known to the police so he uses code names again. "Dangor" and "Nana Muhamed" are the Pan African Congress, and he asks George if he has joined this organization. While on the subject of political organizations, Kathrada wants to know which group another old friend, Barney Desai ("Kader"), might have joined. He asks about other political friends originally from the Cape: May and Dennis Brutus (Maymuna and Dawood) and Alec and Blanche La Guma (Ally and Bilkis). He inquires about "Lalloo" (Lionel Morrison and his sister Sheila, who had taught at the school opened by the Congress to thwart the forced removal of Indians to Lenasia). He has heard from George about "Aunt Waldiya," the World Federation of Democratic Youth (WFDY), and "Ganis" (The International Union of Students). These bring back happy memories of when Kathrada went to WFDY in Berlin. In describing a movie we learn that even the worst movie is "a diversion" and for a group that has been together for

over eleven years, day in and day out, any addition, including the film he described as "junk," can likely become the topic for a lively discussion. As a safety measure he suggests George reply via his niece.

∼

A. M. Kathrada,
Robben Island Jail
22 November 1975

My Dear Tajoo,

Your letter, which arrived on 8th November, was one of the most pleasant surprises of 1975 or shall I say of the decade? I hope it was the herald of many more surprises and not necessarily confined to letters. It is Saturday afternoon about 5 p.m. We've long had supper. I'm sitting in my cell (which by the way I've occupied continuously since 6th April 1965) and settling down to a pleasant evening of letter-writing. There is light music over the rediffusion, my mind is a whirl of reminiscences, wishes, hopes, and thoughts which I want to share with you. Where do I begin? I don't know how much you've been able to gather about us, and I want to avoid boring you with repetition. I take it you have heard of the studies, the sports, music, magazines, food, work, letters, cards, visits and other things that help fill our lives, and make the days less intolerable. Oh yes, and the fortnightly films. We saw a western this morning. Real junk. But most of us sat through it. At least it's a diversion, and it adds to the ever-contracting list of topics on which to voice our opinions. You can imagine how important this is. We are only 30 in our section and most of us have been together day in and day out for over 11 years! During this time we've talked of almost everything one can think of. And any addition is welcome. Needless to tell you, you have featured quite often, especially among the folks you met at my flat. For believe it or not, most of us have now acquired an interest in sports. We keenly follow both local and overseas games, boxing, soccer, rugby, cricket, etc. In fact we've been arguing about your team. I feel certain that, even if you had left them for a time, you are now back with the Endstreeters. Others claim you are with Dangor, Nana Muhamed and the mob. Someone even heard that you were playing for the Trotters 4th team. For whom is Kader [Rustum's father] playing now? Or is he too busy with his practice? Someone mentioned that he was present at Aminabai's commemoration. I haven't heard for ages about Maymuna and her hubby Dawood and their 7 or 8 kids. Is he still lecturing. And Ally (Libby) and his wife Bilkis? I last met him in 1962 at a party at Mom's. Remember Sheila who was teaching at our school in Fordsburg?[1] Is her brother Lalloo still abroad? There are so many others I'd like to know about, but I think this will do for the time being. It was lovely to hear about Veronica. I'm sure she's as charming and nice as ever. Give her my love. Where is Felicity, her mum? How wonderful to hear of Aunt Waldiya. It set me thinking of the pleasant time I spent at her home. I'm afraid I'm not certain if I can place Ganis. Unless it is Waldiya's student brother? It is so long ago.

This year I only enrolled for one subject—Ancient History. I wrote the exams on Thursday. I'm a bit tired of studies. You know I first enrolled in 1965 and except for two years when I was deprived of studies, I've been writing exams every year. So from now on I'm going to take it easy, doing one subject a year for non-degree purposes. Next year I'll do Archaeology. I was fortunate in managing to complete B.A. and B. Bibliography.

Healthwise I've been keeping fit on the whole. About 3 weeks ago I suddenly developed pain in the back and the next thing I was flat out for a few days. Unfortunately I did not allow it to heal completely with the result that I had another attack this week. I'm now going to take it easy for a while. The doctor thought it was probably a strained muscle. Anyway it's not serious.

This is all for today. Let me end with best wishes for the festive season and for a happy New Year. Lots of love to you and all friends & relatives.

Yours sincerely,

AMK

≈ ≈ ≈

Tom Vassen—*22 November 1975*

Letters from London were invaluable in keeping the Robben Island prisoners informed. In this letter to Tom Vassen in London, Kathrada mentions two major sports where politics play a big role. Sports played an important part in the lives

---

[1] When the apartheid government closed one of the two high schools for Indians in Johannesburg, as a way of forcing the Indians to their group area, Lenasia, Kathrada became the prime mover in opening the Central Indian High School in Fordsburg, which would be funded entirely by the local people and in defiance of the government. This was a huge success initially and was known fondly as "the Congress School." Kathrada was its first secretary.

of most South Africans and, as the country became more isolated, the arrival
of any team from abroad willing to break the boycott and play in South Africa
gave a certain respectability to the apartheid regime. For example, in 1990, an
English cricket team broke the boycott and went to South Africa. The pro-gov-
ernment S.A. Cricket Union was delighted, while the anti-apartheid S.A.
Cricket Board did everything in its power to scuttle the tour. Kathrada's
humorous description of Isu Chiba and his team of gardeners going out in the
morning armed with rulers, ballpoint pens, labels, and other instruments is very
typical of Isu. But this type of activity was important because it provided a cre-
ative pastime and a productive one at that. The chameleon story shows how
caring the prisoners were to young and defenseless creatures and perhaps these
young chameleons, in a way, made up for the absence of young people. Their
presence certainly became the subject for lengthy discussions.

∼

Robben Island Jail
22nd November 1975

My Dear Tom,

Well, you've done it this time. Even before my niece from Jo'burg could
inform me that she had forwarded your letter on 18th October, I already
get a reply from you—all the way from London. What shall we ascribe this
to? I'm hesitant to put it down to your newfound abstemiousness (or
abstinence?), for then we would have to compare your record at the time
when you were still a votary of Bacchus. Anyway, whatever it is that drove
you to such promptness, let us hope you shall continue to be influenced
by that force. I suppose it will surprise you to know that the first time I
learned of Tootsie's visit was when you mentioned it. In the early years
Amien, Nassim, etc., used to keep in touch, but now their correspondence has been reduced to birthday and Xmas cards. Do you know that
we are unable to get a clear picture of Federation soccer and S.A. Cricket
Board, etc. The few who do write are unfortunately not interested in
sports and similar activities. Hence the importance of regular letters from
you with wide coverage of the visiting, social and cultural fields. Have you
perchance got any inside information about the events in the Danish
night club that led to Billy Bremner's suspension from Scottish football?
It seems they've been a bit too harsh with him. By the way, thanks for your
offer to subscribe to an international soccer journal. I hope we'll start
receiving copies soon.

I'm very proud to learn of your and Harry's culinary achievements and would like to believe that my contribution towards the early training was not absent. Though some cynics would insist that the main contribution came via the inspiration of Chagan. We've got a little garden patch here which has yielded, according to Isu's statistics, about 2,000 chilies, close on to 1,000 tomatoes, a few radishes, onions, sweet melons (about 6) and 2 watermelons. It was good to see Isu and his fellow gardeners trooping out each morning with rulers, ballpoints, labels and other instruments and carefully taking measurements and making copious notes. One day he even got me to count tomato seeds if you please! Nowadays the garden is Nelson's baby, and he is fanatical about it. As expected, he has read everything he could lay his hands on pertaining to the garden. But one little event of the past month has flummoxed all the gardeners, and indeed the whole community. Early in the year our community of 32 found itself suddenly increased by the arrival, out of the blue, of one chameleon. It caused some excitement, speculation and talk. Now this lady moved from chili plant to tomato and from radish to lettuce—and in vain tried to [match her environment and] her pigment accordingly. To my mind, Lady Chameleon was a singular failure. I virtually dismissed her from my mind. But about 3 weeks ago, this lady did something that forcibly drew attention to herself once more. She suddenly gave birth to 6 little babies and promptly abandoned them. This excited all our parental feelings and our concern for the orphans, the lowly, the helpless. Each morning and throughout the day, you'd find a cluster of chaps around one little baby engaged in animated discussion. The weather took a bad turn suddenly, and the concern for the babies increased in proportion. But the question that hit us the first day and still remains unsolved is: where is Papa Chameleon? If indeed there was one. Some say the Lady is bisexual, others say she came here pregnant. Yours truly has agreed with both sides. Some enlightenment from you would not be out of place. The debate continues. Lady has reappeared. But, incredibly, she's never with her offspring. Some are fed up with her and may have already passed a sentence banishing her. Overt excuse is shortage of insects for her to feed on! But in fact I think everybody is fed up because she abandoned her infants at so tender an age.

I've exceeded my limit almost. Do you know if Dasoo got my letter of August? You omitted to mention whether you did meet up with Yasmin in January. I hope Mummy's health is better. If you have a chance, send a photo of the gang.

Lots of love to you and all from
AMK

≈ ≈ ≈

Rooki Saloojee—*24 December 1976*

This letter to Rooki Saloojee was sent back to Kathrada by a censor telling him to rewrite the correspondence, omitting certain portions. The offending passages include the following: first, a reference to "Mr. Mandela, who takes his gardening seriously"; second, Kathrada writes about his farewell party with many of his friends before going underground and reflects on where those friends are now scattered all over the world. "But worst of all, 3 of our most beloved ones are no more," he continues in a reference to the killing of comrades, one of whom was Rooki's husband, Babla. Rooki was twenty-six and recently married when the Special Branch detained her husband on 6 July 1964. On 9 September 1964, a security officer informed her that her husband had fallen to his death from the seventh floor of the Special Branch Headquarters. Babla's death while in detention, was among the first of the many "suicides." For many years after his death Rooki was to be hounded and harassed by the police and when she was able to find work, the police would threaten her employer and invariably she would be dismissed. The other references are also to people involved in the struggle.

≈

A. M. Kathrada,
Robben Island Jail
24th Dec. 1975

My Dear Rooki,

It is a number of years that I haven't heard from Uncle Amien's wife, Ayesha. Which means I have not been hearing about you either, for she used to keep me well informed about so many of the family members and friends. And it is six years, almost to the date, since you visited me here! I thought I should write a little note & say "hello" to you and the other folks out there. Of course, news about you has not been completely absent, and it has always been most heartening to hear that you are very much in touch with family members and colleagues. Whenever information is received that Rooki has been visiting some family or attending a wedding or a funeral or commemoration, it has always made me feel that we have been adequately represented by you. It has really been very good of you and I assure you it has been deeply appreciated.

What can I tell you about ourselves here? In general things are the same as can be expected. The same dreary routine; get up early, work, supper by 5 p.m., study, sleep. Letters and visits over weekends, film shows every fortnight, games. Every now and then we see a good film; last week we saw *Gengis Khan*, which was very enjoyable. I've been seeing more films and participating in more sports activities than I ever did outside. For the last two years or so we've got a tiny little flower and vegetable garden. ~~Mr. Mandela is our chief gardener, and he takes his work very seriously~~. To me the best item coming from the garden is chilies, then once every 6 weeks or so we manage to have a bit of lovely salad, consisting of tomatoes, onions, cucumber, lettuce. Yesterday, because of the heat, the milk given to one of the ulcer sufferers went sour and, instead of throwing it away, Isu made some *dahin*.[1] It was delicious. All we needed was the *biryani*[2] to go with it. By the way, the next time you see Shireen (my godchild), please remind her to send the recipe for *blatjang*.[3] She promised to get it from her mother. I often think of the lovely food you used to cook. Do you still remember the last little house party we attended ~~just before I "disappeared"? Where are the folks who were present? Tommy and them in England, Yasmin in Germany, Fati in Canada, Mosy (was he there?) in India. Scattered all over. But worst of all, 3 of our most beloved ones are no more. I miss them terribly.~~ I understand Juby was here on a short holiday. Did you see her? I was so surprised when Tommy mentioned in his letter that Tootsie had paid a visit to England last year. Do you see her and the family at all? Please pass them my love. I hope one of these days you will be able to get away for a while and visit the relatives and friends all over.

Are you still doing dressmaking? Are you on your own or do you work in Johannesburg? It would be nice to hear about the people around your way. ~~Do you ever see Mrs. Moodley? I believe her health was not too good. Convey my best wishes to her and to Joyce.~~ Do you know Mohamed Bhana, who lives in Dass Street? He sent me an Eid card a

---

[1] *Dahin*: a spicy sauce using curdled milk and a traditional accompaniment with *biryani*.

[2] *Biryani*: a special Indian rice dish. Cooked rice layered over meat and baked in an oven.

[3] *Blatjang*: a Cape Malay chutney, or relish, made with fresh fruit.

few weeks back. Please thank him for me. Are Ismail and Gene still in Benoni? ~~And Ismail Cachalia? Munga, etc. If you happen to see any of our friends, please convey my fondest regards.~~

If you can find the time, do write. I am posting this letter via my niece. If you are unable to write, please acknowledge receipt of this through Shireen or my niece. This will be all for today. Keep well and look after yourself. Lots of love to you, Hajira, etc., from

AMK

◇ ◇ ◇

Sukhthi Naidoo—*25 January 1976*

In this letter to a young friend, Sukhthi, the daughter of Phyllis and M. D. Naidoo, Kathrada thanks her for sending letters. He always had an ability to relate to young people. Two important pieces of information are contained in this letter: First, he is in traction and is suffering from back trouble; second, and more disturbing, is a new regulation permitting only visits from "blood relatives." Subsequently his "blood relatives" were also refused permission to visit. For more than a year, Kathrada did not have a visitor.

◇

A. M. Kathrada,
Robben Island
25th January 1976

My Dear Sukhthi,

Thank you very much for your letter of 31st December, and also for the one of 2nd July last year. I must not forget the lovely Eid and Xmas cards, especially the one with the photo of the family. You know at first I did not recognize any of you. You have all grown so much since the last photograph I saw a few years ago. I thought I would still see a young lady with a curly head—that is how I remember you. And don't talk about Sha and Sadhan—they are huge. You look so tiny beside them. Mummy too looked different. I think she had long, straight hair. And I'm almost sure she was a bit thinner. Anyway it was very nice to see you all.

I was very happy to see that all three of you have done so well at school. Who will be your new class teacher? You must tell me which school you attend and about your friends and teachers. My congratulations for winning the swimming championship. You must tell me more about it. Also about your music and dancing lessons. I hope Daddy gave you the wrist watch for doing well in Indian dancing.

I'm sure you must have enjoyed going to the circus. Did the clown make you laugh a lot? Were you afraid of the lions? If you go to Johannesburg, you must get Zohra to take you to the zoo. I'm sure you will like it. I remember one day we took Uncle J.N.'s children to the zoo. The monkeys were very naughty and threw a lot of filth at the people. But it was fun watching them.

It would be great fun if you could visit me on the Island. But unfortunately it is not possible. First of all you would be considered under age. And secondly nowadays only blood relatives are allowed to visit us. You must ask Mummy to explain what sort of relatives these are supposed to be. Because of this rule, I have not had a visit for over a year. Zohra and other nieces and nephews of mine were refused permission. So there would have been no chance for you to come.

We had a pleasant Christmas. We had a lot of sweets and biscuits. Our annual games were enjoyable. We have 3 teams. My team, "Aces" came second. I took part in Bridge, Scrabble and a few other games but didn't do too well.

Guess what, I am writing this lying flat on my back—and in a real bed in my cell with crisp white bed sheets and all. My food is brought to me, I'm being helped with shaving and washing, while I just lie in bed and read books and write letters and things. The reason for all this laziness is that I am actually tied down to my bed with 10 lb. weights dangling from each foot. The medical people call this traction. It all started about 3 months ago when one morning I suddenly felt pain in my back, and the next thing I was flat in bed. Within a few days, I was fit again. But a few weeks later I had another attack, just a few days before the exams. Again I recovered after a few days. Now last Sunday I had the third attack. So this time the doctor decided to tie me down. It's the 2nd time in 13 years that I'm enjoying a bed; the first time was in 1966 when I had a little operation. They say I'll be like this for at least 2 weeks, maybe more. It is a bit uncomfortable but not unbearable. By the way, I managed to write the exam—Ancient History—and was lucky to pass.

This is all for today. Pass my love to Mummy and Daddy and Sha and Sadhan. Also to Uncle Deva and Gabby and Aunt Novi. Thank them for their lovely Christmas card. And Zinaida, Nolan, Ravel and their mummy. I believe Uncle Dawood is not well. I wrote to him a few weeks ago. Look after yourself. Lots of love to you.

From Uncle Kathy,

AMK

~ ~ ~

Sukhthi Naidoo—*28 August 1976*

~

On 7 September 1976, this letter to Sukhthi was returned to Kathrada informing him that it could not be sent as the censor had objections to the person—a thirteen-year-old. Although she did not receive this letter, it does have an important message. Apartheid was devastating to the self-esteem of non-whites. They were taught to know their place in society and not encroach on the white person's world, so for them something like competing in the Olympic Games would not even be considered remotely possible. Kathrada encourages this young person to aspire to the highest and he would be proud to see her name in a magazine as one of the Olympic swimmers.

~

A. M. Kathrada,
Robben Island Jail
28th August 1976

My Dear Sukhthi,

You must be thinking that I have forgotten all about you. It is over five months ago that I received your lovely letter; on the 20th March to be exact. That was your second letter this year. I liked the beautiful pink writing pad that you used with the flowers. Did you choose it yourself? I am ashamed that I am using this colourless and unattractive paper to write my reply. I will try to order a nice writing pad one of these days.

I must congratulate you for doing so well at swimming. You must carry on. One day you may be in the South African team at the Olympic games. Earlier today I was reading about the gold medals won by

Kornelia Ender from Germany (D.D.R.), and I was thinking of you. Kornelia was 13 when she first took part in the Olympics, in 1976. I will be so proud if I can open the *Huisgenoot*[1] in 1980 and see your photo as a swimming champ of the Olympics. I am sure you must be keen to see Kornelia and her team in action. If you ever decide to go to the G.D.R. and need a guide, I can volunteer for the job. You see I can still speak a few words of German, and I visited the G.D.R. many years ago. So I can be quite helpful.

By the way, did you see any of the competitions on TV? It must have been exciting. Have you got a TV set at home? It must be nice now that Mummy is able to take you to the pool without having to get permission.[2] Do you also go to Johannesburg? You must tell me about your trip.

Now that your teacher has gone to Canada, are you still continuing with lessons in Indian dancing? I think you said Daddy has promised to buy you a wrist watch if you did well in dancing. You must have got the watch by now.

One of these days you will be writing exams again. And then you will be in Std. 4.[3] What are your favourite subjects at school? Do you also have to do Afrikaans? Do you like it?

When you write again you must tell me when is your birthday. Also, one of these days you must send me your photo. I hope you are allowing your hair to grow longer. In the last photograph it was too short.

It was very sad to hear of Uncle Dawood's death. I knew him for a long time and was very fond of him.

When I was writing to you in January, I was lying in bed with my legs all tied up. You remember? Well they kept me that way for two weeks. It wasn't too painful. My back is better, but not completely normal. I was sent to Cape Town for x-rays. It appears that I have got a bit of arthritis. I did not go to work for a few months, but now I've started going out again. I've been given a bed in my cell and also a chair. The chair is very useful.

Otherwise I am well. This year I am doing only one subject again: Archaeology. I am writing exams on 18th October.

This will be all for today. I hope you are keeping well. Lots of love to Mummy, Daddy and all the family and friends.

---

[1] *The Huisgenoot*: a weekly magazine in Afrikaans.

[2] Her mother was in all likelihood placed under house arrest and could not go to any public place where two or more persons might be gathered. Special permission would have to be obtained.

[3] The equivalent of grade six in American schools.

Lots of love to you from Uncle
AMK

7th Sept.—Told by Chief B—this letter has been withheld. (Objection to person)

≈   ≈   ≈

Zohra Kathrada—*25 February 1978*

The death of Apa Cajee's husband triggers fond memories of the days when Kathrada was still at Flat 13, Kholvad House, the apartment block where the Cajees live. He describes in vivid detail to Zohra how Indian customs prevailed among the community, where it was regarded as improper for a Muslim woman to engage in conversation with him and vice versa. Yet, if anyone required a ride to the next suburb, they would send one of the children to ask "uncle" if he would take them wherever they needed to go. "Uncle" always obliged and they would "travel in silence." In those days, an elder would be addressed by the young as "uncle" or "aunt," even where there was no blood relationship. Whenever these women saw visitors from out of town heading for Kathrada's apartment, trays of food would suddenly appear. When he was placed under house arrest and could not go out from 6:00 P.M. to 7:00 A.M., the women of Kholvad House provided Kathrada with food. Later, the children would go into his flat to break the solitary house arrest. The women argued that not even the Special Branch would be so stupid as to arrest 5-year-old children. Another instance of the warmth and kindness of the women, in this case, Apa Cajee, occurred when the late ANC President, Chief Luthuli, inadvertently locked himself out of Flat 13 and was seen pacing up and down. She invited him in and entertained him until Kathrada appeared.

≈

Robben Island Jail
25th February 1978

My Dear Zohra,
Your last letter of 26th January reached me on 11th February. My last letter to you was on 28th January; hope you received it. When you find the card from Dasoo, please send it along with one of your letters.

It was sad to hear of Dawoodbhai's death. You were the first to inform me. I should have thought Uncle Amien would send me a telegram. It was an unfortunate omission on his part. When you see him, please convey my sympathy. I wrote to Uncle D.I.'s son, Yusuf, on 11th Feb. Incidentally, please check with Uncle Amien if Djamilia got the card I sent in December.

I'm sorry also about the death of Apa Cajee's husband. If you are around that way, please pop in at Kholvad House and convey my sympathy to her and the children. I suppose some of them must already be married by now. Apa herself together with the other neighbours at Kholvad House were tremendous. And I was very attached to all the children. I never tire of remembering about them. There was a strange relationship between the female neighbours and myself. I don't suppose you younger people will be able to quite appreciate it. You'll most probably call it "old fashioned." We never used to talk or even greet one another. Day in and day out, for years, we would meet, but we'd just pass by as if we were total strangers. Apa, Saraban, Mrs. Casoo—all of them. (I think Khuskhala was the only one with whom I conversed.) Yet there was a deep feeling of mutual respect between us. You know, every once in a while, one of the ladies or a group of them would be urgently needing a lift somewhere. Then they'd send the kids to ask if Uncle could not take their mummies to Fordsburg or wherever they'd be wanting to go. And we'd travel in silence. These good people only had to see some out-of-town visitors coming to my place and, within minutes, they'd send trays of food. Only a few days ago I was telling someone of a simple, yet very beautiful and significant, incident. One day Chief Luthuli[1] [who often used to stay at Flat 13] forgot his key inside and could not get in, so he apparently paced up and down the balcony for a few minutes until, as he told me, a kind neighbour invited him in and entertained him. I thought it must have been Babla's brother on the 4th Floor. But when Chief insisted they were people on the 3rd Floor, I asked him to point out the flat to me. Imagine my surprise when he pointed at Flat 11; i.e. Apa Cajee's flat. But the most unforgettable thing to me was when I was placed under house arrest and I had to be at home by 6 p.m. For the first two or three days, just after 6 p.m., there

---

[1] The late Chief Albert Luthuli, president of the African National Congress and recipient of the Nobel Peace Prize in 1961. He died in July 1967 under mysterious circumstances—hit by a train as he was taking his usual walk.

would be little knocks on the door in quick succession, and there would be food from 4 or 5 neighbours! I was living alone and this was too much. Eventually I asked my friend, "Quarter," to thank the ladies on my behalf and explain that I could not possibly eat all that food. They were apparently quite unhappy about this. Nevertheless they felt they had to do something. So they decided to take turns in sending food. And this is where the kids came in. There must have been over half a dozen of them, aged about 2 to 5 years. Now, being a house arrestee, I was not allowed to receive visitors at all, not even my mother. The ladies in their wisdom must have decided that no policeman was going to arrest me for having visitors aged 5 downwards. So every day thereafter, just after 6 p.m., there'd be little knocks on the door and these little ones would walk in, each carrying something. What a touching gesture! I thought one small way in which I could show my appreciation was to give something to the kids. So I began keeping a good quantity of chocolates and handed these out. I didn't realise that these little scamps were better politicians than I was. They must have had a meeting and decided on a strategy. For, on weekends and holidays, the little knocks increased and the delegation would walk in even if they were carrying one roti, the very first one fresh from the stove, and wait for their "reward." I later learned that they would start nagging their mothers early in the mornings to take food for Uncle. Anyhow, talk about this spread and soon it reached the ears of the visiting American TV teams and they wanted to film it. (You see, I was the second person in S.A. to be placed under house arrest, so there was a lot of interest and publicity.) So one day they came at about 5:30 and set up their tripods and lights and cameras. It looked all very bright and exciting. And at 6 o'clock the delegation, much reinforced, came tripping in. At their tender ages, they became TV stars! Of course, there was a humorous side to this episode. One little one—she couldn't have been more than two—decided she too had to have a role in this drama and joined in with a plate in her hands. But, at the crucial moment, something must have snapped in her elaborate feminine garments and little *broekies*[2] started showing—the first stage to falling down altogether. Blissfully unaware of what was happening, she, however, dutifully completed her mission, collected her sweets and marched off. I won't mention her name for she must be 18 now and possibly married!

---

[2] *Broekies*: Afrikaans for "panties for young children."

How I've rambled on and on. And I must have told you of this before. Forgive me, but I do get carried away when I think back of some of these things. Do you know that even after my arrest these kids nagged their mothers to send something; so while awaiting trial I often used to receive some delicacy or other from the kind neighbours.

I was happy to learn that you stopped at Schweizer during your Cape Town trip. I hope all is well. I'm looking forward to the telegram intimating the arrival of Khatija's twins. When is Ismailmota going to start building the new house? Where is Chota's shop going to be? It is a pity he won't break away from Schweizer and move to Jo'burg. But I suppose he is too attached to country life and finds it difficult to get away. I don't blame him.

I'm terribly sorry to hear of little Yusuf's diabetes. I hope he is well. I'm writing a little note to Julie and Samad.

It is nice to hear of the generally good school results. Congratulate them for me. Pity about Zohrabibi.[3] I hope she doesn't get discouraged. I've long given up all hope of receiving letters from them. So you'll just have to keep me informed. Incidentally, Hajou's brother, Mohamed, is he going to continue university here or is he going abroad?

It is a long time that I haven't had any photos from you. I hope you will be sending some soon.

I'm keeping fine. Still in "A" group. Keep well and lots of love to you and all the family.

From

AMK

P.S. It is Papa's birthday soon. Please convey my best wishes to him. I'm sorry I made a mistake about Zinaida's address. It's 15 Jacaranda Ave.

Dasoo Iyer—*Easter, 1978*

It is Easter, and like Christmas time, a period when Kathrada gets nostalgic. He thinks of the friends such as Dasoo Iyer who he might have been with at this time of year. His way of dealing with this nostalgia is to write, for the writing

---

[3] Kathrada's elder brother's daughter.

itself creates closeness. Now that they no longer work at the lime quarry from Monday through to Friday, every day is now the same with no weekend to look forward to. He has taken up sport again and follows music quite closely. This reference to "music" is Kathrada's signal that all references to this topic are in code. "Chotabhai" is the code name for Mac Maharaj who had been released from Robben Island in 1976. When Mac Maharaj was released he smuggled out a copy of the manuscript, Long Walk to Freedom: the Autobiography of Nelson Mandela, *referred to here as the "L.P"; the musicians and composers are political comrades. Kathrada is eagerly awaiting publication and is enthusiastic about the possibility that a special edition to mark Nelson Mandela's 60th birthday might also be published. Kathrada concludes that "this would be something unique and for everyone to look forward to." For the first time ever, he has done poorly in his studies. An even greater setback is that his study privileges have been cancelled. This means that for the rest of his life sentence he will not be able to study again. The "crime" Kathrada had committed that led to the cancellation of his study privileges was that he had proof-read and commented in writing on Mandela's illegally written autobiography, the original of which had been found by the authorities. After fourteen years he and his colleagues can now listen to radio broadcasts, which will be monitored and controlled by the prison authorities. There is also talk that they might be allowed newspapers. On a negative note, he writes that visits are still restricted to "first-degree relatives" only and no longer are the prisoners allowed to receive books, magazines, other literature, or gifts from outside.*

∽

A. M. Kathrada
Robben Island Jail

My Dear Dasoo,

[Your letter of] February reached me on 11th March. I'm [rushing] the reply in the hope that it will get to you before your typewriter cools and renders you lethargic for a long time. Zohra also informed me of your Xmas card, but she had unfortunately mislaid it while she was moving house. Many thanks anyway for your kind thoughts.

It is the Easter weekend, and like Xmas, it is the time when one feels a bit nostalgic. And the best cure for this condition as far as I'm concerned is to write letters. This has become my fixed habit for many years now. In this way I manage to feel closeness with people with whom I might, under different circumstances, be spending the weekend. Otherwise in jail it is like any other time of the year. For the last year and

[a] half almost we have not been going out to work. So you see, weekends have lost their meaning, and every day is like any other. One has got all the time to play, to study, to talk, to read, or just laze away. Yours truly, as you can imagine, chooses the last course. What a colossal waste of time it is to be in prison! Lately I feel I have sufficiently recovered from my back ailment, and I've started playing tenniquoits again. One of these days I may pluck up enough energy to learn tennis, which is by far the most popular game in our section.

You may recall I once made a very brave effort to learn to play the melodica. But it ended in disaster. When the [gods were] handing out music genes, I happened to have been too far back in the queue. So my interest in this sphere is strictly that of an observer. But I do take some interest. I cannot help it; we hear so much of it daily and the younger chaps discuss all the recent developments, deviations, etc. So I have to be with it. I hear of people like Nancy O___, Joan Baez, Jimmy Hendrix and many others, especially Black musicians from America. Then at least I feel a lot of pride in being personally acquainted with people like Chotabhai, etc. I'm so happy that his reputation among musicians and composers is continuously growing. He is someone you can discuss anything with, ranging from the archaeological excavations at Walids Village to the biography of Queen Nefertiti (or Nafisa as popularly known). I'm eagerly looking forward to the L.P. and hope he is able to overcome all difficulties. Incidentally, there was some talk about issuing [the] songs separately as well. This I'm sure would be a wonderful idea; all music lovers would welcome it; in fact would press for it, considering the urgent necessity for that type of folk singing. Some time ago we heard of plans to issue a special birthday edition which would sort of be biographical with music and songs of different periods in the musician's life. Now this would be something unique and for everyone to look forward to. I hope you will make it a point of keeping me informed. I have an idea that you also tried your hand at the violin once. Or am I mistaken?

Anyway, I'm not going to write to Pupli and them, for I'd be saying much the same things as in this letter. So I hope you will show them the letter as you've been doing in the past. By the way, I'm taking it for granted they have reconciled. I believe Dagga's[1] marriage broke up some time ago. Do you see him at all? I know it will be impossible for you to get him to write, but I do want to hear about some relatives and friends,

---

[1] Dagga: the nickname for his nephew, Aziz Pahad.

especially people like Sayyed, Ranjit, Baji, Asmal, etc.[2] Do make it a point to ask and you could tell me about them in one of your letters.

You seem to be doing very well with your studies. Congratulations. For me 1977 was the worst year ever. I ended up by writing only Economics and I went and failed that. Can you imagine it! And my misfortune did not end there. As Zohra has told you, the Prisons Dept. has cancelled my permission to study for the duration of my sentence! The reason is that I had abused the study privilege by using study material to write memoirs. So I must thank you and others very much for your kind offers of assistance. But I shan't be needing it.

Now, for some good news. Since Feb. 27th we are being officially allowed news. The Radio S.A. news service is taped in the morning and afternoon and then is played over our rediffusion system every evening. Imagine after all these years of deprivation. Now with a flick of the switch, we are suddenly in touch with the world. But I must say the news is dismal. Just an example. This evening we heard of kidnapping in Rome and Paris, earthquakes in Japan and the Soviet Union, road accidents in Cape Town, tanker collision and oil spills in France, sentence of death on Bhuto, the pollution caused by a Soviet spacecraft over Canada, etc. All of which, coupled with the dollar trouble and the economic position, generally makes me almost glad that I'm in jail! Anyway, the news service is a step in the right direction. There is talk of further improvements. The Minister was here a couple of weeks ago. He said he was seriously considering giving us two daily newspapers—one English and one Afrikaans. Most probably *Die Burgher* and *The Citizen*.[3] But he made it clear he was not making a promise. Let's keep our fingers crossed.

The position with visitors remains the same. Only first-degree relatives may visit. That, of course, excludes Zohra and all my nieces and nephews. It often makes me regret the fact that I didn't get married. Then at least I'd have a first-degree relative to visit me.

My health is fine. I'm glad about Sally's holiday. Pity she didn't meet Zohra. I hope she has fully recovered.

Oh, yes. Just as well Tommy did nothing about the football magazine. We are no longer allowed to receive anything—books, records, sports

---

[2] Baji: African National Congress; Ranjit: China; Sayyed: The Soviet Union; Asmal: Pan African Congress.

[3] Both papers are pro-government.

equipment, musical instruments—from outside. We can purchase these things by placing the orders from here.

One of these days, I'll have to write to Tommy. That may force him to reply. I hope you haven't forgotten my request about the photos. Send as many as you can. Harry and his spouse, Stretch and his, they can all come. There are no longer restrictions.[4]

I must end now. Keep well.

Lots of love to Sally, Venitha, Vijan and all friends.

All the best to you from

AMK

∿ ∿ ∿

Tom Vassen—*17 June 1978*

Kathy opens with a reminiscence of the old days at Tom Vassen's father's place. Then, he regales Tom with stories of a trip to Cape Town. We learn that a uniform diet has been agreed upon, at least in principle. But even in prison, apartheid was practiced. There were different diets for the different prison populations: Indians and Coloreds fared better than did their African colleagues. This particular piece of information Tom would not have read as the censor sent this letter back instructing Kathrada to leave out all the underlined parts. There is also a library depot with a good selection of books, which is good news for the inmates. Kathrada urges Tom to send as many photos as possible of all the South African friends who are in London.

∿

Robben Island Jail
17th June 1978

My Dear Tom,

I'm sure you must be thinking jail has made me a bit of a sadist; tormenting your conscience as I do. I suppose I'll just have to risk that appellation, especially if it eventually leads to some sort of a response from you. ~~Let's start with a few statistics. On the 13th I completed 14~~

---

[4] Kathrada can, at this time, receive photographs of "mixed" groups, that is blacks and whites in the same image.

years on the Island. On 11th of next month it will be 15 years since Rivonia. In August next year I shall be reaching half a century. Fifty summers! I always think of the little party we attended when your Dad turned 50. Remember? We all wrote our names on his handkerchief, and I think I wrote something about his being 50 years young. Wasn't it the time when you and I bought all those roasted fowls in Hillbrow? And wasn't Sakina also at the party? Yes, I'm almost sure I'm right. I try to picture the occasion, but many of the details escape me. What is confusing me a bit is the New Year's Eve party there when that lady (I think from Rhodes) was kneeling, Indian style, before your granny. What lovely memories.

Anyway, having started with statistics, let us carry on but with the less prosaic 36–18–35 variety. Let me tell you of my night out from Robben Island. It was in May, a bit on the cool and windy side, not an ideal day for a sea trip. I went out with Susan. Having been out with her once before, I wasn't very apprehensive about the weather. She was well togged, elegant, almost luxurious. Well, believe it or not, yours truly sat behind the bar counter, the powers that be having first ensured that all the consumables were safely out of reach. Anyway, thanks to her gentle care, I did not really need artificial supplements in order to brave the heavy seas; and within 45 minutes we docked at Cape Town. I hardly left Susan, and almost my very next step was to plunge myself into a world dominated by the fair sex. My bedroom at the slopes of Table Mountain, a soft rain and mist,—beverages and delicious food, much enhanced by the beautiful ladies serving it. . . . Add to this the kindly interest and care, the tender caresses, the coaxing, the whispers and charming smiles. What's more, I was taken by young ladies to the theater! Yes, there only to be thrust in the company of yet more young ladies. Albeit this time, they being in purdah, I could only derive comfort and satisfaction from watching the smiles in their eyes. Call it a harem, Arabian nights . . . or what you will. But it was very heaven I tell you. And in those brief—alas too brief—hours I was king. No longer a prisoner, I shed the anxieties, the responsibilities and worries which to a greater or lesser degree are concomitants of jail life.

Day dreaming? A little touched? Escaped? No, nothing as dramatic as all that. Let me set your mind at ease. The lady, Susan, I talked about is no female acquaintance of mine but the name of the new Robben Island boat—the *Susan Kruger*. And all the other ladies I referred to were the nurses, staff and theatre sisters of the Woodstock Hospital. You see I had to go there for an examination that could only be done under anaesthetic. They didn't find anything that warranted an operation so they sent me packing to the Island.

Dasoo has told you that my study permission was cancelled by the Prisons Dept. So now I try to while away the time by reading and sleeping. Since February we are being given the SABC news. We are told we may be getting newspapers too. But this is still being considered. Another improvement; all of us now have beds, ~~and apparently it has been agreed in principle to introduce a uniform diet scale. So you see things are looking up for us.~~ We still have films. Also we now have a Provincial Library Depot with a fair selection of books. Sportswise, after being forced to lay off for a couple of years due to a back problem, I've been playing tenniquoits again.

This will be all for now. How are you keeping? How's the gout? Are you still on the wagon? How is Mummy's health and the aunts and the rest of the family? Pass my fondest love to them and to all the boys and girls from back home. I'd love to have photos of you all. You know we are now allowed to have an unlimited number of photos. Do you think you can organize some. And don't leave out the spouses of the chaps who married there. Incidentally, did you get my Christmas card at the end of 1977? Hope to hear from you soon. Write via Zohra. Keep well. All the best to you and all the folks from

AMK

1st July
Informed I should omit underlined portions [indicated by the words being lined through].

≈ ≈ ≈

Zohra Kathrada—*24 June 1978*

This letter was returned to Kathrada instructing him to leave out the underlined parts. The first concerns swimming facilities for the black population. At this time there was not a single place apart from the Huddleston Baths in Soweto. Anglican Bishop Trevor Huddleston was an outspoken critic of apartheid and the government and, before he was "obliged to take up duties elsewhere," he built a swimming pool in Soweto. He was also active in Sophiatown before that "black spot" was removed by the government. People like Molly and Bram Fischer, a white family in the liberation movement, opened their home and their swimming pool to many black families, much to the annoyance of the Special Branch. To mention this to Zohra is too political, hence its deletion. The second deals with visits by "first degree relatives," something mentioned repeatedly by Kathrada without any objection by the censor. Now it is an issue. The only conclusion one can draw is that prison censorship is arbitrary and mindless. The third can be construed as political insofar that even within the black population on Robben Island, apartheid was enforced. There were different diet classifications for Africans, Coloreds and Indians, with the Africans worse off and the Indians and Coloreds only slightly better off. Now, beginning their 15th year, there is talk of creating a uniform diet. When Kathrada got to Robben Island in 1964 and discovered this inequality, he insisted on being treated the same. His colleague Nelson Mandela told him not to reject the Indian diet, as this would be playing into the hands of the authorities who would happily give him what he wanted, namely, the inferior African diet. Rather, Mandela argued, they should fight for everyone's lot being improved. Not only diet but also clothing was two-tiered: Kathrada, being Indian, could wear long pants while Mandela had to wear short pants. The sinister element beneath this ridiculous regulation was that African men, by being forced to wear short pants, were reduced to the status of being "boys." We also learn that only recently they were given beds. Prior to 1978, they slept on concrete floors with two mats for a mattress in their 8 x 8 ft. cells.

〜

Robben Island Jail
24th June 1978

My Dear Zohra,

Your letter of 13th June reached me this morning. It was very nice. It seems all the letters and cards have been reaching. I'll be glad if you'd find out from Dasoo if he got my letter of 25th March and also if Zinaida got the birthday card. I've written to Tommy today. I suppose Dasoo will be able to tell you if the letter reaches. Tommy is a bad correspondent. Just like the Kathrada kids. I had a pleasant surprise this morning. I got a letter from Fareed with 8 photographs! Unfortunately, some of these are not too clear. But at least he's made an effort, and that's important. Now that you've got your new camera, I hope to receive many more photos. Aziz seems to be a mischievous little chap from what I can see in the photos. Aziza and Nazira are lovely. There is one lovely one with their London Farm friends, Anna, Selina and Kleintjie. Thanks a lot also for the R100. I've not yet heard if the Prisons Dept. will be paying anything towards the cost of the specs. But I don't think I'll go for another frame. It would be unnecessary extravagance. Thanks for your offer all the same.

Now that you are going to be a full-time housewife for a little while, I hope you will be able to move around a bit more and do some visiting. For instance, when last were you able to pop in at Aunty Ayesha's and the neighbours? Also Hajoo and the family? I'm longing to hear a few words about them. You must try to see the mother and especially little Mohamed. Do you ever see Rooki Pahad? The last I heard she was divorced and was running a beauty parlour or something. I wonder how Yasmin and Shenaaz are. Also her father. And how are Nassim and family? I'm sure if you can find time to spend an evening or so with Uncle Amien and family, you'll be able [to] find out a lot about friends and relatives. I hope you'll be getting your typewriter back very soon. Then you can write a few long letters. You'll notice if you go through my last few letters, there are a number of questions I asked which you have not yet replied to. Also, tell me what sort of work will you be doing if you take up Public Health. Will you have to undergo special training? What are the prospects of going back to the *Daily Mail?* I'm sure with an active person like yourself, you'll soon get tired of being a housewife. And it must be pretty lonely in the flat.

Next time you go to the coast I hope you'll be able to pop in at my little friend's home. I'm sure it will be nice to meet the family. I share your fears about going into the water. I merely love to watch the sea— from a comfortable distance. By the way, where will you be going for swimming lessons? Is there a swimming bath at Lenasia? It is a lovely form of recreation. But I must say, personally I can do without it. I used to spend a lot of time at the home of the late Molly and Braam, but I never got into the swimming bath. There were occasions during holidays when I used to stay for weeks at homes of friends who used to go away to the coast. And I used to have a swimming bath all to myself. But you'd never catch me going in. You know what we often used to do? Molly was a great lover of curries. So on a Sunday a few of us would go along with pots of food and spend a lovely day at the swimming bath. For my friends it used to be quite a treat; there was no public swimming bath they could go to. There was the Huddelston Bath in Soweto, but

~~then one needed permits to get to Soweto. And it was all to much of a bother.~~ Are there any private baths in Lenasia? I'm sure some of the wealthy doctors and businessmen would be adding a bath or tennis court to their luxurious homes. I was told that Dr. Momoniat has a palatial home. Is it the poshest in Lenz? This Extension 7 that you wrote about, is it officially known as Robben Island, or is that what the people call it? You are right, if I get out of here one day, I'd want to stay far away from the name of Robben Island.

I suppose you too have heard rumours that the Prison will be closing in a few years' time. We heard in the news that there were suggestions for a bird sanctuary or something to be established here. If they move us from here, I hope it will be to the Transvaal so that we can be nearer to you all. ~~And by that time they may even relax on this business of first degree relatives only being allowed to visit us. We're constantly being told of changes and improvements. Let's hope they relax on visits.~~ You know we now have a depot at the Cape Provincial Library here. There are about 2,500 books so far. We've got a few hundred in the section where I live. From a quick look at them I must say they look promising. At least a good start has been made. Unfortunately, so far there are no novels. We hope this will soon be remedied. My first preference is for biographies and then novels. I'm afraid I'm not such an enthusiast for heavy stuff. I leave that to the intellectuals.

~~We also hear that the Prisons Dept. has agreed in principle to introduce uniform diets for all population groups. We have been working and hoping for this ever since we came here. It would be a big step forward.~~ You know, of course, that everyone here now has beds. Unfortunately, the radio rediffusion system has been broken for over a month now, and we are without music. The tape recorder is brought to us for the news. But we are told that an elaborate system is going to be installed one of these days. Each of our cells will be having its own speaker. This will be good.

You are right. We heard of the R61,000 armed robbery on the East Rand. It was quite a daring job. Have any people been arrested? What aspect of it did you see on TV?

We still have our regular film shows. Unfortunately, we haven't had good films of late. Though some haven't been too bad; e.g., *Saul and David, Hennesy,* etc.

Otherwise things are okay. I must say Farida certainly does a lot of shopping. In almost every second letter you tell me Farida had come to do some shopping. Does she come by car? Does she drive? I sent them a card in May and will be writing soon.

My congratulations to your sister on her marriage. It is Shireen, not so? When did she marry? Are they in Jo'burg?

Is Boy still at University? When you get down to writing to Dasoo, how about dropping a line to cousins Essop and them as well. How is Goolambhai?

Hope you recovered completely from flu.

Lots of love to all of you from

AMK

1st July. Informed I should omit underlined portions [indicated here by the words being lined through].

~ ~ ~

Tom and Bob Vassen—*25 July 1978*

A letter of sympathy on hearing of the death of Tom and Bob Vassen's mother, Rangee. She adored and looked upon Kathrada as one of her own. She often remarked to Tom and Bob that Kathrada was the big brother. She knew his favorite dishes, and when she learned that he was coming for a visit, she would make one of these especially for him.

~

A. M. Kathrada
Robben Island Jail
25th July 1978

My Dear Tommy and Bobby,

I was shocked when I heard only this morning that Mummy had passed away. It was in a letter from Dasoo. He had assumed that I had already heard, so he left out all the details. I do recall your telling me in your last letter, which was a couple of years ago, that Mummy's health was not of the best. But I did not realise she was so unwell.

Only yesterday (Friday) I was busy writing my monthly letters, and do you know among the persons I wrote to was Mummy! I thought I should give her a little surprise, and I wrote out a little message on a birthday card for her. All that needed to be done was for it to be handed in for posting which we normally do on Sundays. And this morning I got this letter from Dasoo which contained the sad tidings of her passing away. Can you imagine my shock! Now I have the sad task of substituting a joyful birthday message for a letter of condolence.

Believe me, I've been struggling for over two hours to write this little note. I'm at a loss for words. At last I have decided. Let my tribute to her take an unusual form. Let me enclose the birthday card with its few sentences expressing my sentiments and deep affection for her.

Let me say no more. It has been my pleasure to share many moments of happiness with both of you. Allow me to share also this occasion of sorrow.

Isu and Billy have asked me to express their sympathies.

Keep well. Everything of the best to you, to Dela, Ursula and the children.

From

AMK

≈ ≈ ≈

Zohra Kathrada—*25 November 1978*

This letter was heavily censored; all the indicated portions had to be omitted in the rewriting. In the first part Kathrada recalls how small his quota was in their early days: one letter every six months compared now with six letters a month. The passage where Kathrada discusses a letter from his brother, Solly, being withheld (and having it counted against Kathrada's six-month quota) is what the censor found objectionable. Kathrada mentions this in passing but the censor sees it as being critical of the authorities. The second part is about Kaylash and her mother Luxmibehn. They are the daughter and wife, respectively, of Laloo "Isu" Chiba, a fellow political prisoner who was serving an 18-year sentence. Kaylash, who is of the Hindu faith had fallen in love with a Muslim and both groups frowned upon such a union. Luxmibehn, not having the support of her husband, Isu, feels extremely vulnerable and Kathrada writes pointedly about how religion can sometimes ill-serve the very people it should be helping. This story does have a happy ending. Kaylash did marry her true love and they are still happily married and bringing up a beautiful family in Lenasia. Isu, her father, who is now in the South African Parliament, dotes on his grandchildren and spends as much time as he can with his big family. We learn also that due to the illness of the priest, Kathrada and colleagues will not be enjoying the customary Dipavali food parcel. It is November and the annual sports competition is seriously underway, with Kathrada's team at the bottom but by no means defeated. These annual events were taken very seriously and became highly organized with prizes being given for the various events.

$\sim$

A. M. Kathrada
Robben Island Jail
25th November 1978

My Dear Zohra,

Your letter of 10th Nov. arrived this morning; the R100–00 money order came sometime last week. Many thanks. It seems that my letters and cards have been reaching. I wonder if the card to little Yusuf ever arrived. The one I'm not certain of is my letter to Tommy of 29th July. When next you write to Dasoo, perhaps you can enquire. I'll also be writing one of these days. I owe Dasoo a reply I'm so lazy to write. There was a time when the monthly quota of letters allowed was not enough. There were so many people to write to and always so much to write about. As the monthly quota increased, my list of correspondents was cut down. You'll never guess how many letters we were allowed to write and receive when we first came to jail. It was one letter every 6 months! And now it is just the opposite 6 letters every month. I remember an occasion when Papa wrote something which was deemed to be objectionable, and his letter was not given to me. So I had to wait another 6 months for a letter! It was the same with visits. Now that we are allowed more visits, unfortunately these are restricted to first degree relatives. And my relatives who fall into this category are not of the travelling type. If I had known of the first degree rule, I should have got married long ago! I was amused the other day when I was reminded of some evidence that was given in a court case in 1965. Apparently a certain lady was wearing a ring on her wedding finger. When [a] witness asked about this, he said he was told that she considered herself to be Kathrada's wife. Over the years I have been often teased about this. With the introduction of the first degree rule, I would have been tempted to admit this allegation. But then, of course, another law would have nullified my admissions. So poor me. Whichever way you look at it I remain the loser.

This reminds me. I don't suppose you have kept close contact with Luxmibehn and the girls. So you wouldn't know of the big fuss over Kaylash and the marriage question. Or do you know about it? It is tragic that in these enlightened times, a difference of religion should stand in the way of a young couple's happiness. I, however, have much sympathy for Luxmibehn too. The poor woman is all alone and unable to stand against the pressures. So she is forced to succumb. It is very sad. One would have thought and hoped that, with the tragedies that have accompanied religious conflicts, people would have been influenced to take a sober approach. Things should have been made easier for Luxmibehn and the young couple's marriage facilitated.

But then this becomes a mini-tragedy when one thinks of the curse of religious fanaticism as it engulfs entire sects and nations. Although the basic causes of conflict are much wider, the role of religion has invariably been an aggravating factor. I'm thinking of Indian-Pakistan, Israel-Arab, Ireland and now Jonestown, Guyana. It is unbelievable this madness that can envelop so many people. It certainly bears out the observation of the 19th century philosopher when he likened religion to opium.

Forgive me, my thoughts have strayed again. Just to round up this subject, I was told by the Prison chaplain that their adviser as far as Moslems are concerned is Dr. Kotwal. I was wondering if this is not the same person who used to be in the Transvaal many years ago. I should like to get in touch with him. I'm trying to get his address. Unfortunately, we did not have the Dipavali service this year. The priest, Mr. Govender (of Cape Town) is unfortunately not well and has been unable to come over. This, of course, also meant that our Dipavali was not accompanied by the usual parcels. We missed these because we've been so used to having these Indian delicacies once a year.

Of course, being "A" Group and, thanks to your generosity, there is no shortage of sweet things during the year. But one does long for the Indian variety, especially the sweetmeats, chevda samoosa, etc., which come with Dipavali. This brings me to Christmas. Which means more goodies. And unluckily for me, renewed weight problems. You recall last November the ceiling to purchase "A" group stuff was raised to R12–00 a month. This November, to keep up with the price increases, this has been raised to R17–00. You will excuse me, but I have gone all out with my purchases for Nov. and Dec. In addition, there are the sports prizes and the normal Xmas parcels. So you can imagine what's going to happen. And, by the way, we also are ordering ice cream! To complete the festivities, we have also ordered 2 films at our own cost: *Scallawag* and *Heat of Anger*. We are looking forward to these.

Our annual sports competition has started. My team is still at the bottom. But we hope to improve. I personally will be playing Scrabble, Bridge, Casino, Carrom and possibly Tenniquoits.

I suppose your parents are back. I hope they had a good trip. Please pass my fondest regards to them.

The way you frequent the "Blue Waters," I won't be surprised if one of these days you hire a permanent suite there. Or even acquire a share! Did you manage to see Boy? How is he doing? I don't suppose you had an opportunity to see my little teenager friend.

I'm happy that you will at last be doing some visiting around Jo'burg. Pass my love to Hajoo, Bhai, etc. Will this be the first time you'll be seeing them? I hope you don't forget Aunty Ayesha. I'm sorry about Bhai's accident. Luckily he got away uninjured. Some time ago there was a possibility of his getting married. Do you know what happened. I was supposed to get a photo of the fiancé.

I must end now. I notice in *Fiat Lux* that Fatty won a garden competition. Good for him.

Lots of love to you and all at home.

From

AMK

This letter was returned to me on 9th Dec., to rewrite, deleting the underlined parts [indicated here by the words being lined through]. Resubmitted on 10th Dec.

≈ ≈ ≈

Bob Vassen—*21 April 1979*

Kathrada bemoans the fact that Bob's elder brother, Tom, is no longer writing, but still cherishes the idea that one day he will start again. Kathrada writes about the importance of photos and comments on the two he had received. This would be the first time he would have seen Bob's two sons, Sean and Barry, who were fifteen and twelve, respectively, when Kathrada got the photos. The other photo of the house and garden in London reminds him of the time he had stayed in London in 1951, with his friends, Vella and Patsy Pillay. Kathrada also has a garden and he finds the flowers and greenery very soothing and therapeutic. Kathrada then reminisces about Flat 13, Bob's mom and Ophirton, the suburb where Bob's father lived. This in turn takes him back to those dark days in 1962 and 1963 when people like Bob's parents and Mrs. Pahad stood steadfast and kept an open house, their loyalty and friendship never wavering. This period saw the increasing harassment and intimidation by the police; many people lived in fear that they would be arrested for associating with people like Kathrada. Another person whom he thinks of is Babla Saloojee, whom he regarded as his little brother. Babla was tortured and then killed while in police detention. His was one of the first "suicides." Because Kathrada had mentioned three colleagues by name, the letter was returned with the instruction to delete the underlined part. No fellow-prisoners could be mentioned by name at this time. All the friends listed at the end to whom Kathrada sends regards are all active ANC members.

∽

A. M. Kathrada
Robben Island Jail
21st April 1979

My Dear Bobby,

What a lovely surprise to hear from you! In fact your letter has done a lot to restore my fast-ebbing faith in humanity, at least in that part of humanity personified by brother Tom. While he was still a votary of Mr. Lucas,[1] Tom used to write once in a while. But after he went on the wagon, those frequent letters came to an end. And with that a whole portion of my world—which I hold so dearly—closed on me. I really felt the loss. However, in our circumstances one begins to adapt and acclimatize, and with the passage of time I began to accept the position. Fortunately Dasoo never failed to mention something about you folks, but he could do little more than merely mention you all. Well Bobby, now that you've broken the ice, let's hope we'll be able to maintain close contact. Perhaps brother Tom may come to light again.

You did a lovely thing by sending the two photos. You know, only in jail I really began to appreciate the value of photos. You put it so well when you said they help to narrow the gap in space and time. If you've read my

---

[1] The trade name of a South African brandy.

December letter to Dasoo, you will have an idea of my requirements. I want many photos, all of you and especially the children. I'm not even going to start mentioning all the folks I wish to see. You name them, and I'm sure to want their photos. I must say, Ursula, you and Sean and Barry look very well. Ursula with her new hairstyle and minus a couple of pounds looks lovely. In fact both of you look younger. England must be doing you a world of good.

Your description of the typical London house and the photo fits so well with my memory of Vella's house where I stayed when I was in London. A garden is another thing I really came to appreciate in jail. We've had our little patch here, and it's so soothing just to see flowers and the greenery. It must have a therapeutic effect on us. As you would have most probably guessed, the chili plants became literally the hot favourites. One day I'll write more about this.

There is so much I want to write about and much more that I want to ask you. I'm all mixed up and don't know where to begin. I'm sure I'll be better organized in my next letter.

You mentioned Mia's Farm and I thought of that last picnic we had there, remember? It was lovely. Coral and Basil[2] were with us and so many others. Don't forget to tell me about them one day. My thoughts are just racing on uncontrollably. I think I'll leave off for a couple of minutes and make myself a nice cup of chocolate. Well, I've had the chocolate, but instead of clearing my mind it's got me thinking of food and Flat 13 and Mummy and Ophirton, of so many things. It is Saturday night, and I'm thinking of the russo that I'd been so used to having on Sunday mornings. And I'm thinking of the adversities I experienced in late '62 and '63 and of the loyalty, love and devotion of friends. And Mummy's name and Mrs. Pahad's name would be heading the list and inscribed in gold. But alas those two wonderful human beings are no more. And Babla is gone . . . and so many others.

Bob, I think I better end now and get this away. Otherwise I might just ramble on and on and [get] progressively incoherent.

~~We are all getting on fine. Isu, Billy, Walter (I think those are the only ones you met), all send their regards. Last week Isu's second daughter, Gita, turned 21. For the occasion Isu hired *Gone with the Wind* and bought some eats. It was terrific.~~

---

[2] Coral and Basil; Bobby's sister-in-law and her husband.

Please remember me to each and every one of our mutual friends—
Harry, Herb, Charlie, Dagga, Billy, Issy, Ismail, Stretch, Wikram (the dry
cleaner)[3], everybody.

Lots of love to Ursula, Sean, Barry, Della, Tom, Delia, Boyo, Claude,
Darren, Mrs. Pillay, Mrs. Reddy, Harlene and your good self.

Write soon—and don't forget the photos.

All the best from

AMK

12 May. The original returned to me by censors. Asked to delete
underlined portion [indicated here by the words being lined through].
Resubmitted on 13 May with portion deleted.

≈ ≈ ≈

Poppy Kola—*19 May 1979*

*Kathrada had last seen Poppy Kola, a nephew, in 1961 or 1962, at a time
when life for Kathrada was politically highly charged. His apartment was
under surveillance and his movements were being watched closely. When he met
Poppy he was not being cool or distant he writes, but protective of family and
friends. It was common to be guilty just by association and Kathrada did not
wish to expose Poppy to the security police. Kathrada, Poppy, and a few other
members of the family had broken with the conservative traditions and customs
surrounding Islam, yet they were never victimized or ostracized by the Indian
community, and Kathrada finds this an admirable trait in his family. Poppy,
for example, married an Irish woman and had settled in Dublin and there was
no problem whatsoever. However, in one way Kathrada, Poppy, and a few others had failed in not completing their education. Kathrada, on the eve of completing his high school exams left to work full-time in politics. He is pleased that
no one was following the path of becoming shop owners. Kathrada is keen that
he and Poppy re-establish and maintain contact as he would like to get to know
the family in Dublin. He cautions Poppy not to write anything political.*

≈

---

[3] Wolfie Kodesh.

A. M. Kathrada
Robben Island Jail
19th May 1979

My Dear Poppy,

After all these years, at last I am getting down to fulfilling a promise I've made to myself—which is—to say "hello" to you. Each time I've been wanting to write something crops up and I leave it for another day. And so it went on, and the years rolled by and a quick calculation reveals that I last saw you in 1961 or 1962! I can clearly recall the night you and Broer came to the flat. I advised you not to stay with me, and a few weeks later I deliberately avoided going to the airport to see you off. These actions of mine must have struck you as strange, inhospitable and unfriendly. I think I made some explanation to you, but I'm sure it must have sounded inadequate and unsatisfactory at the time. If you did think ill of me, I feel certain that events that followed soon after your visit will have provided the reasons for my inexplicable behaviour. You see, Flat 13 was already a bit "too hot" and getting progressively hotter and, much as I disliked it, I just had to keep my innocent family members and friends away from there.

So you see, it wasn't as if I suddenly started cooling off towards my near and dear ones. From ever since I can remember, I've had a great liking for you. I can still picture you as a little chap, rather naughtyish, but in a nice way. As you grew up, I began to regard you more as a friend than a nephew. Do you remember one day when you were still at high school, you came up to the flat and found us partaking of victuals which were "unIslamic?" Had it been any of the other nephews, the visit would have been rather awkward. But you did not cause the slightest embarrassment.

Our family has been a bit on the conservative side, but at the same time they have often surprised me with the ease with which they have adapted themselves to and accepted non-conformity by some of its members. I think you, I, Dos and Abdulhaybhai have been about the worst "culprits" in this regard. In our own way each of us has moved away from the norms and traditions which have bound the family, and happily we have not been in any way victimised as a result. One day I must tell you of our experiences when I took the womenfolk from home on a holiday trip to Durban. They were wonderful, and it brought me much closer to them ever since.

I can recall the time you took the "unconventional" step and decided to add a bit of England into our family. From what I was able to gather, the reactions ranged from reserve to enthusiasm. But I heard of no hostility. The one disappointment I did hear of was when you discontinued your studies. This feeling I shared as well. When it comes to studies, our record is terrible. We're such a large family, but in spite of all the encouragement and opportunities, we just have not succeeded in producing a single professional man or woman. That is apart from a handful of teachers. The first hopes were centered on Dos and me. We disappointed. Then it was you and Enver. But you too did not complete. I just hope some of the younger ones will break away from our bad examples. Of course, there is some consolation that some of these young chaps at least are not going to join their fathers behind the shop counters.

Let's get back to you. As I've said, I've been wanting to get in touch with you for some time. I wanted to do so when you got married, and there were other occasions as well. You may put down my keenness to do so to the "old-fashioned" desire to maintain the family connection. I would so much like to know my niece in far away Dublin and Enver and Klena. Unfortunately, apart from a couple of sentences in letters, and a few words at visits, I know virtually nothing about them. What is worse is that I'm ignorant of my niece's name! Can you believe that? Now I'm not going to start casting blame on anyone for this sorry state of affairs. My desire is to remedy the situation by establishing and maintaining contact.

I shall rely on an uncle's prerogative to insist on an early reply from you or, better still, from the better half of the family. With the letter I shall expect photographs of each one of you as well as photos of anyone else, or anything for that matter, that will help to give me a good idea of yourselves. Is this a tall order? I hope not.

There is very much I'd like to write about, but that will have to wait. I'd like to get this letter away. I'm getting on fine. Apart from petty ailments, my health is keeping up. So far I've fortunately been free of the illnesses that frequently come with increasing years and long stretches of imprisonment. My spirits too are tops. I take [it] you do know something about my stay on Robben Island so I shall not repeat "stale" news.

I'm sure it is unnecessary, but let me, nevertheless, sound a word of caution. I am aware you have never interested yourself in politics. When writing, please do not include any political news or comment as these can cause unnecessary delays. I suppose you do know that, for over a year now, we have been allowed to get SABC news as well as an international magazine. So I'm fairly up to date.

This will be the lot. Please pass my love to your wife and to Enver and Klena.

All the best to you from

AMK

≈ ≈ ≈

Aadil Jassat—*28 July 1979*

Coming from a closely knit community, perhaps brought even closer by apartheid laws, lasting friendships developed in the Indian community. These bonds became stronger in the crucible of common political purpose; this was the case with Kathrada and Aadil's father, Dr. Essop Jassat, a veteran of the liberation struggle. Writing to Aadil, now twelve years old, Kathrada wanted to get to know this young person and asks for news about him. This contact was also a way for Kathrada to keep in touch with the father, to whom he was not permitted to write.

≈

A. M. Kathrada
Robben Island Jail
28 July 1979

My Dear Aadil,

I am sure you will be surprised to receive this letter from someone you do not know. You see, I was in jail four years already when you were born. For a few years after you were born, I used to receive letters which had news about you, but for some years now I have not been hearing about you.

I have been regularly receiving the Eid cards sent by you, Mummy, Daddy, Yumna and Zaheera. It has been very nice of you all to think of us, and I must assure you that your kind thoughts and wishes have been greatly appreciated.

But I would really like to know more about you, Yumna and Zaheera. And that is why I am writing this letter to you. I think I am correct that Zaheera is about 6 years old; Yumna, 8 years; and you, 12 years. So you must be in Std. 5 this year, not so? I am sure you will be able to write a nice letter to me and tell me all about yourself and your sisters. About the school, your teachers, the games you play, the bioscope,[1] TV, about the cold weather, the books you read and everything else. And I have another very important request to you. You must send me nice photographs of yourselves and also of Rauhana and Ahmed.

Somebody told me Daddy is fat now. Is that true? It would be nice to see his photo. And also Mummy's.

I have just remembered something now. A few years ago I did have some photos of Rauhana's birthday party at Orient House. And you were in one of the photos. Now I am wondering what happened to these photos. I shall have to look for them. But of course you were all very much younger then. I would like to have the latest photos.

I will end this letter now. Next time I will tell you something about jail. Are you interested?

My health is quite good. I hope Mummy, Daddy and all of you are also getting on well. Please pass my fondest regards to them and to the uncles and the rest of the family.

Also Eid Mubarak to all of you.

Lots of love to Yumna, Zaheera and yourself.

From

AM Kathrada

~ ~ ~

Dasoo Iyer—*17 November 1979*

A moving and eloquent letter to Dasoo. A fellow prisoner, Eddie Daniels, with whom Kathrada and the others had spent fifteen years, had been released a day before; Kathrada is trying to come to grips with this parting of a dear friend. Kathrada wonders if he will ever see him again. At difficult times like these, Kathrada found a certain release in writing letters and "apologizes" to Dasoo for having to bear the brunt of his sadness. All the parts in this letter relating to Eddie had to be left out on orders from the censor.

~

---

[1] A movie theater.

Robben Island Jail
17th November 1979

My Dear Dasoo,

Your letter of 10th September reached me on 6th Oct. On the same day I also received a letter from Bobby. Thanks a lot. I shall be writing to Bobby soon. I'm writing this in the early hours of the morning. It is so quiet except for the rhythmic sound of the waves breaking against the shore as if they were keeping time with the equally rhythmic whistling of the wind. The birds and the crickets and the mosquitoes are all silent. There is not even a stir or a snore from my neighbours. It's as if I'm alone on the island. One feels almost driven towards sessions of sweet, silent thoughts and remembrances of things past. It seems so incongruous to be concerning oneself with mundane things instead of just lying in bed and enjoying the silence and just thinking. If only one were endowed with the talents of a musician, a poet, a writer—any creative artist—then surely this would be the ideal atmosphere.

A door has just banged, a vehicle has come to a screeching stop. And with that we come back to reality. A solitary bird has begun to sing. Soon it will be joined by others. And it will be dawn. That means I better hurry in order to get this away. I've been wondering why I had to choose this moment to write about the wind and the sea and the birds. Is it some form of escapism? Yes, I think it is. Yesterday a very dear friend was released from jail after 15 years! I suppose I wanted to avoid thinking about the vacuum this has created. He came in just a few months after us. We soon became friends. Over the years we shared many experiences together, exchanged confidences, read, played, discussed, worked, differed, argued. We came from two completely different backgrounds and in many respects held differing ideas and outlooks. We were thrown together in the same confined environment to face common problems and, more important, to gear ourselves for the years that lay ahead. In the process, a close bond developed between us. And this week we had to part, perhaps never to see each other again. We were in the original foursome who started playing bridge surreptitiously at first and with hand made cards. We played a number of other games together. Just a few hours before the boat took him away, we played a couple of rubbers of bridge, we drank tea, ate biscuits, sang a few songs, teased each other and said goodbye. It was a very difficult moment, and we let it pass as quickly as possible.

~~I'm sorry that you had to be the victim of my present state of mind.~~

It was very nice to hear from you after such a long time. I noticed that you too are inclined towards nostalgia at times. Yes, the Gettysburg Address brings back memories. We used to make deliberate mistakes like "Four score and seven minus 19 years just to test if the teacher was alert. The headmaster, the party for the handicapped, the powerful voice of our own Paul Robeson, the singing and stamping of feet, the garlanding—I can just imagine the atmosphere. It's good to see you so engrossed in remedial education. I hope you have an equally successful Guy Fawkes evening.

The thought of your headmaster reminds me of *Goodbye Mr. Chips*, which I was reading a couple of months ago. Didn't Mr. Chips also devote his whole life to the profession he loved above everything else! And what powerful bonds of affection between teacher and pupils!

I'm glad that Rookie has been able to visit you all. How long is she staying? It must have been wonderful to see her. She must have told you of her visit to Robben Island some years ago. Nice to hear of Sakina as well. Is she still studying or lecturing! Pass my love to her. Only recently I was reading something that covered similar ground as her thesis. Was it ever published?

~~When you do get down to organizing some literature on the Olympics, please remember that it must be posted to [me] directly by the bookshop. Let it be addressed to the Officer Commanding with a letter that it is meant for me.~~

Hope both Vanitha and Vijan have done well in their exams. There is a slight chance I may be studying again. Will let you know.

Healthwise I'm fine. A few months ago I was sent to a specialist in Cape Town for a general check-up. After a very thorough examination, he declared me fit and said I'd have no problems for insurance. So there seems to be quite a bit of kick left in the old horse.

Keep well. Lots of love to Sally, the children and all friends and relatives. Merry Christmas to all of you and everything of the best for 1980 from

AMK

24 Nov. Original returned with instructions to leave out portion marked in red [Reproduced here as lined-through words].

~ ~ ~

Head of Robben Island Prison—*24 November 1979*

Kathrada, at a low point in his life, writes this letter to the Head of Robben Island Prison. In particular, he complains about actions taken by censors regarding a letter to his close friend, Dassoo Iyer (see the letter, above, written on 17 November 1979). In it, Kathrada mentions a recently released prisoner and is upset by capricious and arbitrary behavior.

~

24th November 1979
The Head of the Prison
Robben Island

Sir,

I am sorry that I have to, once again, refer to you a letter that has been returned to me for rewriting.

As you will notice there are two portions that the censors have found objectionable and have instructed me to delete.

I am aware of the arbitrary attitude of the censors about not allowing me to mention the names of fellow prisoners. This is unfair and has no basis whatsoever in terms of the law or the rules and regulations governing prisoners.

As far as this particular portion is concerned, I respectfully submit that it is not even covered by the prohibition imposed by the censors. I am not mentioning any names, and in any case, the man in question [Eddie Daniels], is no longer a prisoner on Robben Island. I fail to see how this paragraph can possibly be subversive or violate prison security. I have been writing this type of thing in previous letters And there have been no objections. In fact, I can think of at least one time this year in which I wrote about a fellow prisoner who is now out of jail and it was allowed to go through.

I wish to appeal to you to use your authority to restrain the censors. They should be prevented from just being guided by their own personal feelings and likes and dislikes. They should be made to give a rational explanation for their actions, to point out exactly what is wrong with contents which they deem to be unfit.

As for the second portion [of my complaint] you will recall I specifically discussed this matter with you. What I wrote there is no more than what you agreed I could do. I am merely taking the precaution of stressing to my friend that he should not personally handle the literature but place the order through a bookshop.

I am enclosing the letter. It is unfortunate that I have to constantly approach you on matters which are so straightforward, but which are unnecessarily complicated by the narrow outlook of the censors.

I should be pleased if you will let me know your decision with regard to the two paragraphs.

Lest you get the wrong impression, I might point out that I do not refer all similar letters to you. Last month the censors returned a letter to me, and though I did not quite agree with them, I thought they were not being unreasonable, so I rewrote the letter. For quite a few months, I had not been experiencing much difficulty with the censors. But for the past couple of months there seems to have been a radical change in their attitude. They seem to be reverting back to the old days of malicious and arbitrary censorship. Under the circumstances, I must make an earnest appeal to you for your assistance.

Thank you very much
Yours faithfully,
A. M. Kathrada

≈ ≈ ≈

Shamima Kola—*15 December 1979*

Shamima has written to Kathrada describing her family's rejection of Neelan, the person with whom she is in love. Kathrada reminds his niece that this is an age-old problem and cites Romeo and Juliet, Othello, Leila Majnu, *and others who have suffered as she is obviously suffering now. He asks her to be patient and not to do anything rash. He also tells her of his sympathy for her mother, now a widow and unwell and perhaps not strong enough to challenge her family. Summoning his the tact and diplomacy, Kathrada says he will try to get to the root of the problem, but patience is required. That Shamima had been assaulted he finds reprehensible and totally unjustifiable. He gives her hope in telling of her uncle's marriage to a white woman and where they all seem to be living a happy and contented life. If prejudice is the only reason for the family's objection to Neelan, a non-Muslim, then the family will certainly not get Kathrada's support.*

~

A. M. Kathrada
Robben Island Jail
15th December 1979

My Dearest Shamima,

Your most informative, frank and heart-rending letter arrived last Saturday. Although its contents were sad, I am very glad you wrote and poured your heart out. What a great pity that this, our first contact, had to be occasioned by the very unhappy experience that you are going through. How much nicer it would have been had we been able to write and talk about things that evoke feelings of pleasure and laughter and joy, free of worries and cares and complaints; to write about songs and dances, plays, films, books, debates and hobbies, about everything that adds to harmony at home and understanding and good relationships generally.

But we know that, unfortunately, life does not always flow so smoothly for all of us. We encounter problems of one sort or another which we have to face and solve. The problems often caused by love between man and woman have been with us for centuries. They have given rise to acts of chivalry, heroism, nobility, devotion, sacrifice and strife. They have formed the subject of legend, poetry, drama and history. Some of the greatest plays deal with different aspects of the subject. You have been interested in drama. Need I remind you of *Helen of Troy, Romeo and Juliet, Othello, Leila Majnu, Shireen Ferhad* and countless others. Cleopatra of ancient Egypt and her love affair with Antony which affected the destiny of nations.

I am citing these plays in order to remind both you and myself that the problem we are facing is by no means easy to solve. Many parents still cling to the old-fashioned view that they should choose marriage partners for their children. And the range of their choice is, in general, severely restricted by religious beliefs, colour consciousness and, in many cases—social prejudice.

I do not have to tell you that I condemn these prejudices and find them totally unacceptable and abhorrent. On the other hand, I don't want to be unfair to the parents either. Most of them adopt this right attitude because they don't know any better. They have grown up with wrong ideas and wrong concepts, and as they get older, they find it increasingly difficult to shake off their life-long beliefs. They sincerely think that what they do is in the best interests of their children.

Now, let us take Mummy. I don't know what her views are. I'm going to write to her. I would be very hurt if I find that her objections are also based on narrow and unjustifiable prejudices. But I do not want to criticise her out of hand. I realise that she is in a difficult position. Pappa is no longer there, Munira is married and has her own responsibilities; mummy is very unwell and must be feeling too weak and unable to face the hostile attitudes among family members. I sympathise with her. Even if she has the slightest inclination to support you, I am sure she will still need strong backing. Let us find out. If prejudice is there unfortunately we cannot simply wish it away. We will have to use all our powers of persuasion. There is already a precedent in the family. Pappa's brother is married to a white lady and their children are Catholic. These facts have not in the least affected their happiness. I am now in contact with them. They seem to be such a lovely contented family.

So my dearest Shamima, I'm going to ask you to be a little patient. I know how you feel. Your cup of bitterness must be flowing over. You must be finding it difficult to endure the days away from your beloved. Besides, there has been the humiliation of the dastardly assault upon you. You know I'm so upset and angry about this violence, I don't want you to even tell me who was responsible. Even if you were entirely in the wrong there was absolutely no justification for the assault. I find it reprehensible.

From what you tell me Neelan seems to be a decent and responsible young man. He is evidently devoted to you. It is a pity I do not know him. If the family's only objection to him is based on religion and communalism and racialism then they certainly will not get my support. Let's wait and hear what they say.

There is so much more I wanted to write about but I'll leave it for another time. I ask you again to be patient. Do not do anything rash. The next time you write you must include photos of yourself.

My fondest regards to Mummy, Munira and all the folks at home.
Lots of love to you from
AMK.

≈ ≈ ≈

Zohra Kathrada—*22 December 1979*

As 1979 draws to a close, Kathrada finds himself in the middle of a modern-day "Romeo and Juliet" dilemma. His niece, Shamim, coming from an ortho-dox Muslim home, wants to marry her high school sweetheart, a boy from the Tamil (Hindu) community. In this letter to Zohra, he urges his family to "shed the religious and racial prejudice." He goes on to say, obviously hurt, that "in the times we live there is absolutely no place for prejudices based on religion, race or colour. I do not have to elaborate on the tragedies and sufferings these have caused." He offers to help and asks his family to be rational and objective and not to cause pain and possible injury to Shamim. Within the Indian com-munity in South Africa, there are Muslims, Hindus and Christians; the ten-dency for these groups to marry within their own group has been strong. In its extreme form, Hindus married only Hindus from their own village or the vil-lage their grandparents had come from. Within the Muslim group, they had an equivalent practice. Those who married "out" of the community often found themselves ostracized by one or both families. Some left South Africa while oth-ers braved the cold blasts in the hope that reconciliation would eventually come. This would not be the first time Kathrada would intervene in such a situation.

≈

A. M. Kathrada
Robben Island Jail
22nd December 1979

My Dear Zohra,

Your letter of 24th November reached me only today. Thanks also for the R70. It came just in time. My last letter to you was of 1st Dec.; it should have reached you by now.

I received a letter from Shamim and have replied to her already. I have also written to Tahera at your Box number. This is really not an easy problem to solve. I replied so speedily to Shamim because I have fears that she may do something desperate. What is necessary for all concerned in this affair is to exercise patience, caution and understand-ing. I must tell you, as I told her mother, that Shamim's letter has touched my heart. She seems to be highly intelligent, sensitive and tal-ented. She has [handled] her troubles in a calm and forthright manner.

She is obviously very much in love with her boyfriend and wants to marry him. She has known him since she was in Std. 7, and, in spite of obstacles and objections, she has continued her relationship with him. So, in addition to her other qualities, she strikes me as a determined as well as devoted young lady. The family's main objection to the boy seems to be that he is Tamil. I'd be most disappointed and hurt if the only serious fault they find is the boy's religion and possibly his colour. Obviously I cannot side with the family if this is so. It may be that there are other faults; alcohol and drugs have been mentioned. Here I must be very careful not to simply accept anything said by either side. Deep emotions are involved and it is difficult to be free of prejudice. What is absolutely indispensable is a calm, reasonable objective and, above all, a reasonable approach. I have offered in my letter to find out all that I can about the boy. I believe it is essential to get reports from people who are completely impartial.

In the meantime I must appeal to you, and especially to Papa, to take a more positive view of the matter. I know it is very difficult to break from tradition and customs, which have been rooted, in us for years. The first and foremost requirement is to make a determined effort to shed the religious and racial prejudice. Try to accept that Shamim is no longer a kid and that she is determined to go to great lengths in order to marry the boy of her choice. Most important to bear in mind is that Shamim belongs to a generation of youth that is no longer prepared to meekly accept the notions and behaviour patterns and attitudes laid down by the elders. They've got their own views, outlooks, ambitions, desires and norms, which they use as a basis for their behaviour and practices. It is part of a worldwide phenomenon. I'm not for a moment saying that we must just throw overboard all our own beliefs and surrender to every demand and desire of the young people. But it is going to be indispensable to make certain radical adjustments and shake off outdated ideas and practices. In the times in which we live there is absolutely no place for prejudices based on religion, race or colour. I do not have to elaborate on the tragedies and suffering these have caused. We have to understand and come to grips with developments among the youth and try to narrow the gap that is existing between us. Otherwise the young people will grow further and further away from us until they become total strangers. And we will lose them altogether.

I know what I'm asking is not easy; more especially when one's own family is concerned. I say be very careful not to judge the boy on the basis of rumours. As parents and elders, take a more active interest in the affair. Make your own careful investigations in order to ascertain: is the boy responsible? Does he have regular employment? What sort of a family does he come from? Are his intentions towards Shamim honourable? Is it true that he is a drunkard and drug addict, or does he just take an occasional social drink? These are among the things you must find out. But the first prerequisite is to try to get rid of prejudices.

I'm very concerned and anxious because I don't want Shamim to do anything hasty and rash. If your investigation reveals that the boy is not suitable, then let us put our heads together and try to dissuade her from continuing her relationship. But if, apart from religion, there are no negative findings, then we must try to accept the position and give our blessings to the union. Of course, there is no guarantee that the marriage will be a success. But then it is just not possible to prophesy about any marriage, no matter how suitable the couple may seem. This is something that can be worked out and primarily by the partners. We can make things easier for them.

Please try to ensure that no undue pressure is put on Shamim. The horrible thought keeps coming to my mind that she may be driven to do something desperate and harm herself. She is young and needs sympathy, understanding, kindness and love and patience. My anxiety is increased by my personal knowledge of cases where young people have actually committed suicide. At the beginning of 1963 I actually arrived on the scene a few minutes after the wife of a very dear friend of mine had gassed herself to death. There are other cases I've heard of.

Marriages across religious and colour lines are increasingly common. This is the reality of our times and we must accept it. Sons and daughters in prominent Moslem families have already broken this tradition. Most of the cases that I personally know of have had successful marriages.

There is so much that can still be said about this, but I have to end now. I'll have to leave other matters for my next letter. You asked whether I regretted not having got married myself. I'll deal with this too.

Keep well. Everything of the best of all of you for 1980.

Lots of love from

AMK

~   ~   ~

Bob Vassen—*19 January 1980*

*The first letter of the New Year and, in wishing Bob and family a happy 1980,
Kathrada thinks back to a New Year's Eve party in December 1962 at the
apartment of Bob's dad in Ophirton. Going to the Danube Nightclub was not
possible, as Kathrada being a banned person could not attend a public gathering. Even at a private home his being present was still breaking the law. He is
grappling with a family matter involving racial prejudice and this leads him to
a detailed account of visits to Berlin, Warsaw, Auschwitz, and Lidice and the
horrors he witnessed. The authorities have now installed a radio system with a
speaker in every cell and this together with a few magazines, have helped to
make the inmates "feel part of the world." Kathrada teases Bob, the boy from
Fordsburg, and hopes he is not the person smuggling illegal immigrants into
England. He also remembers a young Indian girl at Trafalgar Square in London
carrying a placard, which read, "We are here, because you were there." The
English he maintains are the last to complain about Black immigration.
Although behind bars and cut off from the outside world for so long, Kathrada
and his colleagues manage to keep themselves informed, by all means possible:
both legal and illegal.*

~

A. M. Kathrada
Robben Island Jail
19th January 1980

My Dear Bob,

I hope my delay in replying to you does not influence you to emulate
my bad example. Dasoo must have told you that his and your letters
arrived together on 6th October and that I'd be writing to you later. Well,
here goes. The year being still young, let me start off by saying "Cheers"
to you and all the family and friends. Let this and the years to come continue to bring you happiness and joy and health. My thoughts are so dis-
organised, jumping from one thing to another, enveloping the past, the
present and the future. But I don't want to use this as an excuse to postpone writing. Rather a rambling letter than no letter.

I just remembered the last New Year's Eve that we were together. We
were at the flat for a short while. There was some debate as to whether we

should go to the Danube. For good reasons, I could not go there. So we went to Ophirton. We had an enjoyable time. I can picture that young lady (from Rhodes I think) kneeling oriental style before your granny as if in prayer. And, as the night wore on, she passed into oblivion. It was all quite amusing and in no way offensive. Do you still remember? It was New Year's Eve wasn't it? Little did we know then what 1963 would bring! The watershed which changed so many of our lives. For you, marriage and children—and eventually, England. For me, Rivonia and jail.

While I'm in the past, let me go a bit further back. To 1951–52, to my visit to Europe. This week it all came back to me with such force. We saw the film, Holocaust. Berlin, Prague, Warsaw, it was all there. I remembered the ruins and rubble of Berlin, the massive feeling of guilt that had overwhelmed the German people, the strenuous efforts of especially the youth to hold out their hands of friendship, freundschaft, and to pledge that it will never happen again. There were some moving events that I shall never forget. Social gatherings where young people met and talked, sang, danced, ate, drank, kissed, embraced and pledged everlasting friendship. Thus, Vietnamese met the French—Koreans met Americans—and Israelis met the Germans. Moments packed with emotion and inspiration. I went to Prague where Gauleiter Reinhardt Haydrich was assassinated. The Nazis accused the people of the little village of Lidice of hiding the assassins. For that they shot every male inhabitant of Lidice and virtually razed it to the ground. When I went there Lidice had been rebuilt, but it was a village of widows and children. In Prague, I recalled how bravely Julius Fucik had written his last words, almost until the hour when he was executed. Fucik symbolized the resistance to Nazism and his words published in a book, took their place in literature that will inspire generations to come. Then to Warsaw, to the area where the ghetto had been. Only a monument was there to mark the murder of tens of thousands of Jews and to pay tribute to the handful who fought back and died. But indelibly printed on my mind is the visit to Auschwitz concentration camp. The trench in which dogs mauled and savaged people to death, the gas chambers, the incinerators, the lampshades of human skin, the pillows of human hair, and other gruesome reminders of unbelievable atrocity. The streets outside the crematoria were littered with small pieces of human bones. I brought back a handful of bones with me to South Africa.

Many young people, especially those who were born after the war, find it hard to believe that Holocaust was by and large based on historical fact. Indeed, I've read magazine articles which dismiss the happenings as propaganda. And this only after one generation! How can people have such short memories! This film, with all the reservations one may have, is a necessary reminder.

By coincidence I happened to be busy reading Mussolini's biography, and I had already decided to reread Bullock's study on Hitler when this film came. A few months ago we saw The 5th Offensive. Yesterday we saw a British documentary, *The Face of Famine*. A fortnight back a documentary on Einstein proved to be a suitable prelude to Holocaust.

I'm sorry that I've gone off on a tangent about Holocaust. I suppose to some extent it is because for the past few months my mind has been focussed on a family matter that involves elements of racial and religious prejudice. A Moslem girl wants to marry a Tamil boy. I won't bore you with more of this.

Did I tell you that they have installed quite a good rediffusion system in jail? Every cell has a speaker. We get 2 SABC news broadcasts daily, plus radio plays, quizzes, and radio and recorded music. This plus Time magazine, etc., has made a tremendous difference to our prison life. It's not only the political news that is important. Sports, drama, anthropology, book reviews–all this contributes to make us feel part of the world. This evening there were a couple of Irish folk songs, and I thought of my nephew and his Irish wife in Dublin. (Incidentally, I hope you managed to give my message to my younger nephew in London.) Every time I hear Professor Higgins trying to drum proper English into unwilling Eliza's head, I think of you. One day there was an item that said that some private schools in England which specialized in teaching English to foreigners were also smuggling illegal immigrants into UK on the side. Naturally I thought of a certain Fordsburg boy who is guilty of teaching English. But I don't know about [the] smuggling part of it. Whenever I read or hear of the English complaining about Black immigrants, I think of a photo of a demonstration in London in which an Indian girl was carrying a placard saying, "We are here because you were there." How succinctly and poignantly it sums up the whole position! The British, French and other colonial powers should be the last to complain of Black immigration.

It was lovely to read of your trip to America though, given a chance, I don't think I'd want to visit that place. Somehow I've never been attracted by it. Of course, if I had to visit friends settled there, it's a different matter. It was so nice to hear of Coral and Basil and the kids and to see their photos. I still hope one day Basil will recall the promise he made during a lighter moment and write. It would be most interesting to hear something about the Museum of African Art, of other S. Africans in America, etc.

Coming back to the radio, we've been listening to some chap called Anand Naidoo who reports for Radio S.A. from Brussels. Do you know him? He sounds South African.

I've heard a disturbing report suggesting that the marriage of Govindbhai seems to be on the rocks. What a great pity. Do tell me about it but only if you feel you want to.

I must end now. Lots of love to Ursula, Sean, Barry, the aunts, Tom, Della, Herb, Harry, Billy, Charlie, Harlene and all the gang. Write soon, and send more photos.

All the best to you from
AMK

~ ~ ~

Dr. Karim—*14 June and 30 July 1980*

In this letter to Dr. Karim, a medical doctor and scholar who has written on the effect of Arabic on Afrikaans, Kathrada expresses his views on the common sense and efficacy of preventative medicine. He welcomes the shift of religion from ritual to social obligation but wonders whether this can happen. This reminds him of 1947 when as a young man he was so angered by the hysteria the local Muslim community displayed on the birth of modern Pakistan. More recently this anger returned when a leader in the Muslim community in Durban got "hot and bothered about happenings thousands of miles away" yet did or said nothing about conditions at home.

~

A. M. Kathrada
Robben Island Jail
(First written on 14 June. Returned. After representations to HOP, rewritten & handed in on 30th July 1980. AMK.)

Dear Doc,

I must thank you for your very interesting and informative letter which arrived on 26th April. It gave me a lot to think about and, at the same time, gave rise to further questions and problems in my mind. I have been observing with interest the growing trend of thought among medical men in particular that a great percentage of modern diseases have their origin in social and psychological factors and the consequent emphasis on the preventative rather than curative approach. To a layman like me this appears to be simply a matter of common sense. But, of course, that would be rather superficial. I realise that, in fact, it is a vast and complex problem linked up as it is with the entire socio-economic-political set-up of countries. I doubt it very much if in the whole of the Western world there is a single country where the preventative aspects of medicine has not remained more than an ideal. And the same would apply to the over- whelming majority of third-world countries. I take it that the type of approaches you are advocating has still not gone beyond the thinking stage even in the Moslem countries. You must have been able to get a good idea of the latter at the conference in Qatar. All of this indicates the magnitude of the problem. I believe that any progressive approach towards alleviating disease and illness is to be welcomed irrespective of whether it comes from religious bodies, social welfare institutions or any other groupings. But at the same time it would be unrealistic to build high expectations from the resolutions and aims of such bodies. For with the best intentions in the world, their activities cannot have more than [a] cosmetic effect.

I do not for a moment want to belittle the work you are doing. In fact I welcome very much the move away from the mass of rituals and injunc- tions and the increasing emphasis on the social obligations of religion. Naturally, this has its own implications. I remember as a youngster being very much disturbed and angered by the virtual hysteria that swept the local Moslem community when Pakistan was born. Now, 30 years later, I found myself similarly angered when I listened recently to a radio inter- view by a Durban Moslem leader about another Moslem country. I asked myself, much the same as I did in my youth, whether it would not be more fruitful and constructive for this man to direct his anger and devote his energy towards more immediate local problems. I cannot help but suspect an element of escapism in people who get all hot and both- ered about happenings thousands of miles away and remain untouched about things at home. Social obligations, as I understand them, imply commitment and involvement, not to remote and far-off events but to everyday reality. Here I am not necessarily confining myself to politics. But surely there is such a lot one can do in so many other spheres—law, medicine, education, social welfare, sports, etc.

I was listening the other night to Professor Van der Vyfar of Wits concerning aspects of the judicial process in certain Moslem countries as a violation of human rights: I think he was referring to the events portrayed in *Death of a Prisoner*, the public floggings in Pakistan and the sentences meted out in Iran. I will be interested to hear your views on this.

Let me move to more personal matters. I suppose you have heard of the decision of the government to allow us to study again. I haven't quite decided what to do, but I am thinking of History Honours. Even better than that is the decision to allow us newspapers. I'm really looking forward to this. Up to now we have had no reply on things like *Fiat Lux, Alpha, Bantu*, etc., for S.A. news! Incidentally, I saw your photo in *Fiat Lux*, and recently an article about your studies on Arabic influence on Afrikaans.

Since the beginning of this year, we have an Imam from Cape Town visiting us monthly. The arrangements were made by Dr. Kotwal whom you may know.

There is some confusion here about your thesis and literature. I am under the impression that you had sent these to me. The local authorities say they know nothing about it. Please clarify. I'm looking forward to hearing about your Australian trip. On June 13th I finished 16 years on Robben Island! I'm keeping well except for a touch of cholesterol. Will write more about it later.

My fondest regards to Rahim and all relatives and friends.

All the best to you from

AMK

≈   ≈   ≈

Aziz Kathrada—*19 July 1980*

A charming letter to his grandnephew, thanking him for the letter he had written. Kathrada is delighted that Aziz is taking his sports seriously and offers him every encouragement to continue, pointing out that sport is not only healthy, but it also teaches teamwork. He quotes de Coubertin's famous speech and tells Aziz to remember these words and to adopt them as his code of conduct when he plays any game. He is pleased that Aziz is doing well in his studies. The two, Kathrada says, go together.

≈

A. M. Kathrada
Robben Island Jail
19th July 1980

My Dear Aziz,

I was very surprised and happy when I received your nice letter in May. I am sorry it took me such a long time to reply. I asked Zohrabibi to tell you that I got your letter. I hope she did so. I wrote to her on 28th June.

I was glad to read that you were training hard for your Sportsday at the end of May. I hope the day was a success, and all of you enjoyed yourselves. You must continue to play soccer and other games. Do you have races and long jumps and high jumps and things like that? It is very important to play all kinds of sports. In that way you can keep fit and healthy. You also learn about teamwork. I hope you were selected in the soccer team that was supposed to play against Bloemhof.

I hope you take an interest in the Olympic games which started in Moscow today. The modern Olympic games were started by Pierre de Coubertin in June 1894. A few years later he said in a speech:

The most important thing in the Olympic Games is not to win but to take part, just as the most important thing in life is not the triumph but the struggle. The essential thing is not to have conquered but to have fought well.

You must ask your teacher to explain the meaning of these words. Then you must try to remember them because that is the spirit in which all games must be played. These words appear on the scoreboard on the opening day of all Olympic Games.

I am also happy to see that besides sports, you are also doing well in your studies. This is very good because sports and school work must go together. You must encourage the little ones—Suliman, Ismail, Mohamed—to play sports. Do Aziza and Nazira play?

On 8th September is your birthday. And on 7th September is Ahmed's Let me send both of you my very best wishes. I hope you have nice birthday celebrations. I wrote to Aziza when it was her birthday. I hope she received my letter.

In her letter Zohrabibi told me that Behn was sick and was in hospital. I hope she is better now. I sent her a card wishing her well.

Please give my fondest regards to your father and mother, to Aziza and to all the people at home.

Everything of the best to you and lots of love.
From
Uncle Ahmed
AMK

≈ ≈ ≈

Farida and Ahmed Bhoola—*20 September 1980*

A little girl, whose name he had chosen and who had meant so much to him, had been killed in an accident along with her little cousin, Haroun. In this poignant letter, Kathrada offers his condolences, knowing there is nothing he can say that will lessen the sorrow. He was preparing his letter-writing schedule and had marked 30 November, and Leila's name, not knowing that just hours before her life had ended so tragically. Every morning and every night he would think of all the little ones-their pranks, their mischief and their illnesses. As he had given Leila her name there was that extra bond. He also had chosen a Tswana name for her; Refentse, a name that meant "We Have Overcome"; had shown her photo to a fellow prisoner whose daughter bore that same name and on showing the photo Kathrada was filled with great pride. Overcome with grief, he asks that they remember her for the joy she brought into the lives of so many. What thoughts must have gone through his mind in his stark cell that night: no radio to distract him; no newspaper to take his mind off the tragedy; no one with whom to share the grief.

≈

A. M. Kathrada
Robben Island Jail
20 September 1980

My Dear Farida and Ahmed,

I never ever imagined that I would have to write a condolence letter to you. It is one of the most difficult things to do. What can I say to you after such a major tragedy in your lives? Words fail me, for anything that I do write will never be able to convey to you how deeply I share your grief. And there is nothing I can say that will lessen your sorrow. And yet I must say something.

This morning I was called to the office. I went so happily as I was expecting to be given my first newspaper. Instead I was told of Zohra's phone call informing me of the death of Leila and Haroun! I was stunned. Later I was called again and told of Ismailmota's phonogram giving the same news.

I have a great love for all the little ones in the family. I laugh at their little pranks and mischief, I treasure their little utterances, and I am equally concerned about their illnesses and misfortunes. Every morning and every night I think of them without fail as I think of each and every one of you. But the little ones occupy a special place in my heart. With Leila, however, there was something more. I gave her the name; and that alone created a special relationship. Then, being a girl, there is always that extra soft spot for her.

This week Leila was on my mind more than normally. When she was a little over a year old, I thought it was appropriate that, in addition to Leila, Natasha, she should have a Tswana name as well. I chose Refentse, the same name as the little daughter of a friend of mine here. We do not stay in the same section of the jail, but every few months we get an opportunity to meet and exchange a few words. And invariably we talk about the two Refentses. This week, in anticipation of the meeting, I took along Leila's photo (taken at Fatima's wedding) to show him. He was so happy to see it and this filled me too with joy and pride. You may be wondering why I never mentioned anything to you about Refentse. I did try to do so but failed. Incidentally, Refentse's father is also a doctor.

It was on Thursday that I showed the photo to my friend. On Friday evening I was checking through my schedule of letters that had to be replied to; birthday messages to be sent, etc. When I came to Leila's name and November 30th, I made a little note of something I wanted to tell her or rather to tease her. Little did I know then that she had already died a few hours before.

I know it is impossible to ask anyone to even try to forget such a loss. But let us remember Leila for the joy and delight she brought during the brief span of her life. Try to be courageous. Remember that your tragedy is shared by so many and especially

Your Uncle

AMK

~ ~ ~

Shamima and Neelan Poonen—*4 October 1980*

Shamima and Neelan are the two young people who had fallen in love and had incurred the displeasure of Shamima's family, primarily because Neelan was not of the same faith. Kathrada had taken up their cause and had written a number of letters to Shamima's mother expressing his views on racism and bigotry. We learn that they are now married and that Shamima's mother had stood by her daughter, something of which Kathrada is proud. He assures the couple that in time the others would relent and see the folly of their ways. For Kathrada their marriage was not "merely a victory of two young people in love, but it was a triumph against racism and narrow-mindedness." He acknowledges the shortcomings of letter-writing but in the circumstances, this is the only way they can communicate until, as he puts it, "we are able to meet." He is now in his 17th year and still full of hope that one day they will all be free.

~

A. M. Kathrada
Robben Island Jail
4th October 1980

My Dear Shamima and Neelan,

How wonderful to have heard from both of you. Your letters and photos arrived on 6th September already, and I'm sorry I could not reply earlier. I must thank you also for the birthday telegram. It was very thoughtful of you. I hope you will excuse me for replying to both of you in this one letter. You see, we are allowed to write only a fixed number of letters each month.

Yes, it is a pity that we have to rely on luck and impersonal means of keeping contact. Letters are so restrictive, inadequate and can be so remote. Much more so in a case such as ours where we haven't even met one another. However, circumstances over which we have no control have placed us in different worlds almost, and until such time as we are able to meet, we will have to make do with letters. I must say that photographs help to some extent to add some flesh and bones to people whose shape and form otherwise exists only in one's imagination. They also help to narrow distances. And perhaps equally important, photographs provide colour and considerable joy to the drab and monotonous routine of prison life. You can, therefore, imagine what a great pleasure it was to receive your photos and of your friends. Now at least I have an idea of how my niece and nephew look. Your friends gave rise to a lot of interest, happy comments and speculation. Solly and Rashed are, of course, known to a number of colleagues, though they did not know that Solly had got married. Our congratulations to the couple, not forgetting Rashed and Kaylash. To me personally the Karanis and Randeras are of special interest, and I almost feel certain I'm in the process of discovering some more nephews. You see, there were only a handful of families with those surnames in the Transvaal. My father's sister was married to a Karani. At the time of my arrest their son, Ismail, was working in Evaton. There were other family members whose names I cannot now recall. Then the Randeras. There was only one family by that name, and they were at a placed called Machavi near Potchefstroom. I should very much like to know if your friends are connected with these families. I hope they won't mind my prying into their ancestry. A word about the ladies in the photo. They are all so lovely and oozing with charm. Makes me almost regret that I was born in the wrong generation.

I've just realised that this is my first letter to you after your wedding, and I haven't even congratulated you yet. I'm sure you must have received my messages from Zohra. Please accept my very best wishes. May your future be adorned with cloudless skies, with laughter and song and uninterrupted happiness. I feel so glad and relieved that the family consented to the marriage. It is unfortunate that some family members still remain stubborn and choose to have nothing to do with you. But please don't let this upset you or allow it to mar your happiness. Time and experience are great teachers, and you can rest assured that in the not too distant future the *verkramptes*[1] will wake up to the folly and short-sightedness of their attitude. This letter would be incomplete if I didn't mention my own gratitude and admiration for Mummy. Her decision to relent and then to stand by you was an act of great courage. This must have helped a great deal in influencing the Ottosdal part of the family to waive their objections. I am also happy to know that my little effort helped. It always feels good to be able to contribute towards the

---

[1] An Afrikaans term, that became popular in the political arena during this time. It was used to define a person or persons who were narrow-minded, very conservative, and short-sighted.

happiness of people. But yours was a case nearest to my heart. The fact that you are the daughter of one of my closest friends and relatives made it incumbent upon me to render whatever assistance I could. The issue of racism and religious bigotry made me even more determined. Your marriage was, therefore, not merely a victory of two young people in love, but it was a triumph against racism and narrow-mindedness.

I'm afraid I'll have to end now. There is much more to say, but I'll leave it till next time. Yes, Neelan, I remember your father well. He was a good artist, and I think his anthology books were exemplary. Please give him my fondest regards. And the rest of the family. Everything of the best to the two of you, and lots of love.

From

AMK

~ ~ ~

Djamilla Cajee—*25 October 1980*

In her letter to Kathrada, Djamilla apologized for writing about boring matters. He assures her that what she writes about, school, her teachers, sports, visits, and other people are by no means boring. This is precisely what he wants to read about—things that will help him and his colleagues keep themselves informed and keep them in touch with changing events. The arrival of newspapers changed their lives and they "greedily gobble up" every morsel of news. On hearing of the possibility of Djamilla and her family moving to the new "Indian" township of Azadville, Kathrada says a feeling of sadness went through him. As long as Amien, Djamilla's father and Kathrada's close and most loyal of friends remained in this flat that was Kathrada's, he felt that he too was there in spirit. He goes on to tell Djamilla about the fame of the flat and how tempted he is to one day write the story of Flat 13. This flat did indeed have a proud and long history: it was where Kathrada learned his politics; where Mandela had his law offices for a while; where every prominent opponent of apartheid had at some time stayed or visited. It was an institution in its own right. That it might be empty or occupied by strangers leaves Kathrada feeling sad and uncomfortable. In actual fact, Amien stayed on and when he believed that Kathrada might be released he got Flat 13 ready for him.

~

A. M. Kathrada
Robben Island Jail
25th October 1980

My Dearest Djamilla,

I received two letters from you this month—one on the 4th and the other this morning. Thanks very much. It is always nice to hear from you. It is even better to see you fulfilling your undertaking to turn over a new leaf and writing more frequently. I am keeping my fingers crossed and hoping that this enthusiasm on your part will not wane. What made this morning's letter even more welcome was its length as well as content. It was more than your usual "telegram."

You complain about boredom and not knowing what to write. You would be surprised how the most commonplace everyday things can make interesting reading in jail. Your school and your teachers, the subjects you do, your reading, your sporting activities, the sponsored walk, your trip to Swaziland, your friends, your love for cats—all this is of interest. You see, I've been in jail for over 17 years now and all the time living more or less among the same people. Day in and day out the same faces, the same routine, the same unchanging environment. We have talked to one another about almost every conceivable thing you can imagine. We can recognise one another just by seeing the shoes or hearing the footsteps. Under these circumstances, every bit of information from outside is of importance. Apart from breaking the monotony, letters bring us in contact with new people, with new ideas, different interests, varying habits. All this helps to brighten up things. So you need have no fears that your letters might be boring. Just write about the everyday, mundane things and you can rest assured your letters will be read with great joy. Your mention of cats took me right back to the days of my own childhood. I too was a great lover of cats. Here we seldom see any. A few years ago a warder brought along a kitten. It was a great pleasure to hold it and play with it. Incidentally, a long time ago I read a delightful book called *Jenny*. It's about a boy who dreamed he had turned into a cat. It's by Paul Gallico. I'm sure you'll enjoy it. Do you read the cartoons about Catastrophe? They're quite good at times.

I must say that with the coming of newspapers, a great change has taken place in our lives. We greedily gobble up as much about the outside world as we can. You know since about 3 years or so we are no longer sent out to work. We have the whole day to read or play, or talk, sleep—anything. But now suddenly we find there is no time to do many things that we were doing before. It's because of the newspapers. Since my last letter to you, we received the *Sunday Post, Sunday Express, Tribune* and the *Rand Daily Mail*. I have heard of the *Daily Mail Extra,* but it doesn't seem to be available in Cape Town. We are trying to make arrangements to get it. You know what—the *Daily Mail* costs 35 cents in Cape Town! But in spite of that, it is the most popular paper.

I'm sure you must have enjoyed your trip to Swaziland. It is a lovely place. I was last there in 1962. I was so glad to hear about Aunty Rookie. The folks in England wrote to say how pleased they were to see her. I was so surprised as I didn't even know she had been away. Please give her my love.

I am also surprised to hear about the house in Azadville, Does it mean you all will be moving away from the flat? Who is going to take over? You know, I still seem to be so attached to the flat. With Daddy staying there I always felt I too was there in spirit. A feeling of sadness went through me when I read of the new house. I'm sure many people will miss the flat. We so often talk about it. It has a kind of history behind it, which can even form the subject of a book. In fact I was toying with the idea of writing it when I get out of here one day.

I must end now. Please say a big "thank you" to all your lovely friends for remembering me. Lots of love to them. Also to Mummy, Daddy, Iqbal and all friends.

Tons of love to you and a happy birthday.

From

AMK

This photograph with trade unionist S. V. Reddy was taken shortly after Ahmed Kathrada's release from prison in 1946 where he had served a sentence for participating in the Passive Resistance Campaign.

Ahmed Kathrada on the rooftop of Kholvad House in 1953. In the background is Moulvi Cachalia. This and the photograph of Nelson Mandela (below) were taken by a young American student, Herbert Shore. Today, Professor Shore teaches at the University of California.

Nelson Mandela on the rooftop of Kholvad House in 1953.

REGISTER VAN ALLE PERSONE (a) Wat vir Aanh

evangenis No, Prison Number.	Polisie/ Hof No, Police/ Court No.	Naam en Ras. Name and Race.	Geslag. Sex.	OPNEMING IN GEVANGENIS. ADMISSION INTO PRISON.		Misdaad waarvan beskuldig. Crime charged with.
				Datum. Date.	Op wie se gesag. On whose authority.	
8/64		AHMED MOHAMED KATHRADA	I/m. Moslem	13/6/44	Officier Pretoria	Sabotage in contaven... tion of section 21(1) of act N. 76/62. One count being count two in the indictment
7/64		GOVAN MBEKI	c/m	13/6/44	Officier Pretoria	(1) Sabotage in contav. of Act 21(1) of a. 76/1962 (Two counts) (2) Contra. Act. 11(a) r.w

The admissions register to Robben Island, 13 June 1964.

Robben Island Prison,

....

The Officer Commanding,
Robben Island Prison.

    Sir,

        I No............., NAME......................................,
am fully aware of the fact that to study while I am in prison is a
privilege granted to me personally.

        Should I misuse this privilege by using my study material,
stationary , books and time for any other purpose except for my
studies, or allow that it be used by any other person for any purpose,
I shall forteit the privilege to continue with my studies for the
full duration of my incarceration.

                  Yours faithfully,

                  ....
                  Date............... ....

Witness:..............................
Date:..............................

A request form for permission to study, circa 1965. As with most things,
prison authorities tried to control the prisoners' every activity.

A. M. Kathrada,
No. 468/64,
Robben Island
5th October 1967

Lt. Van Tonder,
Robben Island.

Sir,
   You will remember that when I raised with you the question of our Christmas orders, you stated:-
   (a) That every prisoner is allowed to order:-
      (i) 1 lb sweets
      (ii) 1 lb dried or fresh fruit
      (iii) 1 lb cake or biscuits.
   (b) That there was no restriction on the cost of these items as long as the stipulated weight is not exceeded;
   (c) You agreed to my request that we be given a wider list of items from which to choose.
   (d) You agreed that I submit such a list to you for your consideration.

   Attached herewith is the list. I shall be very grateful if you will please:-
   (a) inform me whether you approve the items suggested;
   (b) ascertain whether the items are available in the weights stated.
   (c) arrange for us to be given the prices.

   I wish to reiterate that last year's orders were most unsatisfactory. I sincerely hope you will do all in your power to comply with the suggestions contained herein, more especially since it is only once a year that we enjoy this privilege.

      Thanking you,
         Yours faithfully,
            AM Kathrada

A 1967 request for sweets. The receipt of candy once a year was considered a privilege by prison authorities.

A. M. KATHRADA,
468/64
Robben Island
11th March 1968

The Officer Commanding,
Robben Island Prison.

Sir,
   Kindly order on our behalf, the games as per attached list, and deduct the money from the following accounts. Any money left over should be kept in a separate account for the Single Cells, in order to facilitate future orders.

         Thank you very much,

            AM Kathrada

Number	Name	Amount	Signature
8/65	L. Chiba	R8-00	
864/64	E. Daniels	R3-00	
9/65	S. Maharaj	R2-00	
764/64	F. Bam	R2-00	
129/67	M.D. Naidoo	R2-00	
60/64	B. Nair	R2-00	
466/64	N. Mandela	R1-00	
~~341/67~~	~~S. Sholu~~		
	~~M. Dingake~~		
20/67	W. Mkwayi	R1-00	
363/64	N. Alexander	R1-00	
64/64	J. Zulu	R1-00	
471/64	W. Sisulu	R1-00	
		R14-00	(Twenty-four Rand)

A 1968 request order for board games from "social secretary" Ahmed Kathrada sent to Robben Island prison authorities.

The guard tower at
Robben Island Prison.

Visiting Mandela in Victor Verster Prison. This photograph was taken
shortly before Ahmed Kathrada's release in 1989. Seated (from left to
right) are Nelson Mandela, Wilton Mkwayi, Elias Motsoaledi, Andrew
Mlangeni, Oscar Mpetha, Raymond Mhlaba, Ahmed Kathrada, and
Walter Sisulu. Subsequently it was discovered that prison authorities had
planted listening devices under the chairs and even in the bark of a tree.

A few days after his release, in October 1989, Ahmed Kathrada traveled to Soweto where he visited with Walter Sisulu.

In 1990, Rivonia Trialists Ahmed Kathrada (extreme left), Nelson Mandela (third from right), Walter Sisulu (extreme right) and others, visit the site of their arrest twenty seven years earlier.

Andrew Mlangeni, Walter Sisulu, Elias Motsoaledi, and Ahmed Kathrada on the Rivonia grounds in 1990.

Eddie Daniels and Ahmed Kathrada at the entrance to their cell block on Robben Island in December 1995.

This photo was taken on 13 February 1995, the day after the Robben Island Reunion Conference. From left to right: Ahmed Kathrada, Andrew Mlangeni, Walter Sisulu, Dr. Moreillon (from the International Red Cross in Geneva, Switzerland), Govan Mbeki, Raymond Mhlaba, and Wilton Mkwayi.

Ahmed Kathrada visits his former prison cell in 1995.

In 1996, old friends and compatriots Ahmed Kathrada and President Nelson Mandela greet each other in front of Genadendal, the President's official residence in Cape Town.

Kathrada chats with American actor Sidney Poitier outside Tuyhuys, the President's Cape Town office.

Ahmed Kathrada, ex-prisoner, chats with his ex-warder (prison guard) and current member of the Robben Island staff, Christo Brand, in 1997.

President Nelson Mandela and Member of Parliament Ahmed Kathrada during a parliamentary recess in 1999.

1981—1989

~ ~ ~

Tahera Kola—*14 February 1981*

A moving and eloquent testimony to the courage and bravery of Shamima's mother, Tahera. In this letter to Tahera, widow of his old school friend and relative, Ahmed Kola, Kathrada expresses his admiration for the tremendous courage she showed when, alone, she stood by her daughter who wanted to marry a non-Muslim. The rest of the family, outraged at the thought of one of their women marrying "out," resisted with all their might. Through her courage, Tahera has given happiness to many and Kathrada points out that "happiness is contagious and is much more rewarding than a host of sullen, angry, complaining dissatisfied faces." He hopes that with the passage of time that the part of the family still opposed will accept this marriage.

~

A. M. Kathrada
Robben Island Jail
14th February 1981

My Dear Tahera,

I have been meaning to write to you for some time now but kept on postponing it. I must confess it has been very negligent on my part. I hope this letter finds you in good health.

As you know, I am now in fairly regular contact with Shamima and Neelan. Their letters are a real delight, oozing with happiness. Naturally

133

they are still young and adjusting to each other amidst the whirlwind of excitement. But they appear to be settling down very nicely. They have set up their own home, they have jobs, they have a motor car—and, most important of all, they have your love, good will and blessings. Each time they write, they mention how grateful they are to you for standing by them.

I must really congratulate you and, at the same time, express my own gratitude and admiration to you for the manner in which you have acquitted yourself. It was undeniably a difficult situation which required a maximum of patience, tact, objectivity and, above all, courage and big-ness. You have been truly remarkable, and you can rest assured that Kola would have acted the same way as you have and would have been proud of you. I can imagine your plight. You had to combat racist attitudes, reli-gious bigotry, colour consciousness, family ostracism, gossip, slander and a lot more. And you stood virtually alone. Once you took a stand, a lot of others who were undecided, wavering or fearful were given courage and swung around to your point of view. Today, as compensation for your unselfishness and courage, you have given happiness to two young peo-ple as well as relief and joy to many more. And as you know, happiness is contagious and is much more rewarding than a host of sullen angry, complaining dissatisfied faces. Let us hope with time the hardness of the folks in Schweizer will mellow and they will accept Shamima and Neelan.

Shamima sent me some wedding photos. She is a lovely girl. What a surprise to see among her friends are two couples who are also related to us—the Karanis and Randeras. She told me she had intended coming to Ottosdal to help you make achaar. I was so pleased about this. I feel good when I hear of young people still engaging in traditional and "old-fash-ioned" activities like achaar-making. At least I know that when I come out one day, I'll still be able to enjoy some of the things of the good old days. Things like achaar-making, papad-making, stock-taking, etc., were lovely social occasions that provided opportunities for family and friends to come together. This type of thing must be getting less and less these days.

Last month I had a letter from Marie in Dublin. She also loves com-ing to Ottosdal. She told me of Poppy's illness. Fortunately he was well on the way to recovery. The past few months have been very harsh on the family with so many deaths in quick succession. Leila, Haroun, Apa and now Solly. Before that there was Abdulhay. How very sad. I sent a telegram when I learned of Solly's death. I hope it was received. I was telling Zohrabibi that from childhood we looked upon Apa as a sort of mother-figure, someone we respected and loved. And now she is no more. I shall miss her.

I hope Mahmud is well. Please convey my best wishes to him.

Today I had lovely visits from Zohrabibi and Yasmin. This was Yasmin's first visit, and it's been really nice to see her. I last saw her when she was 3 or 4; she was shy and unfriendly towards me. Zohrabibi I don't remember having seen at all. She must have been just born when I was last in Schweizer. Today they are lovely young ladies, full of charm and confidence. And no longer shy. Shamima and Neelan may visit me at the end of the year. That will be wonderful.

Please convey my fondest regards to your mother and father and to all the rest of the family in Schweizer, Ottosdal and elsewhere.

Lots of love to you

From

AMK

≈ ≈ ≈

Dasoo Iyer—*28 March 1981*

A number of people, all of them involved in the freedom struggle, have died since Kathrada's incarceration, and he writes about some of them. B. T. Naidoo and his brother Roy Naidoo were committed and dedicated Congressites from an early stage in liberation politics. Roy Naidoo was an adopted son of Mahathma Gandhi. Mr. M. "Murvy" Thandray was Kathrada's teacher when Kathrada was ten years old and their paths crossed often later in life. The two found themselves in jail during the Passive Resistance Campaign of 1946 and in 1953, when Kathrada was one of the key people in setting up a school to thwart the forced removal of students to the "Indian ghetto." Murvy gave up his secure post in a government school and went to teach in the Congress School. Kathrada pays tribute to them; to all the others he mentions in "a roll call of honor." He is saddened by the passing of his old political buddy, Ismail Bhana, who has died in London. He asks Dasoo to pass on his condolences to Ruth First (Rabia) and to her husband Joe Slovo (Jawahar) on the death of Ruth's father, a staunch member of the South African Communist Party. One paragraph is in code. MacMaharaj (Mannikum), on his release, smuggled out the autobiography (music) of Nelson Mandela (Uncle Soapy) and Kathrada

*writes about how happy he and Walter Sisulu (Uncle Jokotea) will be to know
that Maharaj is successful in his work related to the autobiography.*

~

A. M. Kathrada
Robben Island Jail
28th March 1981

My Dear Dasoo,

Thanks a lot for your letter, which arrived exactly a month ago. I
haven't had a reply from Bob to my letter of 15th November. I suppose
I'll hear from him one of these days. I always look forward to letters from
you all, to the bits of information about the friends and relations who are
abroad. And you'd be surprised at the number of items even about people who are still at home that are contained in your letters and about
which we are ignorant. I suppose the people at home just assume that we
are up to date about the folks at home. It was good when chaps like
Nassim and Doha were able to keep in touch. Do you know that the first
time we heard of the death of Thandray and B.T. was from Zoya's father!
We have no idea how long ago they died nor the circumstances of their
death. And worse still, I want to send my condolences but don't know
who I can write or where. You see how cut off one can be in jail.

What a wonderful chap old Murvy was. I wonder if one can easily find
people like him among the younger generations. My first contact with
him was in 1939. After having spent only one term in Std. 2, I was promoted to Std. 3c—to Mr. Thandray's class. Besides the 3Rs, I'm almost
sure I received a fair share of hiding from him. I say almost sure because
when this was put to him in later years, he was a bit cagey. However, anyone who knew Murvy could not fail to be impressed by certain of his
outstanding qualities–discipline, utter selflessness, devotion, courage, a
rigid morality, modesty, honesty and a remarkable spirit of sacrifice. Do
you know that he gave up a £50-a-month post as school principal to
work for £12 p.m. in End Street! In the process he lost his pension.
Often he did not get even the £12 on time. On occasions he used to walk
to Denver, and many times there was no food at home. But he never
complained. For some reason he and I never managed to shed the
teacher-pupil relationship, and for all the years I could not refer to him
as anything else but Mr. Thandray. We were in the same batch [of Passive
Resistance Campaigners] and spent a month together in Durban. There

were many embarrassing moments as you can imagine. But we survived, and the respect remained. What a man! He has joined Roy, Nonbhai, Fakirbhai, Sulimanbhai, B. T., Sooboo, Aminabai, Miriambai, Ismail, Babla, Monty, Jack—the salt of the earth.

When Zohra wrote in January and told me of Ismail's death, I just could not believe it. I said I hope the folks in London tell us more about it. Then came your letters. What a tragedy. I don't even want to start writing down the host of memories and thoughts that came to mind—that would take up many letters. I wish I'll have an opportunity one day to write about him and about all the others. I was also shocked at the reference to the late Gloria. This was the first I heard that she too is no more. I hope you will elaborate. In the meantime, please convey my deepest sympathy to Ismail's widow and the children. Another bit of shocking information was the death of Rabia's father. That whole family is often in our thoughts. Please make a point of telling Rabia that we all share her loss. My sympathies also to her hubby, Jawahar, her mom and the children.

So far I've written only about the dear friends who are no more. Let's move on to other matters. I enjoyed reading about your roots trips. It must have been a wonderful experience. I learned that there are 72 cousins who are nuns or priests! I won't be surprised if the South African part of the family was responsible for driving a good number of them to the church. What with the formidable catalogues of sins ranging from one brother actively propagating atheism in Fordsburg in the forties to a daughter shacking up with a larney in London in the eighties! One can hardly blame the good people in India for turning to religion. They certainly have a lot to pray for.

Talking of shacking up reminds me of the wolfman, an ancient votary of this mode of living. Having accumulated experience in at least two South African cities, he must have undoubtedly transported this evidently profitable practice to London. It's nice to hear about him. Just the other day someone recognized him among my photos, and this led to a nice old chat. Please pass my fondest regards to him. Incidentally, I suppose you all heard of the death of Esther who used to work in the hampers office.

I haven't been hearing about Mannikum for some time. Is he still so peripatetic? Somehow I got the idea that he had settled at the late Anand's place. Or am I wrong? It's good to hear that his musical ventures are meeting with such phenomenal success. I'm sure his Uncle Soapy will be very happy and proud of him. Not to speak of his soccer-playing Uncle Jokotea. One can just imagine the reaction of the latter. Mannikum was always a great favourite of his. The two of them were forever engaged in analysing some topic or other.

I didn't know Abe was back in London. Do you ever meet him? I take it he, Hussein and Barney still form an inseparable trio. Please pass my regards to them. I take it all three of them are practicing law. I think I once asked you about Moosajee. Where on earth is he? Many years ago I heard he was somewhere in the tropics. That was the last. I understand Zainab and Aziz are also in London. Do you ever see them? You must have heard of the very posh wedding of Amina's daughter at the Carlton Hotel. Apparently it cost many thousands.

Let's come to yours truly. I've been given permission to study again and have registered for History Honours. I haven't received any study material yet from the university. It is not going to be easy to get back to studies. I had just settled down to a routine of reading newspapers, magazines and novels and finding it very pleasant. To make it worse, the first two papers of the course don't appear to be my cup of tea. You know, they deal with philosophy, historiography, methodology and what not. However, there's no way I can escape it so I'll just have to get stuck in. If not for anything else than for the huge amount of money involved. It is unbelievable. You know it cost me much less—books and all—to complete my whole B.A. than what I had to pay just for two papers this year! I feel very guilty each time I have to write home for money. I was reckoning the other day that in February alone I must have cost them close to a thousand rands! Can you believe it? Two of my nieces had come to visit me. These air trips plus stay in Cape Town couldn't have cost less than R500. This plus the study money plus other incidentals . . . it's prohibitive. Thanks a lot for your offer to assist. Don't be surprised if I take advantage of it one day.

We've been seeing some good films lately. *The Champ, Odessa File, The Sandpiper*, etc. Also a lovely documentary, *Olga*, about the Soviet gymnast. It's unforgettable. I'm beginning to become a fan of a small group of actors, including Peter Finch, Jane Fonda, Vanessa Redgrave, Meryl Streep. And, believe it or not, I thoroughly enjoyed John Travolta in *Saturday Night Fever*. But please don't talk too loudly about the latter among serious guys like Hanuman, etc. And while I'm about it, let me utter a heresy. I very much enjoy and prefer a singing group called Joy (currently in London) to a woman called Nina Simone. I'm sure many will want to shoot me for this.

I better end now before I get myself into a bigger mess. My health is fine. I hope the same goes for all of you. Lots of love to Sally, Vijan, Vanitha and to the rest of the family and friends. Just in case I don't write before then, please say happy birthday to Mota and Sakina.[1]

All the best to you from

AMK

≈   ≈   ≈

Dr. Karim—*24 October 1981*

A combination of letters from people, such as Doctor Karim, newspapers, magazines, radio, and visits are helping to narrow the information gap. One day, should he be released, Kathrada will not feel so cut off. He pursues his interest in diabetes and mentions the high incidence among Indians. Kathrada raises the issue of an Islamic Centre in the context of it being available only to Muslims. He notices the trend to have such sectional projects, and what he finds shocking is that they are being initiated by the younger and more educated members. "Could it be that our fathers were more broadminded and farsighted than us," he asks.

≈

A. M. Kathrada
Robben Island Jail
24th October 1981

Dear Doc,

Thanks a lot for your letter which arrived on 12th September. As usual, it contributed greatly towards narrowing the information gap in various fields. With the aid of letters, newspapers, magazines, radio programs and visits, slowly but surely we are catching up with things. Naturally these cannot completely make up for almost two decades of deprivation but they certainly go a long way. If ever I have to go out of jail, at least I won't feel like Rip van Winkle.

---

[1] Mota is Dr. Y. M. Dadoo and Sakina is Sylvia Neame.

Your remarks about diabetics being able to live a normal life span are most encouraging. Let's hope one day they will be able to transplant the pancreas. Or manufacture artificial ones. I suppose one can say that the insulin pump is virtually an artificial pancreas. There appears to be a widespread belief among medics that there is greater prevalence of diabetes among Indians. I remember many years ago Professor Seftel, pursuing this line of investigation, especially went to India to carry out some research. I don't know what his findings were. I have had the experience with a number of doctors who, immediately on learning that I was an Indian, start off with a urine test. Have you any opinion on the question of Indians and diabetes? With regard to the transplanting of organs, I notice that the medical profession is by no means unanimous—especially when it comes to the heart. Every now and then one reads of some criticism of Chris Barnard[1] by eminent doctors in different parts of the world. It makes one wonder.

It is good to hear of the growing number of Indian specialists. I suppose most of them are young and I wouldn't know them. But I'm sure I would know some of their parents—after all we were a very small community in the Transvaal. I'd appreciate it if you mention a few names of the specialists. As for rendering good service, especially among the poor, our medics have a proud record. I'm glad to hear this is still continuing.

I was interested to read that you were toying with the idea of doing psychiatry. But it wasn't quite clear whether you were going to practice it or merely in order to prove or disprove existing theories. Whatever it is, I must say you are a real glutton for work. I just don't know how you manage it. Do you relax at all?

I've heard a lot about the late Ismail Coovadia but I don't think I ever met him. In fact I think it is most unlikely that we did. We wouldn't have been the best of friends. I am sure your becoming chairman of the Jamaat must have added greatly to your burden of responsibilities. It is gratifying to note that the type of secular activities and positions that Kaka was associated with are being vehemently opposed, particularly by the younger people.

A thought has just struck me. Let me go back to diabetes. A close friend of mine, the late Solly Nathie from Evaton, suffered from it. His

---

[1] Dr. Christian Barnard was the first to carry out a heart transplant at the Groote Schuur Hospital in Cape Town, South Africa.

daughter married a doctor from your area. If they are still living there, please pass my regards to them.

Sorry for the diversion. In a previous letter you mentioned the extensive plans being made to build and Islamic centre in Lenasia which would cater for a wide variety of activities. I got the impression that the school library and recreational facilities would be for Moslems only. I must confess it is painful to learn that in this day and age, instead of broadening our horizons to encompass more and more peoples and a variety of ideas, we are actively propagating and practicing outlooks that tend towards the opposite direction. The philanthropy, the sacrifices and devotion of our parents for community upliftment is traditional. One needs but to recall that, until recently, the bulk of the schools catering for our people in South Africa were built with money donated by the community. This applied also to country hospitals and other institutions. Of these, very few, if any, were exclusively for Moslems or Hindus. I remember how very disturbed we were about the existence (or the proposed setting up) of Moslem and Hindu sportsfields in Pretoria. I can also vividly recall the tremendous efforts that were made to avoid the splitting of the community on religious lines after the establishment of Pakistan. What is most disturbing about recent developments is that the initiative for sectional projects comes from the younger and most educated people. Could it be that our fathers were more broadminded and farsighted than us? To bring it to a personal level; in my social circle there were Hindus, Christians and Moslems. (I'm confining myself for the moment to the Indian friends.) Some were intensely religious, others not. We were a very close group and were in and out of one another's homes. We respected the beliefs of the group and celebrated Eid, Dipavali and Christmas together. I'm just trying to think what would happen today if on a Sunday afternoon we were to decide to go for a swim. Does it mean that we would have to split up and go [to] the swimming pools catering for each religious group? What a tragic situation we would be facing!

I'd hate to think that our ideas and practices of two decades ago would now be regarded as "old-fashioned." With respect, to me it seems as if we are going backwards.

For over a year now an Imam from Cape Town has been visiting us about once a month. I am the only Moslem in the section in which I stay and there are only a handful in the rest of the prison. Whenever Imam Bassier comes, I am invariably accompanied by Hindu and

Christian colleagues to his services. I too have been going to Christian and Hindu services. I am wondering if such a thing would be possible outside.

I am sorry if I've gone off on a tangent on this issue. Please do not regard any of my remarks as being criticisms levelled against you. But I do have strong feelings about it. Incidentally, do you know Dr. Kotwal in Cape Town who is also an official of the Islamic Council?

My studies are getting on slowly. We write in January and I haven't yet succeeded in obtaining three of my textbooks. I'll be writing two papers. If all goes well, I'll most probably register for three next year. I notice UNISA fees have gone up again; it is now R90 per course! And the books are so expensive. The family has really been marvellous–the way they have seen to my needs.

Thanks for your offer for the translator. I'd really love to have it. But unfortunately the local authorities cannot give me permission to receive it. What are the chances of your finding time to contact Pretoria and try for the permission? With your contact in influential circles, you may just succeed. And while you're about it, you can also ask about your thesis. I have a feeling they will be more amenable to an approach from outside.

Otherwise things are fine, health and spiritwise. I hope the same obtains with you and the family. My regards to all.

Everything of the best to you from
AMK

≈ ≈ ≈

Zohra Kathrada—*17 July 1982*

Kathrada cherishes a story about Yusuf, his grandnephew, sending R20 for Kathrada to pay the police and so save himself. He and his colleagues enjoyed the story very much. Kathrada writes about the people in Kholvad House where he had his apartment and how, even after so many years, they still regard him as part of the big family. Following these warm recollections, Kathrada denounces the "new rich" Indians for alienating themselves from their humble origins, for being snobs and racists and often forsaking the less fortunate. He congratulates Zohra for stepping into her old role as a midwife and offering her services free of charge. He hopes she will be there to assist his favorite, Shamima.

~

A. M. Kathrada
Robben Island Jail
17th July 1982

My Dear Zohra,

Thanks for your Express letter which I received on 26th June. If I could arrange it, I'd like to give you a typewriter. As I've told you before, your typed letters are generally longer and more informative. It seems in your case too the typewriter enhances the thinking process. I'm sure Papa must have a collection of typewriters, and you should be able to store one of them for him at your flat. You must have received my letter of 12th June. On the same day I also wrote to Shamima.

I asked the authorities about the card I sent to Yusuf on 3rd April. They insist that it was posted. I wonder what went wrong. It's a pity he didn't get it. I and my colleagues thoroughly enjoyed ourselves with that bit about Yusuf sending me R20 which I should pay the police in order to save myself. You should continue to send me these little remarks he and other kids make. They are cute and clever. You know kids are very down to earth, and they have a way of getting directly to the point. One day when they are grown up, it will be nice to remind them of their childhood utterances and doings. I've just been reading a book by an English woman teacher who specialised in child education, and she's been writing about her travels and especially describing her experiences with children. It is most enjoyable. It is a pity that in the earlier years of my imprisonment the folks who wrote did not include the type of things you've been mentioning in your letters. Today we would have had a lovely record of the young adults in the family.

Talking about kids reminds me. Last week I received a surprise letter from my neighbour's daughter in Kholvad House. You may know the parents, Salim Nanabhay, whose wife is an Akhawaya. Their daughter, Fatima, is about 24. She must have been about a year old when I was arrested. She wrote as a result of my letter to Djamilla following the death of Sarabai. She is thanking me on behalf of Sarabai's family and neighbours. Having lived in Kholvad House for so many years, many inhabitants of the building have come to regard themselves as part of one big family. It is nice to know that they still think of me as a family member. When Zohrabibi was coming to visit me, it was Khuskhala who phoned her to tell me of Sarabai's death.

I've been thinking of your chance meeting with the Kathrada couple at the Metro Cash and Carry. Some years ago I told you how we accidentally landed at a garage in Verulam only to discover that it belonged to a Kathrada and how the old man would not let us go once he came to know who we were. It was quite a spontaneous display of enthusiasm and hospitality and genuine too. I must add, however, that I was surprised by his warmth. This was because over the years the richer Natal Indians gained a reputation for their unfriendliness and inhospitality. It is not wise to generalise, but in the case of this class of Indians, I think their reputation was well deserved. They were such snobs and racialists. All they could think of and talk about was money, motor cars, their exclusive clubs, their posh houses and such things. Of course, if you were rich and had similar interests, you would be able to gain entry into their society. Their behaviour was typical of what the French call the *nouveau riche*, which literally means the "new rich"—people who had come into money relatively recently and who develop attitudes which set them apart from the rest of the people. Basically they were trying to escape from the poorer state from which they had just emerged. In their desire and hurry to gain status, they could outdo Oppenheimer. Fortunately we had a lot of friends in Natal and did not have to frequent places where we would meet these types. In this respect the richer Transvaal Indians were much better. They had not yet become snobs— it was only the odd individual here and there who would emulate his Natal counterparts. I often wonder what the position is like today in the Transvaal. I am sure if you come across the type of people I'm writing about, you would never want to have anything to do with them. There were tragic cases where these "nouveau riche" would become so alienated from their humble past that they would even ignore or neglect the plight of their kith and kin.

Let's get on to something else. It was good to read that you were able to acquit yourself so well as a midwife after not practicing for so many years. I can imagine how grateful the parents of the baby were for your assistance. And all for gratis! You certainly are most generous. You better be on hand when Shamima's Leila or Ahmed makes its debut. Is it usual for psoriasis to clear during pregnancy? And does it return after the child is born? I hope Shamim's has cleared for good.

Though you're not practicing as a midwife, you certainly seem to be doing well in the kitchen as a professional cook. It's good that you were able to rope in Enver's assistance to prepare snacks for the unexpected number of guests. Is he able to do any more than make snacks? I suppose he learned a bit of cooking while in England. In one of my future letters we will discuss the question of being always ready to provide food to unexpected guests. I'll relate an experience or two.

If all has gone well, I suppose Enver has got his passport by now. If so, you'll soon be jetting your way to the East. All my best wishes. Pity I haven't close friends in that part of the world whom I could ask you to look up for me.

There has been a slight hitch about my books. You see, being in jail, we have lost contact with the reality of things outside. When I decided to send my books per passenger train, I didn't give much thought to the cost. Last week a friend wanted to rail his books to Durban and discovered that the 82 kgs would cost R71–00! That shocked us. Now we are waiting to find out the cost by goods train. If that too is too much, the books will just have to stay here. If and when the authorities move me from here to another prison, they'll have to transport my things. You see, my boxes are over 82 kgs. And those are just part of my books—the ones I won't be using again in jail. The big problem will come if they decide to release me one day.

You must have seen that some Robben Island prisoners have been freed. I hope this hasn't excited you folks unduly. As the Minister said, they are giving priority to those doing short terms. It is no use speculating about what is going to happen to us. Mr. Omar saw me on 28th June. He will be seeing me again sometime. At present there is nothing for me to add to what I said in my last letter.

It is nice to hear that Dr. Karim is a grandfather. He hasn't written for some time. I believe Fatoo's mother had broken her leg. I hope she is well again.

I better end now. Keep well and lots of love to you and all at home.
From
AMK

Zohra Kathrada—*21 October 1982*

On Thursday, 21 October 1982, at 10:00 A.M., Kathrada was told that he was to be moved that afternoon. By 2:00 P.M. he packed belongings accumulated over the last eighteen years into "12 boxes of different sizes." He writes about the sadness he felt at not being able to say farewell to his comrades. At 3:30 P.M. he was on a boat, headed for he knew not where. It was only at about 6:30 P.M. that he was satisfied that they had deposited him at Pollsmoor. The food is much better and more varied but he cannot get used to the huge servings. He will have to watch his weight. Why he has been moved he does not know. In his autobiography, Long Walk to Freedom, *Mandela hypothesizes that "the authorities were attempting to cut off the head of the ANC on the island, by removing its leadership."*

∿

A. M. Kathrada
D 790/82
Pollsmoor Maximum Prison
Private Bag X4
Tokai
7966

My Dear Zohra,

You noticed I have changed my address. On Thursday morning, 21st October, at about 10 a.m., I was informed by the Commanding Officer of Robben Island that I was going to be transferred from the Island that afternoon. He did not indicate where I would be going to. I quickly packed my stuff, mainly books, and was ready by 2 p.m. All in all there were 12 boxes of different sizes! I'm sure I must have left a few things behind, but my colleagues will send them along. It was quite sad to part from there, especially from people with whom I had lived for over 18 years. But it could have been worse. The rush and excitement was so great that I did not have time to ponder and worry. In the 3 hours or so there was so much to pack that I didn't have a proper opportunity to say farewell to each of my colleagues. Then at 3:30 I was on the boat. The sea was very rough, but I didn't feel it. After a long time I had discovered that the best way to avoid sea sickness is not to eat for a few hours before travelling. Anyway, it was only when I was deposited at my new abode at about 6:30 p.m. that I was satisfied that I was at Pollsmoor. As sad as it was to leave friends behind at Robben Island, I was equally happy to be reunited with friends who left me behind when they came to Pollsmoor on 31st March. I am adjusting to the new environment. I find the hardest thing to adjust to is the food. You won't believe it, but we are getting huge quantities of meat and vegetables for lunch—it is impossible to finish. I keep a portion of it for supper, but still it is too much. At supper there is lovely thick vegetable and chicken soup. For breakfast there is porridge, bread, jam, peanut butter and coffee. We also get a fruit daily. Yesterday I had to take a firm decision to cut down drastically on my eating. The food is so tasty that it is no longer necessary to buy foodstuff from the shop except for things like mango pickles and a few little things. In addition to the food, generally things are okay.

Of course, you all must be curious to know the reason for my transfer. Well, I do not know a thing and haven't the faintest idea. Nobody has given me any reasons and nobody is likely to. So we'll just have to settle down and wait. I take [it] you folks did receive a letter from the Pollsmoor authorities about my transfer. They say they had written on the 22nd October.

The last letter I received from you was on 18th September, and I received the R100 on 9th October. I wrote to you on 18th September as well; that is, after receiving yours. I'm sure there must be a letter from you at Robben Island. They will send it along.

I was thrilled to receive the telegram from Shamima about Leila's birth. I hope she received my telegram and letter. I take it their visiting arrangements will now automatically be transferred to Pollsmoor. Just for safety's sake, they should just write and confirm with Pollsmoor. I understand there were also applications from Zohrabibi and someone else. I was told of this before I left the Island. But I haven't any details. How far are you with your visit? I think you should apply to Pollsmoor.

Between now and the end of the year, I have to be extremely careful about writing letters. Otherwise my quota will be full. So I will only be replying to some of the folks next year. I hope they will be patient and understand.

Because of the position relating to letters, I have to ask you to do me a big favour. Could you please send a postcard or short letter to some of my correspondents just to tell them of the change of address.

I am writing to Zohrabibi to tell her and others. This will be all for now. I hope this moving will not have an adverse effect on my studies.

Lots of love to you and all the folks at home.
From
AMK

≈ ≈ ≈

Bob Vassen—*29 January 1983*

Examinations are over, and Kathrada is thinking of doing a Master of Arts Degree but is aware of the obstacle he has to overcome. Only prisoners who have two years or fewer to serve qualify to do an M.A. As there is "no ceiling" to his sentence, he does not qualify. The authorities would not budge on this issue. Using a code, he says he is still trying to find out whether Aziz Pahad (Dagwood) ever received his message about assistance for the ANC people (Amrit's children) who were on Robben Island (at Nallabhai's place). For the first time in twenty years he is able to be close to a baby, the daughter, of Shamima and Neelan, and despite the glass barrier that separated them, he got a great thrill out of the visit. The words, "Hillman," "Spain," "Portugal," "Monaco" had been part of a code, but in the move from Robben Island to Pollsmoor, Kathrada lost many papers, including the code. He informs Bob of this loss by writing that words like "Hillman," "Spain," etc., are just names. He hopes that Dasoo and Tom would write, and he inquires about other political friends: Billy Nannan, Mac Maharaj (code name, "Cyclopse"), Herby Pillay. He especially would like to know about Dennis Brutus (code name, "Denichand"). He would like to know whether Dennis has overcome immigration problems that he had been having with the United States (Uncle Samad) and what his relations with the ANC (Amrit) are like. Unfortunately this letter was not sent and was given back to Kathrada six months after it was written.

≈

A. M. Kathrada
29th January 1983
[Returned to Kathrada in July 1993]

My Dear Bob,

Thanks for your letter of the 8th December which reached me on 20th Dec. I delayed replying as I was busy with exam preparations. After my lectures arrived in May last year, I realised I had taken on too much. Then came the sudden move from Robben Island in October; and this greatly increased the pressure. However, I finished exams yesterday and am spending the next few days writing letters and reading. I expect results in a month's time or so. If I manage to get through, I'd like to do an M.A., but there are hurdles which won't be easy to overcome. The Prisons Dept. will only allow M.A. to prisoners who have two years or less of their sentences remaining. With yours truly there is no ceiling on the sentence so no one knows how much longer I have. Anyway, I am hoping to negotiate with the authorities in order to try to overcome the hurdles. But first I must get through.

Thanks for your Xmas card. I hope you got mine and the one I enclosed for Coral and Basil. Unfortunately I do not have their address. I hope they are getting on well. You recall I mentioned a young chap on the Island who was simply determined to take away Jacqueline's photo. Well, I couldn't save it; he carried out his threat, and now I'm minus Jacqueline. Which is a great pity. So please try to devise some means of getting a fresh supply of photos from the States.

Bob, I'm sorry to raise the question again about scholarships for Amrit's children who are staying at Nallabhai's place. Thanks for the information that assistance will be available. But what I really wanted to confirm is whether the late Rabia[1] and/or my nephew, Dagwood, ever received the list of the names of the children, details of their study plans, etc. In the same letter I had also suggested it would be a good idea to send Xmas cards, etc., to the other members of the families. I sent this information about the same time as I wrote to Ursula a couple of years ago. If it is not too much trouble, please try to check and let me know. You see, I never got an acknowledgement. My nephew should be able to remember.

Now that the exams are over, I am in a better position to assess what the move from Robben Island has meant. I was just given a few hours to pack and take the boat. In the process, I left behind, misplaced or destroyed many things—study material as well as personal stuff such as notes on letters, addresses, etc. With the result that I no longer have simple information such as the background on Prem. Lawrence, etc. And it is only now I'm realising how bad my memory is.

---

[1] The code name for the late Ruth First, the wife of Joe Slovo. She had been assassinated by the apartheid regime in 1982.

For the last year or so we have been allowed visits from children. At Xmas time I had a most thrilling experience when my niece, Shamima [Kola's daughter] and Neelan [Poonen's son] brought along their 3-month-old baby, Leila. Can you imagine what it is like for the first time in 20 years to be so near a baby and to watch its various antics! We were separated by a glass window, of course, but in spite of that it was an unforgettable experience.

You folks sure seem to have had a lovely holiday in Europe. I'm glad Ursula was at the wheels. I'm afraid I can't comment about Hillman nor, for that matter, about Spain or Portugal, Monaco, etc. You see, these are just names to me now. Is Ursula going to teach you to drive?

Brother Tom seems to have embarked on another six-year silence! And this time Dasoo appears to have joined him. I've written to Dasoo to shake him up. See if you can't pass a quiet hint to Tom. You haven't written for some time about Billy, Cyclopse, Herb, etc. How is Denichand? I hope he overcomes his problem with Uncle Samad. Is he still friendly with Amrit? (I mean Denichand.) Do you ever hear anything of Sakina?

I must end now. Sorry to hear Sean didn't make it. When I last wrote to you, I told you about the rumours of my death.[2] Well, I'm still very much around.

Keep well, and lots of love to Ursula, Sean, Barry and all the folks from

AMK

     ≈ ≈ ≈

Mammie Seedat—*29 May 1983*

Kathrada recalls the warmth and hospitality of Mammie's home, with all its generosity and kindness. These qualities, he writes, are reflected in her letters. He reminisces about the various people who frequented their home and others he knew in Durban. Two of his "heroes," Ismail Meer and J. N. Singh, he still holds in the highest esteem to this day.

≈

---

[2] On at least two occasions, on Robben Island and at Pollsmoor, there had been reports in South Africa that Kathrada had died. The origins of these "reports" have never been traced.

A. M. Kathrada
Pollsmoor Maximum Prison
Private Bag X4
Tokai 7966
29th May 1983

My Dearest Mammie,

Your lovely letter of 26th April (and completed on 4th May) reached me on 26th. You won't believe how nice it is to hear from you. It takes me right back to Hampton Grove and to all the wonderful people who lived there. That house had a wonderful atmosphere about it; it exuded warmth, kindness, hospitality, generosity, friendship, love. What was unique about it was that all the people were part of the general atmosphere—from Daddy's mother down to the smallest child. Everyone welcomed visitors and strangers alike—with open arms. Naturally it was the stamp of your and Daddy's personalities that was the dominant influence.

Like in the house, so also in your letters, one can see your personality. The sentiments expressed on those pages are so genuine and straight from the heart. When I read them, it is as if the walls of the jail are no longer there and I am speaking to you in person, and I want to go on listening about all the things happening in Durban about all the family members and friends. However, after all the years of separation we have learned to take the bad with the good. For instance I was so very happy to hear about the visit of Radhie and J.N. to you. You know, in the days when I was at high school there was a very small number of our people at university so that we youngsters looked upon all university students with admiration. Since about 1943 or 1944 when J.N. and Ismail were at Wits, they became my "heroes." To this day my admiration for them and their wives and families remains as strong. It is always a great pleasure to hear about them and their children. Now for the sad news that came with this item, and that was the health of Prem. Yes, I remember her so clearly as a very pretty and attractive person with great charm and grace. It is so sad and distressing to learn that her health has broken down to such an extent that she is immobile. What can one say but only hope that medical science can still come up with some drugs to relieve her of pain and restore her mobility and good health. In the meantime if you do have a chance, please convey my very best wishes to her and my fond affection. You said Radhie was going to write to me. How I wish she does as there is so much I'd like to know about the children and the other members of the family. Is Nesyah still lecturing at the university? You know, the very first time I came to Durban, 1945, was with J.N. and Ismail. We stayed at Pinetown and Mansfield Road.

I was also very happy to hear about Dr. Mohamed and Babu. I still have a hazy recollection of the time Mohamed and his friend, Mac, came to Ike's place in Jo'burg; they were hitchhiking to London to go and study! I was very happy when I learned that Mohamed fulfilled his ambition and became a doctor. And by the look of things he is a successful practitioner. Good luck to him and my very best wishes. Is Housein still practicing in Durban? I was also happy to hear about Babu. Until a few years ago, he used to send me an Eid card or Xmas card, then he suddenly stopped. Give him my regards as well. Also, whenever you meet other family members and friends, please pass my warmest greetings. I notice Hassen has done well with an S.C. Do you ever hear anything about Chota and Choti?

One of these days it will be Ramadan. My supply of Eid cards has not yet come and I'm getting worried they won't arrive in time. So I must apologise in advance if you do not receive a card from me this year. Let me, for safety's sake, wish you and all the family a Happy Eid. I will be thinking of you. Mammie, can I ask you to do me a favour please? You remember I once asked you to phone Dr. Mayat's widow for me. Could you ask her whether she received my letter of 30th January in which I commented on her book about Indian clothing fashions.

This will be the lot today. I hope your sugar and pressure are under control. Does Stella stay in Durban now? My regards to her.

I have been following with great anxiety the drought position. Being a "farm boy," I am perhaps a little more conscious about the importance of water than urban friends.

Mammie, look after yourself. Lots of love to you, all the children and grandchildren and the friends from

AMK

Roshan Dadoo–1 October 1983

A letter of sympathy to Roshan from Kathrada after receiving news of her father's death. Dr. Y. M. Dadoo was one of Kathrada's great heroes. He was a

"leader, colleague, father, older brother, guide, mentor, friend," Kathrada declares. When he was nine, Kathrada writes, he first heard of Roshan's father. Dadoo was the person who began to mold Kathrada into the political person he would become.

∽

A. M. Kathrada
Pollsmoor Maximum Prison
Private Box X4
Tokai 7966
1st October 1983

My Dearest Roshan,

Having heard about two months ago of your father's grave illness, the news of his death did not come entirely unexpectedly. Yet, how does one prepare oneself for such a calamitous event? I was about 9 years old when I first heard of him. And since that time, he has always been there. In my childish eyes he had become larger than life, and I never contemplated that puny death could remove him from our midst and that I would never see him again.

I grew up trying to memorise whatever I heard and read about him, and I was clinging to his every utterance and statement.

By the time I was 10 and at school in Johannesburg, he had already become a legendary figure, and he was my special hero. Oh yes, there were others too: cricketers and boxers and film actors, authors, artists, poets, scientists, etc., about whom we talked at school and in the afternoons and evenings after school. And we also did all the things that school kids do; we played cricket and soccer, went to [the] cinema, tried to sing the songs of the day, boasted about things we did and also about things we did not do, we played truant, gossiped about our teachers, did all the naughty things that kids do, and we got our share of punishment.

But at that time already I found myself drifting away from my peers and becoming more interested in the doings and sayings of your father. Soon I became friends with kids whose fathers were colleagues of your dad's. At their homes I began to see him. And it was at one of these places that one day he actually said a few words to me! Can you imagine what that must have meant to me!

My little life began to get increasingly intertwined with things with which your father was associated, and over the years a whole spectrum of relationships crystallized between us. He became my leader, my colleague, my father, my older brother, my guide, my mentor, my friend. And I like to think there was an occasion or two when he was my doctor! In 1946, during my matric year, it was he who came to fetch me from school one day in order to do something for him. Since that day, I never went back to school. He was now my guardian.

I think it was in 1941 (or 1943?) that the greatest modern poet of India, Rabindranath Tagore, died. There was a memorial service at the Gandhi Hall, which I attended, more to hear your father speak than to pay homage to Tagore who was no more than a distant name to our young minds. I can still remember your father telling the gathering: India—poverty-stricken and miserable as she is—has been further impoverished by the death of Tagore. Can I do better today than to borrow those very words to describe our condition as a result of the death of your father.

I am sure that everything that I can say about him and much more has been said. I associate myself with all the glowing tributes that have been paid. Those of us who had the privilege to be associated with him will remember him for his courage, his devotion, his patriotism, his concern for the underdog, his love for fellow beings, his ability as a doctor, his brilliance, his generosity, hospitality, modesty, his sense of humour, his powerful oratory, his leadership qualities, his familiarity with theory, his charisma.

To you and Shireen, above everything else, he was a father. Gentle, loving, caring, devoted father. My heart, therefore, goes out to you at this dark moment in your young life. Please be assured that there are many, many people who share your sorrow and loss. I can only express the hope that the days and months to come will heal the wound and help you to adjust yourself to life without your loving father.

Needless to say that my feelings of sympathy apply equally to Shireen, your mummy, and to all other family folk and friends.

My colleagues, Walter, Nelson, Raymond, Andrew and Patrick have asked me to convey their condolences.

Lots of love to you
From
AMK

∽ ∽ ∽

Zohrabibi Kathrada—5 *November 1983*

Kathrada wrote to his niece, Zohrabibi, upon receiving the news that her father, Kathrada's elder brother, Ismail, had died suddenly from a massive heart attack. This news came all the more as a shock because Kathrada had believed his brother was on the road to recovery. When Zohrabibi's mother died in 1976, Kathrada had then tried from his cell to comfort her. Now her father has died and he tries to be with her "at least in spirit at this dark hour." Kathrada writes that the government's forcing his brother to leave the home in which he had been raised and later came to own, had hastened his death. The Group Area Act, an apartheid law, which removed thousands, if not millions of people from their roots and their birthplaces at the stroke of a pen, wrought havoc with human lives; it was an act totally bereft of any human feelings.

∼

A. M. Kathrada
Pollsmoor Maximum Prison
Private Bag X4
Tokai 7966
5th November 1983

My Dear Zohrabibi,

Once again tragedy has struck the family, and it is with heavy feelings that I have to address this letter to you. Warrant Officer Gregory informed me early this morning that Zohra had phoned to say that Pappa passed away at 3 o'clock this morning after a massive heart attack. For a while I was stunned and it took a few moments for the news to sink in. I was shocked because the most recent reports about him were so positive and encouraging and I, too, accepted that the worst crisis was over.

I got Zohra's letter on the 1st Nov. and she gave me details of the latest position. I was relieved to learn that he had been allowed to go home from the nursing home. His condition must have improved so much that he even asked Zohra to tell me that he'd be visiting me as soon as he was well. Yesterday I had Shamima's letter. She said she visits Pappa every day and she was happy about his positive attitude towards getting better.

These reports greatly helped to set my mind at ease; and while I would have liked to see him, I was going to advise him to wait a while until he had completely recovered. Then I was thinking he should spend a few months in Cape Town just resting.

While these and many more things were going through my mind, I got the shocking news of his sudden death. And now we all have to adapt ourselves to this new reality. Naturally the first person I thought of was you; the same as in 1976 when your mummy passed away. I know how attached they were to you and, as in 1976, I am once again writing a few words to you to be with you at least in spirit at this dark hour.

My mind goes back to May 1982 when I last saw him on Robben Island. Already at that time he must have had some premonition of his approaching death. Never before during all his visits did he speak so much about death. How he was hoping that by some miracle I would be able to spend the last few remaining years together. Unfortunately that was not to be.

I feel certain that what hastened his death was his having been forced to move from the house to which he was so attached. I could imagine how very hard it was going to be for him, and I think I mentioned to you about the traumatic experience he must have gone through. I knew he was never going to be happy and settled in any new house no matter how big and beautiful or comfortable. After having literally grown up in the old house, it became part of himself. Baji lived here, Ouma lived there, your mummy lived there—all of them are no more. Some of the kids were born there and everyone of them grew up there. Pappa must have been living there with millions of happy memories. Indeed, those memories became part of himself, part of his life. And when finally he was wrenched away from that house by cruel, unfeeling people, he was suddenly a lost man. Little did they care that they were destroying not just bricks and mortar but they had passed a slow death sentence on a healthy, live, guiltless human being.

When I first heard of the heart attack, I was convinced that the house affair must have had something to do with it. In fact I told my colleagues exactly that. How tragic that, through the unscrupulous, selfish and callous actions of some people, other human beings have to suffer—and die.

Anyway, what can I tell you at a time like this—you who are the carrier of so much sorrow? I don't want to sing Pappa's praises—his qualities are well known. He was calm, patient, hospitable, generous, devoted, kind, caring, sensitive, considerate and loving. He had a fine temperament and a keen sense of humour. We will miss these qualities and much more.

The tragedy is greater for you as it came on the eve of a great occasion in your life. I can imagine how keen he must have been to see you married. But alas, it is not to be. I don't know if the date had already been arranged. My feeling is that once the normal period of mourning is over, it is not necessary to have a long postponement. I'm sure Pappa would have preferred it that way.

You are a strong and determined person, and I'm sure with time you will master the crisis. I can only appeal to you to remain strong and resolute and calm. You will need these in the days ahead.

I hope you and all at home are keeping well. Please convey my heartfelt sympathies to everyone at home. I'm sure you must have received my telegram.

My last letter to you was on 10th October. Do write when you feel a bit settled.

Keep well, and lots of love from
AMK

P.S. I'm posting this letter to Jo'burg so that it reaches you sooner.

My Dear Zohra,

I'm posting Zohrabibi's letter to you Express Post because I think it will reach Johannesburg quicker than Schweizer. Please send it to her as soon as possible. Or phone her as soon as you receive it.

Thanks for your letter of 21st October. It reached me on 1st November. I'll reply after hearing from you.

Yesterday; i.e., 4th November, I had a lovely letter from Shamima and Neelan with 19 photos. They're lovely. I'll be writing to her.

Although the main letter is addressed to Zohrabibi, it is naturally meant for the whole family.

≈ ≈ ≈

Shireen Patel—*28 January 1984*

Kathrada sees one of his godchildren, Shireen, after twenty-one years. This visit of Shireen and her mother, Khatun Patel, "wasn't just a visit, it was an event." So thrilled was he that his colleagues, noticing his joy, said the event called for a celebration to which Kathrada readily agreed, and as "chief cook" the arrangements and preparation had been left to him. It is on visits such as these that Kathrada picks up information and news that no one provides in letters, probably because the assumption is that he will get to know about them or that there are other more pressing things to write about. But, for Kathrada, the little things mean a lot. When he went to jail, racial discrimination in the workplace was a given and would have been carried out to the letter. Hence, he is pleasantly surprised to learn that this was not the case at Shireen's company. Now, in 1984, with skilled labor and educated people in short supply, the government is forced to relax its Job Reservation Act, which prohibits blacks from certain jobs, and also to relax or even abandon the degrading workplace conditions that exists for blacks.

~

A. M. Kathrada
Pollsmoor Maximum Prison
Private Bag X4
Tokai 7966
28th January 1984

My Dearest Shireen,

Your visit, together with Mummy, was one of the nicest things to happen to me in all the years that I've been in jail. It wasn't just a visit, it was an event. Heaven knows for how long and how often I've been trying to build a picture in my mind of the little girl I last saw in 1963. Photographs I have seen, but they are grossly inadequate. At best they convey some idea of the physical likeness of a person but little, if anything, of the personality. Oh, yes, they most certainly have their value, more especially in the prison environment. But photographs can never be a substitute for the real person. Now at last, for two whole sessions of 80 minutes each, I was accorded the pleasure of standing face to face with Shireen. And I enjoyed every second of your presence.

It is exactly 12 o'clock on Sunday morning. Your plane will have just taken off, and by the time I finish writing, you will be landing at Jan Smuts Airport. Back home—to Zaheda, Yusuf, the kids and to all the other near and dear ones. Back to "normality." We will be obliged to once again revert to the impersonal letters to continue contact. Hopefully now it will be on a more regular basis. However, I'll take a realistic view of this and say I'll be happy if you are able to write about 3 times a year. More letters from you are always welcome. But you do have a full and active life to lead, and it is not fair nor practical to expect you to spend too much time writing letters. As we agreed, it will be good if you write a paragraph or two one day and then add a bit now and then until the letter is completed. I know this is more easily said than done. For one thing, there is the bother of putting away an unfinished letter and finding it again! But it is worth a try.

Let's get back to you. Both you and Mummy looked lovely. What surprised me most is that Mummy looked the same as she did twenty years ago. Of course, she has put on a bit of weight, but she seems to have lost some again since the last photo of hers. And it was so good to see her as cheerful and jolly as ever. It was when we spoke of old friends that I realised how cut off one can be in jail. To think that I hadn't heard of the death of Aunt Snowy, Aunt Bibi, Queresh, Dr. Mia, etc. I was really shocked to get the news so many years after. Please convey my condolences to Jean and the children. On the other hand, it was exciting to talk about so many friends and relatives, some of whom I had even forgotten about. I was also surprised to learn that Mummy had visited Zaheda and Ebrahim in Canada. It's good that she has been travelling a bit.

I was very interested to hear of your work conditions, especially the fact that there was no discrimination. I forgot to check with you, but I suppose your firm also sells video machines? In which case I won't be surprised if one of these days you'll be buying a video camera.

I had to interrupt the letter in order to prepare some snacks: canned fruit, jelly, etc., to celebrate your visit. You see, when I returned from the visits, my colleagues saw how thrilled and happy I was, and they said, "This calls for a celebration." To which I readily agreed. I had to prepare the jelly on Saturday to allow it to set. So we have just finished our celebration. It is 5 p.m. (Sunday), and I'm back at the table to continue the letter. In the absence of anyone better, I have to act as chief cook. Small things, things that one would not give a second thought to outside, become important in jail. It is with the help of such seeming trivialities, plus visits, letters, studies, newspapers, games, etc., that the 20 years have passed by so quickly.

Let me end now. Don't forget to get Dr. Essop to arrange an appointment for you with Professor Seftel so that you can get a second opinion. Tell Mummy to try to find the time to visit Ouma Bhayat or to

phone her. Also, pass my fondest regards to all the family and friends in
Benoni, Johannesburg, etc., especially to Rookie, Ismail, etc.

Lots of love to you, Mummy, Zaheda, Yusuf and the families

From

AMK

If you see Amina, tell her thanks for the birthday card.

Zeenat Cajee—*27 May 1984*

*With the death of her father, which followed the death of her mother, Kathrada
can appreciate that Zeenat Cajee is thinking of marriage. Kathrada's main
concern is her studies. He has been following her progress over the years and
always cherished the notion that she would go on to university and distinguish
herself. Now with the thought of marriage, he is concerned that she might
abandon her studies completely and so throw away a wonderful chance forever.
Kathrada is convinced that her grandfather would have given the same advice.
In the extended family, which was still very strong, this plea would be seen as
"sound advice from an elder" and not as intrusive. To strengthen his case, he
reminds her of the time he left university and points out that he never went back
to his studies until prison twenty years later.*

A. M. Kathrada
Pollsmoor Maximum Prison
Tokai 7966
27th May 1984

My Dear Zeenat,

Thanks for your letter of 13th April which reached me on 24th April.
I assume you were writing in reply to two of my letters: (1) of 4th
February; (2) of 28th February.

I quite appreciate the heavy responsibilities that have been thrust
upon your shoulders and those of Feroza. But both of you seem to be
very determined young ladies and full of self-confidence, and I feel certain that you will be equal to your new responsibilities.

Let's come to your decision to get married. Naturally it comes to me as a great surprise. You see, for the last few years I have been keenly following your progress at high school, and my mind has been all geared towards seeing you graduate one day from university with flying colours. In my thoughts I did not allow for any radical changes of direction. At my age there are not many shock-absorbers in the system, and here you come like a bolt from the blue and announce to me that you have decided to get married! Anyway, I have survived the shock, and I am able to look at the position objectively.

The first thing I would like you to clarify is: will you still continue with university after marriage? Secondly, is the young man also at university? Thirdly, if you have no objections, can you tell me a bit more about him—his name, age, interests, etc.?

I have no intention of delivering a lecture on the subject of youth and marriage for the simple reason that I am not qualified to do so. Moreover, I have seen numerous couples who married young and went on to lead long and happy lives. On the other hand, I know of as many couples who married at mature ages and who quickly messed up their marriages. But this is on the basis of personal knowledge and not scientific. Unfortunately I cannot readily recall scientific surveys on the question of age and marriage. I'm sure there must be many.

I'm, of course, not asking you to start looking up statistics of successful and failed marriages before taking the steps. In the state of mind in which you wrote you obviously appeared to be sure of your decision, and under those circumstances no amount of statistics will influence you. But I do have one important matter which I would urge you to very seriously consider. And that is your university career. If marriage is going to mean you having to abandon your studies, then I would appeal to you to please wait. At this stage in your life the most important thing should be your studies. Quite apart from gaining a degree and profession, the mere fact of spending a few years at university can be one of the most profound and valuable experiences. It is a whole world in itself, and the knowledge and experience gained there will place you in a strong position to face the future. I do fully appreciate how lost you must be feeling without your Dad. With him alive you felt motivated to study, to make him feel proud of you. Now you think that motivation is no longer there, and you feel that a husband may help to fill the vacuum that has been left by your father's death.

I know that nothing can replace a father or mother or the love that they could shower upon you. But I want you to know that I for one—and I'm sure there are others—look upon you with a love and affection and concern that is close to that of a parent. You may find it strange, but my attachment to you arises from my great affection and respect for your grandfather. Had he been alive, I know he would have agreed with my appeal to you to give first priority to your studies. You cannot imagine how much importance I attach to your education. For a number of years I talked about you to my colleagues on Robben Island. In fact I boasted to them about my brilliant little girl, and I felt proud each time you wrote and gave me your results.

I am not suggesting that you should break off your relationship. In fact a steady relationship can be an advantage to your studies. Especially if your boyfriend is broad-minded, patient and understanding. So by all means continue your relationship, but postpone the marriage until you complete at least the first degree.

Am I asking too much? I don't think so. Do you know that in 1951 I registered at Wits, and after a few months I chucked up studies and went overseas. I never studied again till I came to jail. Up to now my greatest regret was not to continue at Wits while I had the opportunity. I want to save you from similar regrets in later years.

Think about what I have said. I must end now. My studies are going on slowly. I managed to get through and am busy with my finals which I'll write in January. My health is also fine.

Lots of love to you, Feroza, Miriambai, Aunt Sarah, Bibi, Uncle Yusuf and all the family from

AMK

Essop Jassat—*15 July 1984*

Essop Jassat, friend, political colleague and personal physician, who had him-self suffered at the hands of the apartheid regime, has sent Kathrada a little gift for which Kathrada thanks him. He sympathizes with Essop upon learning of the death of Essop's eldest brother. After thirteen years Kathrada sees Rooki again and pays tribute to her courage, her fortitude, and her inner strength. Even after twenty years Kathrada has not come to terms with the brutal killing of Babla, whom he regarded as his "little brother." One day he hopes he will be able to pay proper tribute to him and also to Mrs. Pahad, who was his "second mother." In writing about reaching his twenty-first year in jail, Kathrada provides an insight into what has made it possible for him and his colleagues to emerge from prison, not only unscathed and without bitterness and regret, but triumphant and as committed as ever to the struggle for freedom. He sums it up in one word: "apprenticeship." Throughout the years of struggle he and so many others knew precisely the difficult road that lay ahead. A road strewn with obstacles, armed forces, resistance to change, dogma, and an enemy that was powerful and felt it was invincible. Kathrada's ultimate goal was to reach and achieve justice, equality, dignity, and freedom for the oppressed. These were the ideals for which he was prepared to sacrifice everything. There were no illusions that achieving them would be easy. Every time he spoke at a rally or addressed a meeting or wrote slogans on walls or helped smuggle some comrade out of the country, he knew what the dangers were. This became the credo by which he lived. When he was arrested and sentenced to life imprisonment he had completed his apprenticeship and was ready, armed with a belief system that was unshakable and unbreakable. Jail became for him a continuation of the struggle but on a different terrain. He congratulates Essop on his service to the community as a doctor.

∼

A. M. Kathrada
Pollsmoor Maximum Prison
Private Bag X4
Tokai 7966
15th July 1984

My Dear Essop,

Thanks for your lovely letter, which arrived on 4th July and for the R25–00. It was a very kind thought on your part to send the "eidy."[1] Please accept my condolences on the death of "Truman." My sympathies also to Isa and Nez and to the rest of the family. I had a letter from England this week in which I learned of the death of Checker Jassat. Had he settled in England? Or were they perhaps referring to "Truman?" And just imagine how cut off one can be in jail; the London letter also told me that Magan Mitha had died some years ago! I wouldn't have got this information even now had I not enquired about him.

---

[1] Eidy: a gift given on the day Eid is celebrated.

You've probably heard from Zohra that I'd be writing to you later. That was actually my intention, and I wrote and asked her to convey my message to you. But I decided during the week to change my plans a bit and reply to you now. Yes, we are allowed a fixed quota of letters and visits, but please don't feel that by my corresponding with you someone else is being deprived of the opportunity. I have planned my program for the rest of the year in accordance with the number of letters I still have left, and I had included you among the persons I had to write to. All I'm now doing is bringing your letter forward by a few weeks. But I really don't want to trouble you to reply. I know how very busy you are, and I suggest you just phone Zohra to tell me that you have received the letter. I shall be perfectly happy I assure you. You can reply to me at Eid time next year.

It was lovely to see Rookie again after about 13 years. She doesn't seem to have changed one bit nor aged a single day. She's so full of life, and I admire her courage, loyalty and spirit of independence. Before I came to jail she was simply Babla's wife. But since his death I began to discover the personality in her own right. Letters and visits from friends and her own visits to me revealed a side of her I never knew. She has refused to be crushed by Babla's cruel death; instead she appears to have filled the vacuum with vigour and determination. It's really been an inspiration to see her. Moreover, to me she represents Babla, whom I loved as my little brother and dearly admired and whose death I still have not been able to fully accept. Over the past 21 years I have lost many near and dear ones—I have a list of almost 80—but if I were to come out of jail today and asked who I missed the most, I'd reply without hesitation, "Babla and Mrs. Pahad." The one was more than a brother to me and the other a second mother. Someday I hope I will be able to pay a proper and more adequate tribute to them. If I ever manage to implement a plan to write a book—*Flat 13*—the stories of these two will occupy high positions.

I suppose you know that Rookie brought along a turkey and biryani for Eid, but unfortunately I was not allowed to receive it. You see, Shehnaaz [Fatima Meer's daughter] had already arranged to bring food, and on Eid Day she delivered biryani, samoosas, kebaab, roti, chicken, mithai,[2] etc., etc. Some of it came by air freight from Durban and the

---

[2] *Biryani:* a rice dish with lentils, meat, potato, saffron, and other spices, a specialty for Eid (the celebration after the month of Ramadan); *samoosa:* a savory triangular shaped meat pie; *kebaabs:* spicy meatballs; *roti:* a round flat bread; *mithai:* Indian sweetmeats served after dinner or with tea.

rest was prepared locally by Shehnaaz and Dr. Ayesha Arnold. So we had a real feast—for 2 days. It was the biggest and best feast we had in 21 years. Mrs. Mayat (widow of Dr. Mayat) from Durban also sent a parcel of mithai, but it was returned to her.

On Wednesday 11th July it was 21 years after Rivonia! But unluckily for us we did not receive the symbolic key which should have brought freedom and other privileges. The only keys we know are real ones and they are used to keep us in, firmly and securely, so that we may continue to give our days and weeks and months and years to feed the insatiable appetite of retribution. A situation of this nature is tailor-made for negative responses, and if one enters jail in a frame of mind bent on looking at the dark side of things, then every minute of one's stay would be intolerable. It would be impossible to contemplate a lengthy period of imprisonment. Fortunately for us, our apprenticeship had prepared us for the jail situation—and for worse. So that it is possible to look back at the 21 years, not only without bitterness and regret, but in many ways as a continuation of the apprenticeship. For undoubtedly jail is a great teacher.

I interrupted this letter to listen to "Test the Team," my favourite radio program. I note that one of the original team, Prof. Bleksley, died last week. He must have been your professor, not so? Anyway, this program is followed by the 9 o'clock news. And that means that I must start winding up my work and prepare for bed. Let me end with my very best wishes to you. Although we haven't been in frequent direct contact, it has been a source of great satisfaction to see you emerge as a pillar of strength and a towering figure in the community and beyond. Your work as a doctor and in public affairs continues to be an inspiration. Lots of love to Shireen, Aadil, Yumna, Zaheera and all the family and friends. All the best to you from

AMK

Pass my regards to Effie when next you see her.

Leila Issel—*1 December 1984*

Kathrada explains why he cannot always reply to the letters he receives. There are regulations that determine how many letters he can write, regulations invented by adults as a means of control. He wants to know all about her

school, her class, her favorite subjects and at the end he reminds her to please send him a photo the next time she writes. He describes a typical day in the life of a political prisoner.

~

A. M. Kathrada
Pollsmoor Maximum Prison
Private Bag X4
Tokai 7966
1st December 1984

My Dearest Leila,

I apologise to you for not sending you a greeting card this year. I thought it is better to write a little letter to you instead.

Let me star off first of all by wishing you, Mummy and Daddy and the rest of the family and all the friends my very best wishes for the holiday season and especially for the coming year. I am sorry I can no longer remember the names of all the members of the family, but I think your brother's name is Yasser. Am I right? But I remember you very well from the time that you went and gave the flowers to the lady from Johannesburg because your daddy was unable to do so. We thought that was very sweet of you.

I hope you are enjoying your school holidays. I am sure you must also be helping Mummy with the housework. One day you must write and tell me about yourself. What class are you in? Do you enjoy going to school? What is your favourite subject? What do you want to do after you finish schooling? Do you like to read? Do you like T.V.? You see, there are so many things I would like to know about you. Unfortunately I will not be able to write to you again for a long time. We prisoners are only allowed to write and receive a fixed number of letters every year, and these are not enough. Just to give you an example. If I decide to write only one letter to each member of my family, my quota for the year will be finished. So when you write to me one day, and you don't receive a reply for many months, you will understand it is not because I am too lazy to write or because I have forgotten my responsibility. But it will be because of the Regulations that control our lives.

I know it is not easy for a young person like you to understand laws and regulations and all things that we adults invent in order to control the world. The child's world should be filled with fun and laughter and song and dance and games. Here we come along and try to get you to understand about something called Regulations which lay down that a prisoner can only write a certain number of letters! We are real spoilt sports are we not? You may turn around and ask why is Uncle in jail in the first place. It would be a good question. But it needs a long explanation. I am sure as you grow older, you will readily understand.

In the meantime let me tell you a few little things about our life in jail. I came to Pollsmoor from Robben Island just over two years ago and joined my friends who came here earlier. We all stay together. We get up early in the morning, and we do our exercises. This is very important to keep fit and healthy. Then we shave and shower and get dressed. After breakfast we clean our place. After that we are free to do what we want to. We read newspapers, books, or do our schoolwork. We have our own little FM radio so we listen to the news and other programs. Or we can walk about in the yard till lunch time. The afternoons are quite short. We are locked up again at 4 o'clock till the next morning. Once a week we see films, mostly from the Cape Provincial Library. Some of them are very interesting. We are only 6 so we cannot play many games. Two of my friends play tennis. On Robben Island I used to play Tenniquoits, but there is nobody to play with here. Every day in jail is the same. Except the times when we have visits. Jail is very boring and a big waste of time. Luckily we have studies, newspapers, books, magazines and the radio which help to pass the time.

I must stop now and go to bed. I will be writing exams next month so I have to study hard.

Keep well and look after yourself. Give my fondest regards to Mummy, Daddy and the family, to Uncle Trevor, Jonathan, Edward, Wilfred, and Aunts Cheryl, Lynette and all your other uncles and aunts.

Lots of love to you from

Uncle Ahmed

AMK

P.S. When you write one day, don't forget to send a photo of yourself. I almost forgot to thank you for the lovely card you sent me last Xmas.

P. W. Botha—*13 February 1985*

In a House of Assembly debate sometime in late January 1985, the state president of South Africa, P. W. Botha, indicated that he was prepared to release Nelson Mandela, the Rivonia Trialists, and all the other political prisoners, provided they unconditionally renounce violence as a means for furthering their objectives. This letter is the response from Messrs. Mandela, Sisulu, Mlangeni, and Kathrada, who were housed at Pollsmoor Prison at the time. Messrs. Mbeki and Motsoaledi were still incarcerated on Robben Island; Dennis Goldberg was locked up in Pretoria. Contact between and among the prisoners at these three locations was prohibited.

∽

The Commissioner of Prisons
Pretoria

The subjoined letter is for the attention of the State President, Mr P.W. Botha

The State President
Cape Town

Sir,

Copies of the Hansard Parliamentary record of 25th January to 1st February 1985 were delivered to us on 8th February.

We note that during the debate in the House of Assembly you indicated that you were prepared to release prisoners in our particular category provided that we unconditionally renounce violence as a means of furthering our political objectives.

We have given earnest consideration to your offer, but we regret to inform you that it is not acceptable in its present form. We hesitate to associate you with a move which, on a proper analysis, appears to be no more than a shrewd and calculated attempt to mislead the world into the belief that you have magnanimously offered us release from prison which we ourselves have rejected. Coming in the face of such unprecedented and widespread demands for our release your remarks can only be seen as the height of cynical politicking.

We refuse to be a party to anything which is really intended to create division, confusion and uncertainty within the African National Congress at a time when the unity of the organisation has become a matter of crucial importance to the whole country. The refusal by the Department of Prisons to allow us to consult fellow prisoners in other prisons has confirmed our view.

Just as some of us refused the humiliating condition that we should be released to the Transkei, we also reject your offer on the same ground. No self respecting human being will demean and humiliate himself by making a commitment of the nature you demand. You ought not to perpetuate our imprisonment by the simple expedient of setting conditions which, to your own knowledge, we will never under any circumstances accept.

Our political beliefs are largely influenced by the Freedom Charter, a program of principles whose basic premise is the equality of all human beings. It is not only the clearest repudiation of all forms of racial discrimination, but also the country's most advanced statement of political principles. It calls for universal franchise in a united South Africa and for the equitable distribution of the wealth of the country.

The intensification of apartheid, the banning of political organisations and the closing of all channels of peaceful protest conflicted sharply with these principles and forced the ANC to turn to violence. Consequently until apartheid is completely uprooted our people will continue to kill one another, and South Africa will be subjected to all the pressures of an escalating civil war.

Yet the ANC has for almost 50 years since its establishment faithfully followed peaceful and non violent forms of struggle. During the period 1952 to 1961 alone it appealed, in vain, to no less than three South African premiers to call a Round Table conference of all population groups where the country's problems could be thrashed out, and it only resorted to violence when all other options had been blocked.

The peaceful and non violent nature of our struggle never made any impression on your government. Innocent and defenceless people were pitilessly massacred in the course of peaceful demonstrations. You will remember the shooting in Johannesburg on 1st May 1950 and Sharpeville in 1960. On both occasions, as in every other instance [of] police brutality, the victims had invariably been unarmed defenceless men, women and even children. At the time the ANC had not even mooted the idea of resorting to armed struggle. You were the country's defence minister when no less than 600 people, mostly children, were shot down in Soweto in 1976. You were the country's premier when the police beat up people again in the course of orderly demonstrations against the 1984 Coloured and Indian elections, and 7,000 heavily armed troops invaded the Vaal Triangle to put down an essentially peaceful protest by the residents.

Apartheid, which is condemned not only by blacks, but also by a substantial section of the whites, is the greatest single source of violence against our people. As leader of the Nationalist Party, which seeks to uphold apartheid through force and violence, we expect you to be the first to renounce violence. But it would seem that you have no intention whatsoever of using democratic and peaceful forms of dealing with black grievances [and] that the real purpose of attaching conditions to your offer is to ensure that the NP should enjoy the monopoly of committing violence against defenceless people. The founding of *Umkonto we Sizwe* was designed to end that monopoly and forcefully bring home to the rulers that the oppressed people were prepared to stand up and defend themselves and to fight back, if necessary with force.

Note that on page 312 of Hansard you say that you are personally prepared to go a long way to release tensions in intergroup relations in this country, but that you are not prepared to lead the whites to abdication. By making this statement you again categorically reaffirmed that you remain obsessed with the preservation of domination by the white minority. You should not be surprised, therefore, if in spite of the supposed good intentions of the government, the vast masses of the oppressed people continue to regard you as a mere broker of the interests of the white tribe, and consequently unfit to handle national affairs.

Again on pages 318 and 319 you state that you cannot talk with people who do not want to co-operate, that you hold talks with every possible leader who is prepared to renounce violence. Coming from the leader of the Nationalist Party this statement is a shocking revelation, as it shows more than anything else, that there is not a single figure in that party who is advanced enough to understand the basic problems of our country, who has profited from the bitter experiences of the 37 years of NP rule and who is prepared to take a lead towards the building of a truly democratic South Africa.

It is clear from this statement that you would prefer to talk only to people who accept apartheid even though they are emphatically repudiated by the very community on whom you want to impose them, through violence if necessary.

We would have thought that the ongoing and increasing resistance in black townships, despite the massive deployment of the Defence Force, would have brought home to you the utter futility of unacceptable apartheid structures, manned by servile and self seeking individuals of dubious credentials. But your government seems bent on continuing to move along this costly path and, instead of heeding the voice of true leaders of the communities, in many cases they have been flung into prison.

If your government seriously wants to halt the escalating violence, the only method open is to declare your commitment to end the evil of apartheid and show your willingness to negotiate with the true leaders at local and national levels. At no time have the oppressed people, especially the youth, displayed such unity in action, such resistance to racial oppression, and such prolonged demonstrations in the face of brutal military and political action. Students in secondary schools and universities are clamouring for the end of apartheid now, and for equal opportunities for all. Black and white churchmen and intellectuals, civic associations, and workers' and women's organisations demand genuine political changes. Those who "cooperate" with you, who have served you so loyally throughout these troubled years, have not at all helped you to stem the rapidly rising tide. The coming confrontation will only be averted if the following steps are taken without delay.

1. The government must renounce violence first.
2. It must dismantle apartheid.
3. It must un-ban the ANC.
4. It must free all who have been imprisoned, banished or exiled for their opposition to apartheid.
5. It must guarantee free political activity.

On page 309 [of Hansard] you refer to allegations which have been regularly made at the United Nations and throughout the world that Mr Mandela's health has deteriorated in prison and that he is detained under inhuman conditions.

There is no need for you to be sanctimonious in this regard. The United Nations is an important and responsible organ of world peace and is, in many respects, the hope of the international community. Its affairs are handled by the finest brains on earth, by men whose integrity is flawless. If they made such allegations they did so in the honest belief that they were true. If we continue to enjoy good health and if our spirits remain high, it has not necessarily been due to any special consideration or care taken by the Department of Prisons. Indeed it is common knowledge that in the course of our long imprisonment, especially during the first years, the prison authorities had implemented a deliberate policy of doing everything to break our morale. We were subjected to harsh, if not brutal treatment, and permanent physical and spiritual harm was caused to many prisoners.

Although conditions have since improved in relation to the sixties and seventies, life in prison is not as easy as you may suppose, and we still face serious problems in many respects. There is still racial discrimination in our treatment, we have not yet won the right to be treated as political prisoners. We are no longer visited by the minister of Prisons and other officials from the headquarters and by the judges and magistrates. These conditions are cause for concern to the United Nations Organisation, the Organisation of African Unity, Anti-Apartheid Movement and to our numerous friends.

Taking into account the actual practice of the Dept. of Prisons, we must reject the view that a life sentence means that one should die in prison. By applying to security prisoners the principle that life is life, you are using double standards, since Common Law prisoners with clean prison records serve about 15 years of a life sentence. We must also remind you that it was the NP whose very first act on coming to power was to release the traitor, Robey Leibrandt (and others) after he had served only a couple of years of his life sentence. These were men who had betrayed their own country to Nazi Germany during the last world war in which South Africa was involved.

As far as we are concerned we have long ago completed our life sentences. We are now being actually kept in preventative detention without enjoying the rights attached to that category of prisoners. The outdated and universally rejected philosophy of retribution is being meted out to us and every day we spend in prison is simply an act of revenge against us.

Despite your commitment to the maintenance of white supremacy, however, your attempt to create new apartheid structures, and your hostility to a non racial system of government in this country, and despite our determination to resist this policy to the bitter end, the simple fact is that you are South Africa's head of government, you enjoy the support of the majority of the white population, and you can help change the course of South African history. A beginning can be made if you accept and agree to implement the five point program on page 3 [above] of this document. If you accept the program our people would readily co-operate with you to sort out whatever problems arise as far as the implementation thereof is concerned.

In this regard we have taken note of the fact that you no longer insist on some of us being released to the Transkei. We have also noted the restrained tone which you adopted when you made the offer in parliament. We hope you will show the same flexibility and examine these proposals objectively. That flexibility and objectivity may help create a better climate for a fruitful national debate.

Yours faithfully
Nelson Mandela
Walter Sisulu
Raymond Mhlaba
Ahmed Kathrada
Andrew Mlangeni

≈   ≈   ≈

Helen Joseph—*17 March 1985*

Helen Joseph, secretary of the South African Women's Federation, co-accused in the Treason Trial and the first person to be placed under house arrest in South Africa, was until her death a staunch and committed anti-apartheid activist. She was born in England but settled in South Africa at an early age. Kathrada wishes her a happy seventieth birthday and reminds her of the time she refused to tell Nelson Mandela her age. This is a letter written with great warmth and affection to a person who has always put the cause first. Kathrada and his colleagues will raise their imaginary glasses and toast a remarkable woman. He tells her about his health and his studies and how, after completing four degrees, the authorities will not allow him to pursue a masters degree.

≈

A. M. Kathrada
Pollsmoor Maximum Prison
Private Bag X4
Tokai 7966
17th March 1985

My Dear Helen,

When I decided to write to you to join in your birthday celebrations, I was overwhelmed by a thousand thoughts which began to flood my mind. I, therefore, invoked the aid of a few pithy quotations in the hope of saying what I would have attempted to do in many paragraphs (and most probably failed).

I deliberately chose to head the list with the quotation from Olive Schreiner, primarily for its content but also because I am aware of the esteem in which you hold her. The little that I've read by and about her leaves me in no doubt that, had she been still alive today, the feeling between you would have been mutual. Indeed, if I were asked to single out someone who most closely resembles Olive Schreiner in her ideas, her loyalty and devotion, her breadth of vision and courage, I would unhesitatingly declare that mantle can only fall upon your shoulders.

Robert Frost once wrote that a diplomat was a man who always remembered a woman's birthday but never her age. I am going to be undiplomatic and take advantage of the safety of prison walls to make the bold observation that when Olive wrote those words in 1906, you were a toddler of one!

Time was when we wouldn't have dared to be so flippant. Nelson and I were just recalling an occasion during the Treason Trial—the time when we were conducting our own defence. At one of the evening consultations in Pretoria Prison, Nelson, as part of the preparations, asked a certain lady what her age was. To which he received the terse reply: "What has that got to do with the case?" No explanations could move her from that position, and the matter was left there. I wonder if she remembers the occasion?

Twenty-five years have rolled by since then. So much has happened to all of us. There is so much to talk about, so much to reminisce. Where does one begin? Even to try to do so through this impersonal manner would be to rob many a precious moment or experience of its colour and meaning. Let us keep the hope alive that one day we will be able to meet and revel in the memories of a rich and eventful past and discourse about the future.

In the meantime remember that you are never absent from our thoughts. And especially on 8th April we will be with you in spirit. We will lift our imaginary glasses and toast a really grand and wonderful young lady whom it was our pleasure and honour to know. (Oliver

Wendell Holmes was so right when he said that to be 70 years young is sometimes far more cheerful and hopeful than to be 40 years old.) You continue to be a source of inspiration and encouragement to us and to countless others.

I have seen some recent photos of yours and have also read your letters to Nelson, including the one which arrived last week. It was almost as if I was looking at the Helen I always knew, and your letter confirmed it.

Now a few things about us. All 6 of us here are well. Just to clear the confusion caused by the papers, Govan, Wilton and Elias are not at Pollsmoor; they're still on the Island.

The Red Cross arranged that we should be given a general check-up annually by a specialist. In February we we[re] taken to Cape Town for this purpose, and after a thorough check-up we were found to be in good health. Naturally there are the little ailments, but they are relatively minor and under control.

To be only 6 can be quite boring and constricting, especially since it virtually precludes meaningful sporting and recreational activities. Fortunately we have a few facilities which go some way towards compensation. For instance, there are the newspapers and periodicals which are a real boon. Then we have an FM radio. You won't believe it, but starting from 5 in the morning, we listen to 20 news bulletins a day—right up to 11 at night. In addition there are favourite programs such as *Test the Team, Venture,* sports, etc.

We also have a little library with some readable books. Perhaps a major boon over the years has been our studies. When I was outside I never imagined I'd be studying again one day. I hope I'm not being immodest if I tell you of what I've been doing. I managed to complete a B.A. with majors in History and Criminology; B. Bibliography with majors in Library Science and Native Administration (now called African Politics). I also did a B.A. Honours in History. Last year I got my results—I've now completed Honours in African Politics.

I've been trying to do M.A. History, but the Prison Regulations don't allow me to do it. Only prisoners who have two years of their sentences remaining may be permitted to do Masters or Doctorate.

Apart from keeping our communal cell clean, we do no other work. To keep active we all do regular exercises.

This is how we pass our time day after day and year in and year out. But our spirits remain as high as ever.

This will be all for today. Please pass my fondest regards to all our friends and family. They are all in our thoughts.

Keep well. Lots of love and Happy Birthday once more

From

AMK

≈   ≈   ≈

Navi Joseph—*23 March 1985*

The letter opens with Kathrada's sympathies to Navi on the death of his mother. Kathrada pays a moving tribute to a grand old lady and to all those people of that generation who had a sense of justice, were selfless and generous with the little they possessed, were kind and thoughtful, and above all, were people who showed courage and fortitude in difficult circumstances. Kathrada hopes that Navi has recovered from his heart attack. He was shocked to hear that Navi who neither drank nor smoked should have fallen prey to this "infirmity." He obliquely and in jest reminds Navi of his younger days.

≈

Pollsmoor Maximum Prison
23rd March 1985

My Dear Navi,

Tommy must have told about your and Dasoo's letter which failed to arrive. Well, they have since come, and I'm hastening to reply.

Firstly, about your mother's death. Zohra wrote and told me about it; in fact she kept me informed about her throughout her illness. And she also made it a point to attend the funeral. So in a sense I was represented there. I'm glad that Zohra has been in touch with the family, and she and Latchmee appear to have struck up a good friendship.

It is strange how one can never adequately prepare oneself for news of death. Your mummy's failing health and advanced age should have been enough to indicate to us that the end was imminent. Yet when it did come, the first reaction to the news was one of shock. Yes, another member of the grand old generation has gone and left us all the poorer. Apart from her unique, unforgettable and lovable characteristics, your mummy belonged to a generation which consisted of many wonderful men and women. It was our privilege to know and be associated with a number of them, and each has made an indelible impression on our memories. I will always remember your mummy for her hospitality, her keen sense of humour, her frankness, her courage, her unbounded love for her fellow beings, her deep concern for the deprived and underprivileged. We shall have done well if we succeed in emulating them—even if only to the slightest degree.

Please accept my deepest condolences and also pass my sympathies to the rest of the family, especially to the South African branch.

Before I get on with other matters, let me thank you and the family for the Xmas card. Unfortunately I am not able to pass your greetings to Govan, Elias and Wilton[1] as they are not with us at Pollsmoor. We left them on Robben Island when we were transferred here.

In my last letter I mentioned something about the sartorial metamorphosis which you had undergone and suggested that it may be regarded as a betrayal of your class. A little while thereafter Zohra wrote and told me that you had had a heart attack! We just couldn't believe it. I notice that three times in your letter you refer to your ailment by some name which we don't seem to have come across before. But all the surrounding information in your letter confirms our suspicion that "infaret" has a lot to do with the ticker. Now, how come you go and contract a cardiac infirmity which we have generally come to associate with affluence? You've always worked hard and led an active life; you've avoided at least two debilitating vices; namely, alcohol and cigarettes (unfortunately I can't include one other vice specifically prohibited by one of the Commandments—I think it is. No?). Or was Stanley Uys right when he said in an article a couple of years ago that the working class in England is a fast-dwindling phenomenon?

Anyway, it's good to know that you're on the mend. After the traumatic experience, I can't blame you if you lie back and enjoy some of the pampering. It must feel good for a change to be at the receiving end of visitors, flowers, chocolates and other goodies. After all, you have spent a lifetime as a dispenser of such and many other favours to countless numbers of people.

In this respect, there is much in common between a patient and a prisoner. The other day I was mentioning to my Irish niece (Did you know that Kola's younger brother is married to a lovely Irish lady and

---

[1] The Rivonia Trialists who stayed on Robben Island.

has been living in Dublin for years?) how nice it feels—even at my age—to be mothered and pampered. I was referring in particular to a visit I had in December from my eldest brother's wife (whom Dasoo met). I must have been about 10 or 11 when she and my brother got married. I had to leave home when I was 8 to go to school in Jo'burg, because I was not allowed to go to the white or the African schools in Schweizer. It must have been quite a traumatic experience for me, because my young mind simply could not comprehend these prohibitions. After all, all our neighbours were white, my godmother was an Afrikaner, my playmates were Black and white, the man who taught me my ABC was Mr. Mtshali [Principal of the African school] who used to come to our place in the afternoons to teach me. At home I was never taught that there was any difference between me and any of these others. And so when I had to wrench myself away to go all the way to Johannesburg, I resisted, both mentally and, to a lesser extent, physically. It is this business of staying in Jo'burg that was responsible for my mother and the elders regarding me as the baby of the family. And that's how it has been through the years. Being in jail has simply accentuated the position. Of course, the jail situation naturally lends itself to the perpetuation of such attitudes. Everybody wants to do something for this poor, helpless being! Khatun and Shireen want to bring cakes and other goodies; Babla's Rookie brought a turkey for Eid.; Dr. Bismillah's sister from Durban sent sweet-meats; the Meer family sent so much food for Eid that we ate for two days; a five-year-old son of a niece of mine got his mother to send R20 to "Uncle so that he can pay the police and get out of jail." Others come and leave money; many want to send books. Believe me, this big "baby" of 55+ doesn't exactly dislike this attention and acts of kindness.

I suppose this collective, spontaneous expression of sympathy is where the similarity between patient and prisoner begins—and ends. Our particular patient in this instance is soon to be up and about and back into the humdrum of everyday life, while this here prisoner is still to remain for many years, to endure the harsh institutional routine and of course at the same time, continue to enjoy all compensations—the attention, the concern and [the] kindness.

I assume you are well up with the recent drama which momentarily catapulted Pollsmoor into the limelight—the visit of Lord Bethel and his subsequent report; the visit of some American law professor (I forget his name) concerned with human rights; the attempted visit by Senator Kennedy; and the so-called "offer" of conditional release made by

President Botha and our refusal to accept it. To many it may have seemed as if we were a hair's breadth away from freedom. But in fact, from the very moment that the announcement was made, it was already a non-starter. Now I don't want to indulge in any false modesty when I say that I haven't got the stuff that heroes are made of; but really I didn't have to go through any sleepless nights to arrive at the decision. It was so patently designed to humiliate us that there just could be no other decision for me but to reject it. But please understand that I'm not for a moment holding it against anybody who has accepted the offer. In matters such as these, it is unwise to ignore individual cases; for one may find that there may in fact be differing circumstances which may lead individuals to take another approach. So it is not advisable to point fingers and condemn without taking into account all the factors involved.

I'm afraid I have to bring this letter to an abrupt end; I'll leave some matters for next time or perhaps include them in my letter to Dasoo.

My best wishes to Harold and Billy[2]—your co-heart patients. Don't forget to get the list from Harold and my regards to Annemarie and the kids.

Congratulations to Alan for his continuing success in the music world. Lots of love to Zoya and also to Tanya and Nadia, and Adie of course.

It's good to hear about Tilly.[3] Lots of love to her. I just can't get over the tragedy of her daughter's death. I'll write more about this another time. Helen turns 80 on 8th April.[4] Try and send her a message. She is a grand old lady. Hope Sadie[5] has fully recovered. Love to her.

I'm fine otherwise. Got my results a couple of weeks ago. I managed to complete Hons. in African Politics.

Keep well. Lots of love and good wishes to all, from

AMK.

P.S. I'm just starting a book, *A Vision of Order*, which is a study of Black S.A. literature 1914–1980, written by Ursula Barnett. Who is she? And don't forget to answer my questions in my last letter to you and Bob.

---

[2] Harold Wolpe (married to Annemarie) and Billy Nannan.

[3] Tilly First, mother of Ruth First. Ruth had been assassinated by the South African regime.

[4] Helen Joseph, one of South Africa's great heroes. She was the first person to be placed under house arrest in South Africa.

[5] Sadie Foreman, political activist, also in exile in England.

~ ~ ~

Dullah Omar—*31 May 1985*

In an earlier letter to Dullah Omar, his lawyer, Kathrada had asked him to obtain the Educational Journal, *as he wished to study the article on black consciousness. He now feels that he has to explain, or at least rationalize, why it was so important to get this journal. To exemplify his case he cites the different teachers' organizations and argues that to really understand the current situation, every aspect has to be studied in depth. He then hints to Dullah that because of the continual refusal to allow Zohra and Enver Kathrada to visit him, and also the refusal to allow him to study for a Masters, these matters might end up in court. Kathrada writes of his disappointment at the number of inaccuracies that are to be found in South African history books and the very few black contributions made. On this point, he hopes that people like Neville Alexander will get more involved and thus begin to redress the balance. The last part of the letter is a window to why people like Kathrada were able to endure the long sentence and emerge triumphant. He writes that their ever-present awareness of why they were in jail helped restrict their incarceration to the physical being only; his mind and thoughts cannot be imprisoned.*

~

A. M. Kathrada
Pollsmoor Maximum Prison
Tokai 7966
31st May 1985

My Dear Dullah,

How lovely to hear from you. You needn't be inhibited about encroaching on my quota of letters and visits. Maintaining contact with you is, to me, as valuable as with the rest of the family and friends. I'm, however, only too well aware of the busy life you are leading and your innumerable commitments, and it would be selfish of me to expect you to carry on regular contact with me. Let's say a letter and/or a visit once or twice a year would be terrific. But I appreciate that even this would not be very easy. Please remember that a visit or letter from you is most welcome.

You know we prisoners are a peculiar breed of people. We live in a very small and confined world, but often our worries, anxieties and demands on folks' time are in direct contrast to the smallness of our world. An example that immediately comes to mind is the manner in which I nagged you about the *Education Journal*. Let me try to offer an explanation, or a rationalisation, for my behaviour. Or perhaps I should say I offer this as a plea in mitigation! You see, in our little world we have all the time and opportunity to read, listen to, speculate about, and "analyse" any news item/s or topic which may attract our attention. You may not believe it, but on our little FM radio, starting from 5 a.m. (news headlines on Good Hope) until 11 p.m. we listen to over 20 news broadcasts every day! In addition we read *Cape Times, Die Burger, Sowetan, Star, Sunday Times, Rapport, City Press, Cape Herald, Leader, Graphic, Guardian* (U.K.), *Time, Frontline, Die Suid Afrikaan, Drum*, etc., etc. Then, in my African Politics we dealt with African Socialism, Marxism, African Nationalism, Liberalism, Black Consciousness, Negritude, Political Organizations in S.A., Biography of Buthelezi, etc. This gives you an idea of the scope for discussion. Naturally, depending on circumstances, timing, relevance, some topics arouse more interest than others. Thus, when I was doing an assignment on B.C.,[1] I came across Mildred Poswa's article on the subject which I found to be very interesting. My professor strongly recommended the *Education Journal* and sent me Mrs. Kies's address. Unfortunately UNISA could only supply me with Part III of the Poswa article. I, therefore, decided to subscribe. Since Poswa's approach was the only one available which differed from the others, I became more and more anxious to get hold of the complete series. I also hoped that other issues of the *Journal* would contain articles on B.C. I might add that the very existence of the *Journal* came to us as a surprise as did a more recent item that the TLSA[2] itself is still about. In the sixties already, in the absence of reports to the contrary, we had come to accept the facetious remark that the biggest branch of the TLSA was in Toronto!

Over the past few months we've been following the trials and tribulations of the CPTA,[3] the emergence of a new Teachers Body in the Eastern Cape under Uren, and the challenge by Pitt. Now the question is if the TLSA is still there, why Uren's outfit? And who is Pitt? etc., etc. Add to this the news of the revival of the NUM under Dudley, and you will understand our desire for information other than that contained in

---

[1] Black Consciousness (Movement).

[2] TSLA: a teachers' organization.

[3] CPTA: the Cape Province Teachers' Association.

the material which we receive. Have I made out a case?

When my nephew, Nazir (Kemal knows him) visited me in April, I said to him that I hoped I hadn't left you with the impression that I was worried about the R4 involved in the subscription. He was immediately able to assure me that that couldn't be.

I've checked with W/O Swart, and he informs me that no copies of the *Journal* had arrived. He also had not yet received your application to visit me. Let's hope I'll be seeing you one of these days.

I also asked Nazir to inform you that the "missing" letters from London (Joseph and Moonsamy) via Ramesh had arrived. He obviously failed to contact you. I have in the meantime sent Ramesh's new address to the friends abroad and am hoping to hear from them soon. I hope Ramesh is not too much inconvenienced by this. Incidentally, could I ask you to do a bit of detective work for me? I should like to get hold of Priya's birthday. Could you assist? Priya still remains the only child whom I was able to touch, cuddle and kiss. Since then I've had a number of visits with children, but I had to see them all through the glass. You see, because of the antediluvian "first-degree" rule, I may not get contact visits from my nieces and nephews and their kids.

I suppose you are aware that the refusal to allow Zohra and Enver to visit me, plus the refusal to allow me to do M.A., may end up in court. I've already had several consultations with Attorney Ismail Ayob in this regard. I expect to see him again soon.

Let me come back to reading matter. One thing that has struck me forcefully, especially in the course of my studies, is the inordinate number of inaccuracies, distortions and significant omissions relating to our history, contained in the textbooks, periodicals and newspapers. One reason for this is that most of the material is written by whites and foreigners. Not because of racial considerations but because of the peculiarities of the country, most people in this category are automatically excluded from writing authentic history. But a more disturbing thing is the virtual absence of substantial Black contribution, apart from an occasional periodical article. Unfortunately, among the younger contributors, there is a tremendous ignorance of our own history. Many years ago we had discussions with Neville [Alexander] about aspects of this problem. We had in fact hoped—some of us in fact said to him in so many words—that he should devote himself fully to research and writing. And at the same time, of course, rope in others to do likewise. I don't know how much he has been able to do, but I must confess I felt saddened and disappointed when I saw him emerging, not as the academician, transcending the numerous groupings and interests, but as an active partisan and spokesman of a section. I shall keep on hoping to see him and others, who are similarly intellectually endowed, make their contribution in the various disciplines which are virtually untouched by our people.

On the more general level, I cannot but share your optimism. Age and incarceration largely prevent us from physically experiencing Wordsworth's "bliss" first hand; I suppose we can turn to Milton for solace and remind ourselves that "They also serve who only stand and wait." In a sense, jail is one long wait. Fortunately the ever-present awareness of the reasons why one finds oneself here helps to restrict the incarceration to one's physical self. One's mind and thoughts cannot be imprisoned, and they remain free to mingle with the folks outside and share their little pleasures and joy and to join them in their travails and tribulations. Under the circumstances it didn't cost any sleepless nights in order to turn down the "offer" of the State President.

In our line of business jail is something one expects. I can still picture the days in 1963 when the decision was taken that I should go underground. I know that to be underground and active reduces one's survival time to a matter of months. As I was walking away from the flat to go to Rivonia, I bumped into Georgie Gamiet in Market Street. Whether it was my somewhat bulky briefcase or "womanly intuition," but she stopped and asked me whether I was also on my way to join my fellow house arrestees in exile. I gave some facetious answer, we exchanged pleasantries and said goodbye. She was the last "free" person I met. A few months thereafter I was in jail. Come July 11th, it will be 22 years! I hope you will forgive any element of immodesty if I invoke the words of Henley to describe the state in which two decades of imprisonment finds us:

> In the fell clutch of circumstance
> I have not winced nor cried aloud.
> Under the bludgeonings of chance
> My head is bloody, but unbow'd.

I must end now. We continue to follow the various cases in which you and other mutual friends appear. But I suppose there are so many cases these days that only a handful get any mention in the press. Anyway, carry on with your good work.

I had no idea that Shahieda and Johnny were divorced. I just hope I didn't make a faux pas in my letter to Leila. I will definitely write to Jenny soon. Thanks for conveying my greetings to various friends. I've heard from Shehnaaz and have replied.

Keep well. Lots of love to Farida, Fazlin, Kemal, Rustim, the rest of the family and friends.

All the best to you from

AMK

≈   ≈   ≈

Essop Jassat—*2 June 1985*

On the subject of incarcerations and trials, Kathrada recalls the long association he has had with Messrs. Mandela and Sisulu. He recounts in detail the strategy the thirty Treason Trialists adopted during the State of Emergency of 1960. This account provides us with a wonderful insight into the "apprenticeship" he wrote about earlier to Essop, on 15 July 1984. Experiences such as these equipped him with the wherewithal to endure this present life sentence. He writes that Botha's so-called offer was an offer that would strip them of their dignity and self-respect.

≈

A. M. Kathrada
Pollsmoor Maximum Prison
Tokai 7966
2nd June 1985

My Dear Essop,

Soon it will be Eid again—and time for my annual letter. I hope it finds you, Shireen and the children in good health, especially Shireen who I had heard a few months ago was not too well. I was hoping that whatever ailment there was connected with your absence, and now that you are reunited it has disappeared. I hope the children's studies were not in any way affected.

It would be unrealistic, of course, to expect that these lengthy "shows" do not cause disruption. But I suppose by now the families have learned to accept it as an invariable concomitant of public life. The important thing is to do everything possible to ensure that the morale is kept high. This is a two-way process, and it is imperative that the "victim," and his family and friends make their full contribution.

Let's pass on to something else; it is quite unnecessary to lecture to you on morale. Apart from you being a veteran of many years of personal experience, in the course of your professional life you must have come across countless cases of disruption and dislocation where you had to counsel affected parties on the importance of morale and confidence.

We here often recount some of our experiences in this regard. You know that Messrs. Mandela, Sisulu and I, apart from four decades of personal friendship, had the common experience of being co-accused in the 3 famous trials of the fifties and sixties; viz., the Defiance Campaign trial of 1952–1953 (20 accused), the Treason Trial 1956–1961 (156 accused at the start ending up with 30) and the Rivonia Trial 1963–1964. These were all lengthy trials and caused considerable disruption—and even tension. Of course, things never got so serious as to adversely affect the smooth conduct of the trials. Let me give you an example of the type of thing I'm referring to. In 1960, during the State of Emergency, the 30 Treason Trialists were also taken into custody. We, together with our lawyers, felt that in the atmosphere prevailing at the time, there was a real danger that even the courts would not remain unaffected and consequently we would not get a fair trial. So we instructed the lawyers to apply for an adjournment until after the Emergency. This was refused. The accused then fully discussed the matter and came to the conclusion that, under the circumstances, it would be squandering the meagre resources of the Defence Fund if we continued to retain the services of our legal team. We unanimously (and enthusiastically) took the decision to instruct the lawyers to withdraw from the case. We would only retain an attorney and conduct our own defence. Adv. Maisels announced our decision to the court (i.e., Justices Rumpf, Kennedy and Bekker) and withdrew. This meant that each accused now appeared for him and herself. We decided that each accused would call his own witness/es. (This all took place while the defence case was on.) Fortunately, of course, we had two lawyers among the accused—Mr. Mandela and Advocate Nokwe, who, while they could not represent us, were able to advise us. I was Accused No. 3 and I called as my first witness, Moulvi Cachalia (who was not an accused). Before me Accused No. 1 had called as his witness, Mrs. Helen Joseph, who was Accused No. 2.

Judge Bekker expressed his shock at our decision and asked whether we appreciated the seriousness of what we were doing in asking the lawyers to withdraw. We replied that we did. Not a murmur of discontent from any of the Accused who were still full of spirit. After the initial drama, we settled down to the usual court routine. It so happened one day when Accused No 1, in leading Mrs. Joseph's evidence, ran out of questions. He unilaterally decided to ask the Court for an adjournment on the grounds that he was "feeling very tired, My Lords." Thereupon the judges jumped at us, reminding us that they had warned us of the consequences of our action. No adjournment. Please continue, Mr. Adams (i.e., Farid). Now the first murmurs began. After the usual adjournment, some of the Accused demanded a meeting that night (in jail). At least one was heard asking "where did Mandela get the idea from about asking the lawyers to withdraw." Many had now completely forgotten where the suggestion emanated and that the decision was unanimous. So that night a lot of words flowed, lot[s] of things were forgotten, and things were recalled which never took place. However, after painstaking explanations and discussion, calm and unanimity were once again restored. We continued without the lawyers until we thought the atmosphere was right, and we recalled them just before the end of the emergency.

I could give a number of similar experiences. The important thing was that, after all the disagreements and tensions, we were always able to successfully and satisfactorily resolve the problems. These experiences helped us tremendously on numerous occasions during our 22-year stay in prison.

How I've gone on about something that may be of little or no interest to you. Please forgive me. When I wrote to you last year, I think I mentioned that we had completed 21 years but were not given the symbolic key that would have led to our freedom. Earlier this year the world was told that the State President had proffered some sort of a key to us. But as you've no doubt heard, we regarded it as a key of humiliation which would be taking away our dignity and self-respect. So it seems that I'll still be sending you many more Eid cards.

Fortunately our health remains good. And our spirits likewise. I miss all my friends on Robben Island. You know, though I'm almost 56, there are things I want to discuss and reminisce about with chaps of my age group. At present I'm the "baby" among the 5 of us here and I feel a bit inhibited about discussing certain matters (all of them of a frivolous nature, of course). Even in relating jokes I have to draw the line. You know, some of the *madalas*[1] are mission-school educated, and they can be real "squares." This doesn't mean that I don't rag them. Old man Sisulu (who turned 73 on 18 May) for instance, is a real sport. I'm often obliged to draw him into all sorts of little pastimes. For instance I'd record his opinion about who is going to win the July.[2] But even better than that, I manage to coax him into choosing his favourite for Miss South Africa. He is always obliging and forever cool and smiling. I've threatened to report him to Mrs. Sisulu, but he shrugs it off good naturedly. Can you believe it—he still runs around the yard every morning and has two sessions on the exercise cycle. He's fantastic.

It took jail to get me started on exercises, and I don't regret it one bit. In fact I'm convinced that our continued good health is to a large extent due to regular exercises. As for our spiritual well being and self-discipline, I've found that our studies have been very important. Whenever new prisoners arrived on Robben Island, I used to advise them to (1) keep warm; (2) start exercising regularly; (3) immediately apply to study. These basics still apply.

Reminds me. I've managed to complete my Honours in African Politics. The Prisons Dept. won't allow me to do M.A. We may be challenging this in court. I've already consulted with Attorney Ayob and am expecting to see Adv. Mohamed. That is, if he can get away from his commitments.

This is the lot for today. I take it you'll be trying to find a locum. I'm sure after 4 [P.M.] and over weekends, you'll be able to fit into Chota's outfit which should keep you busy. Please convey my warm regards to all your colleagues. Tell Cassim that I've been following his work with Nelstop for a number of years and admire his achievements.

Lots of love to Shireen, Aadil, Yumna, Zaheera and all the family and friends. Fondest regards also to Choti and Chota, Shireen and Fuad, Vassoo and all the folks on the Coast. Also Ram, Isu, Rookie, etc., etc.

Keep well and all the best to you from

AMK

---

[1] *Madalas*: elders.

[2] A prestigious South African horse race.

Farieda Omar—*1 September 1985*

On 25 August 1985, while reading his Sunday paper, Kathrada discovered that his lawyer and friend, Dullah Omar, has been detained indefinitely. Shocked, saddened, and disappointed, he now writes to Farieda, Dullah's wife, expressing his sorrow at this terrible news. In this type of detention, the police have wide-sweeping powers and do not have to divulge the whereabouts of the detainees. Where they are, how long they will be held, their condition—all these remain unknown to the families. "In our type of work, we are taught to be prepared for all eventualities," Kathrada writes, but adds that in practice there is still the element of surprise. For so many South Africans, fighting for an end to apartheid, indefinite detentions, and continual harassment had become a way of life.

∾

A. M. Kathrada
Pollsmoor Maximum Prison
Tokai 7966
1st September 1985

My Dear Farieda,

I was taken aback when I learned last Sunday that Dullah was among the persons detained under Section 29. My thoughts immediately went out to you and the children and, of course, to all the families who have been similarly affected.

It is remarkable how, after so many years and such varied experiences, one can never become immune to surprises. In our type of work we are taught to be prepared for all eventualities. One accepts the wisdom of this lesson, but in practice things don't happen without an element of surprise.

On Wednesday 21st August I received the birthday card from you and Dullah and also the ones from Fazlin and Rustum. It was a lovely thought on the part of all of you, and I really appreciated it. I was also told that Dullah had phoned in connection with hiring of *Passage to India,* and at the same time he enquired whether he could bring me some birthday food. The previous week I received a message that Dullah would be consulting with me together with my attorney, Mr. Ismail Ayob, in connection with my studies and visits—matters on which there is a dispute between me and the Prisons Department.

These and similar matters were on my mind when I opened the paper last Sunday (25th August) and saw that Dullah had been detained. Under the circumstances, I believe I cannot be entirely blamed if I reacted to the news with a degree of surprise, mingled with disappointment and sadness. To think that, in a matter of hours or a couple of days, life can take such a dramatic turn! A loving husband and father so suddenly removed from the comforts of home and from the warmth of family to spend an undetermined time within the cheerless, regimented and unsociable confines of a police or prison cell.

Uppermost in my thoughts was Fazlin who is old enough to know that her father is in custody, yet not quite able to understand the workings and machinations of the adult world which is able, without any apparent rhyme or reason, to take her beloved daddy away. The hurt and sadness that overwhelms a child in such situations is something that we adults cannot appreciate. In the child's mind a grave injustice has been perpetrated, and no amount of adult explanations can assuage such feelings. One can only speculate whether, with the passage of time, she will, in her wisdom, find it possible to forgive and forget her childhood trauma and anguish.

I do not, for a moment, imagine that the deprivation which you, Kemal and Rustum feel is any less than that of Fazlin. It is, therefore, my fervent hope that, for the sake of all of you and for countless numbers of others, Dullah is returned home as soon as possible.

In the meantime, keep strong and courageous. Do not allow anything to lower your morale and determination. Remember always that nothing that Dullah has done should cause you to lower your heads in shame or regret. On the contrary, there is nothing but cause for honour and pride.

I believe that the family of one of the Cape Town detainees has been informed of his whereabouts. I hope that you and the other families will also soon know and that you will be allowed to visit Dullah. I assume that you have already sent him the Koran (in English) and the Bible. Perhaps they will be allowed to receive other literature also one of these days. During my detention in 1963, they only allowed me the Bible, and it was a great help. I hope they will also allow you to take food and clean clothing regularly.

But my greatest hope, of course, is that they release him and his colleagues as soon as possible so that they can be reunited with their near and dear ones.

This will be all for now. I have also written to Mammie today. I'm sure you'll hear from her soon.

Please pass my fondest regards to all members of the family and friends. Lots of love to you, Fazlin, Kemal and Rustum. A big hug to Fazlin from

AMK

$\approx$ $\approx$ $\approx$

Nazir Kathrada—*26 October 1985*

Kathrada asks his nephew, Nazir, to give him news of the family in Schweizer Reneke, especially the younger children and also to send photos. The court case regarding his studies and the continual refusal to allow his niece, Zohra, to visit has come to a temporary halt as Advocate Omar, his lawyer, also has been detained by the government. He tells his nephew how he had joked with Advocate Omar about preparing a place for him and now it was a reality: he is in police custody. This reminds Kathrada of a similar incident that occurred in January 1962, when Barney Desai, a friend, pointed out Robben Island to a visitor from England, saying jokingly that it was to be Kathrada's home. By June 1964 Kathrada was on the Island for life. We learn that Kathrada had been arrested four times in four different places for not having the permit Indians required for inter-provincial travel. In October 1962 he was placed under house arrest—the second person in South Africa to receive this strict order. When Kathrada says it was difficult but interesting, he is no doubt referring to the 101 times he defied this house arrest and continued to live as normal a life as possible.

$\approx$

A. M. Kathrada
26th October 1985
Pollsmoor Maximum Prison

My Dear Nazir,

I thought I should give you a surprise by writing before you've even thought of replying to my letter of 1st July. So when you have finished with your exams and after a reasonable period of rest when you finally summon up enough energy and enthusiasm to write, please remember that you'll be owing me replies to two letters.

The main reason which prompts me to write now is to take the opportunity of wishing you a "happy birthday" and at the same time to request that when you do write, you should tell me about the Schweizer folks, especially the little ones. If you still have my last letter, you'll be reminded of your undertaking to send photos—of Leila, Haroon, Mohamed, Ferhad, Amina, Suliman, Ismail, etc.

The next thing concerns visits. I had a message that Khalil wished to visit me in December. Apparently he is coming to Cape Town for a wedding. I shall be very glad to see him. Please contact him to get the particulars from Zohra. Or you can give him the particulars yourself. He must state our family relationship. The important thing is to apply immediately as the first applications generally take some time. I don't suppose anyone else from the family is coming in December. But you can check on that as well. Cassim's brother-in-law (the lawyer) has now been granted permission. But he hasn't fixed a date yet because he wants to come along with someone from Schweizer. I suppose it must be Cassim. I suggest you check with Cassim as well.

I take it you had no plans to come. At the visit you were not too sure when you'd be coming again. Please try to send me the information as soon as possible as I'd also like to accommodate my local friends. I'd also like to know if the wedding arrangements have been finalised for February and who all are planning to come.

When you contact Khalil, please check if Shereen received my letter. I also want to know if your mother received my birthday card. You may be able to help me solve a mystery. I received a birthday card signed "Amina" and posted in Lenasia. I don't know who this person is. Zohra suggested it could be your mother with the card written by you or Yusuf and posted in Lenasia.

Since my letter to you, I have had several consultations with Mr. Ayob and Adv. Omar in connection with my studies and Zohra's visit. In fact I saw them last Monday and Mr. Omar came again on Thursday. Unfortunately on Friday he was detained. We had been making good progress with the court documents. I hope Mr. Ayob comes along next Wednesday (30th Oct.) as planned so that we can discuss the new situation. The case itself will be argued by Adv. Ismail Mohamed, who will be coming to see me one of these days.

Poor Mr. Omar. On my birthday he and the family sent me cards. He also contacted the Prison authorities for permission to bring me birthday food. Two days thereafter (on Kemaal's birthday) he was detained.

I was joking with Mr. Omar last week that I should prepare a place for him here. We all had a good laugh and thought no more about it. Only to hear over the air yesterday that he was in custody. This reminded me of an incident in January 1962 while I was in Cape Town on holiday. A friend of mine, Barney [Desai], and I were entertaining an English author who was visiting South Africa. We drove up to Signal Hill and were admiring the scenery. Barney then pointed to Robben Island and told this lady that that was "Kathrada's future home." In October of 1962 I was placed under house arrest; in July 1963 I was arrested at Rivonia; and in June 1964 I was on Robben Island. How true Barney's joke turned out to be!

By the way, you were not even born when the incident took place! Let me tell you a bit about my Cape Town trip. You see, at midnight on January 15th 1962 my 5-year ban (which had confined me to Jo'burg, etc.) had expired. And I made a dash for Cape Town, together with 2 friends. We landed at Hessie in the early hours of the morning to have a bit of sleep and to pick up *padkos*.[1] Ismailmota and others came from Schweizer with more padkos and to greet us. He also told me that the police had been to Schweizer a couple of days before; they were looking for me, presumably to renew my banning order. You see, for about two weeks before the expiry of my ban I had been staying away from the flat, precisely to avoid the new ban. Anyway, after Ismailmota's information, we hurriedly packed up and were soon on our way. I stayed in Cape Town for about 6 weeks, but the police did not interfere. They did not even bother to check if I had the Inter-Provincial permit. (I suppose you know that until mid 70's, Indians required special visiting permits to travel from one province to another. No matter how urgent one's business was, you just had to have a permit. Failure to produce a permit could mean imprisonment for up to 3 months. There was no provision for fines. I was arrested for permits in Durban, Uitenhage, Cape Town, Bloemfontein. I'll write about this some other time.)

After returning from Cape Town for some reason the police did not re-impose the ban. After my first ban expired in October 1956, I was left alone for about 3 months. In 1962 I took the fullest advantage of my "freedom" and travelled all over the country; 3 times to Cape Town, P.E. East London; half a dozen times to Durban; to Botswana, Lesotho, Swaziland, etc., etc. Then on 22nd October 1962 they placed me under house arrest. I was the second person in S.A. to be placed under house arrest just a week or so after Mrs. Helen Joseph.

---

[1] *Padkos*: Literally "food for the road." There being no restaurants or cafes open to the black population, it was common for people to pack food hampers to last the entire journey.

It was while I was under house arrest that you made your entry into the world. The house arrest order was very strict; I was allowed to have <u>no</u> visitors at the flat—not even my mother! I couldn't leave Jo'burg; no gatherings; report to police every day; no communication with another banned person. It made life very difficult but also very interesting. I'll tell you about it in another letter.

It's because I was under house arrest that I didn't see you and had to wait 21 years for the opportunity!

I think I should end now. I'm getting on fine. I'm sure everybody is interested in Mr. Mandela's health. I must assure you all that he is quite fit. It is only that he has to have this operation which is not serious. He is up and about and carries on all his normal activities—exercises, gardening, etc., etc. There's nothing to worry about.

Write soon. Keep well. Hope your exams went off well. Lots of love to Yasmin and to all the folks at home. I hope Uncle Isu is back home.[2] My fondest regards and good wishes to him and the family.

All the best to you from

AMK

⁓ ⁓ ⁓

Shireen Patel—*10 November 1985*

An informative letter to Shireen on the occasion of her birthday. Kathrada recollects the "old days," and especially those people who had given him so much and for whom he has the greatest affection, love, and admiration. He cautions Shireen not to dismiss out of hand some of these people who certainly might have been old-fashioned and "backward." In his years in prison he has learned that "condemnation on its own served no purpose; in fact it mostly turned out to be counter-productive." What was needed was patience and education, and to back up these words of wisdom, and to prove his point, he cites in graphic detail the occasion when the late Chief Albert Luthuli, president of the ANC and an African, while staying at Kathrada's flat had inadvertently found himself locked out.

⁓

---

[2] Isu (aka. Lalloo) Chiba, a former Robben Island political prisoner who had been detained by the police.

A. M. Kathrada
Pollsmoor Maximum Prison
Tokai 7966
10th November 1985

My Dearest Shireen,

I always feel happy and proud to have a bevy of such lovely godchildren, but unfortunately there is one failing common to them all—they
are such hopeless correspondents! On the rare occasions when they do
write, they solemnly promise to rectify the position, but for some reason
they don't succeed.

Fortunately, however, these failings are not so serious as to in any way
lessen my regard and affection for them. And as proof thereof, here am
I once again getting down to my end-of-the-year routine to send my
warmest birthday wishes to you my dearest Shireen. I write in the fervent
hope that my letter finds you and all the members of the family and
friends in the best of health. Being your birthday and being your godfather, my thoughts are naturally focussed on you, but whenever I give
myself over to revel in reminiscence of the good old days (which happens
quite frequently in jail), my thoughts encompass a whole lot of families
with whom I was closely connected. I think of them with a great deal of
love and affection and admiration and above all with a deep sense of
gratitude. There is so much that they did for me, so much that I learned
from them and I'd like to believe that there was a little that I was able to
impart to them. You know, you young people would be inclined to criticise and condemn some of these families as "old-fashioned" or "backward." And I dare say that in many instances you would be justified,
especially when it came to some social attitudes of the "oldies" which did
not fit in with modern trends and developments. But hard realities and
experience taught me that condemnation on its own served no purpose;
in fact it mostly turned out to be counter productive. What was needed
was consistent, patient, discussion and education. You'd be surprised
how some of the hardest and seemingly impossible cases could change
as a result of education and discussion. You'd discover that wrong attitudes are most often as a result of ignorance and prejudices with which
we grow up.

Uncle Walter [Sisulu] and I were having a walk in the yard just now
and discussing some of these very things and the persons involved. We

recalled the story of some of my neighbours at the flat. At the flat we used to have people popping in all hours of the day and night; men, women, children; workers, teachers, doctors, lawyers, students; whites, Africans, Coloureds, Indians; men and women of all hues and religions. Quite early on we realised that some neighbours were not taking kindly to this traffic, and a few of them even subtly displayed their hostility. Racial prejudice was very much evident; but, worse still, even religious prejudice raised its ugly head. Of course, none of the neighbours spoke to me directly, nor were my visitors openly insulted or abused. Everything was done behind our backs but in such a way that we would get the message, loud and clear. The problem was the old and familiar one—they had been brought up to believe that Africans and, to a lesser extent, Coloureds, were prospective robbers, gangsters, rapists, etc.; that all non-Moslems were somehow different and inferior. This included whites. We, however, carried on with our normal life. Some friends who had closer relations with the neighbours talked to them on and off about their wrong attitudes. My biggest surprise was still to come. Unknown to us all, the neighbours were carefully watching the visitors and the goings-on in the flat and in the process they were learning. A lot of events and incidents, discussions, etc., contributed towards changing their attitudes.

It was a Saturday afternoon. The late Chief Luthuli often used to stay at the flat, and whenever he came I used to give him a spare key. This particular day I came home at about 5 in the afternoon and found Chief pacing up and down in the passage outside the flat; he had forgotten to take his key with him in the morning and could not get in. When I enquired how long he had been there, he said he had come at about 3:30 p.m. but some very nice people, seeing his predicament, invited him to their flat and entertained him with tea and cakes, etc. We took it for granted it must have been Babla's brother, who lived on the 4th floor. But the Chief insisted that it wasn't on the 4th floor; he pointed at one of the flats on my floor. We were dumbfounded, and just to make sure, we actually got him out of the flat again to point to the flat. Do you know that the occupants of that flat were the most conservative and narrow-minded and racialistic of all the neighbours. And they actually invited the Chief and entertained him! There were experiences with other neighbours which, though not exactly like the Chief's, were also indica-tors of changing attitudes. What had actually been happening is that it was the first time that most of the neighbours were thrown into a situa-tion like ours. They had entered it with all their ingrained prejudices and attitudes. However, by merely watching my visitors over the years and seeing that these were just ordinary human beings like themselves, they gradually began to change their attitudes. After some time all the neighbours, without exception, became the greatest friends of Flat 13. And they remain so to this day.

I'm sorry that I had to bore you with all this. I suppose in a way I was merely continuing the discussion I was having with Uncle Walter.

I suppose you all must have been keenly following the media reports relating to Uncle Nelson's health, and as you will have noticed, he has undergone a successful operation. At this stage, we know no more than what has been reported. We're looking forward to his return which we hope will be in the next few days.

A few months ago I was told by a friend that Barney's[1] health was not good at all and that his sister had especially gone to London to be with him. I haven't heard anything further and hope that he is well again.

When last did you hear from Daddy? How is his health? And Zaheda? I understand she has been here again. I hope her sugar is under control. And yours too.

This will be all for today. In my last letter I asked you to remind Auntie Rookie about the photos she promised. Do remind her.

Lots of love to you, Mummy, Yusuf and family, the folks in Canada and all family and friends here from

AMK

≈　≈　≈

Khatoon Patel—*18 January 1986*

Kathrada appeals to Khatoon, Shireen's mother and Kathrada's old and dear friend whom he regards as a sister. He appeals to her to re-assess her opposition to her daughter's marriage and to rise above any prejudice she might be harboring. He states that if the marriage were opposed solely on religious and "racial" grounds, he would be unhappy and disturbed. Above all, he was writing because Shireen was so saddened by the lack of support and understanding on the part of her family. The epitome of tact and diplomacy,

---

[1] Barney Desai, an old friend and political colleague who had settled in London. On his return to South Africa after the release of all the Rivonia prisoners and others, Barney joined the Pan African Congress (PAC).

*Kathrada presents a balanced and impartial picture and hopes Khatoon will
provide the support her daughter yearns for and for her to conquer any prejudices that may have contributed to her opposition.*

∼

A. M. Kathrada
Pollsmoor Maximum Prison
Tokai 7966
18th January 1986

My Dear Khatoon,

I am sure you will be surprised to receive this letter from me; but it
won't be difficult for you to guess. Yes, it is in connection with my godchild, Shireen. You know, of course, how much I have been attached to
her ever since she was born, and throughout the years I have tried to
keep close contact with her, and to keep myself well informed about her.

A few months ago I heard that she got married and that you and the
family were not happy about it. But since I had no direct news from her,
I decided not to say anything about her marriage in my usual letter and
birthday card that I send every year. But I was worried about the matter
all the time.

It made me sad to hear about any tension or unpleasantness in the
family. Although Shireen has a special place in my heart, it does not
mean that my affection for the whole family is any less. You have always
been like a sister to me, and Aggie, a brother. And you know, the children were like my own.

This is why I am not writing to you as an "outsider" but as one who
considers himself part of the family. I hope you too will regard me in that
spirit.

A few days ago I received a letter from Shireen in which she informed
me of her marriage and added a bit of information about her husband.
Of course, I had already known of the family's attitude so she didn't
really say anything about this which was new to me. What really struck
me about her letter was her sadness and disappointment that the family
has not supported her in [her] decision to get married to Vincent. It is
her sadness which also makes me sad and which made me decide to
write to you.

Obviously I am unable to say that Shireen has made the right choice.
I don't know Vincent at all; the first time I came to know his name was

in Shireen's letter. But she tells me that they know each other for a few years and have been going out for some time. She also tells me that he is 9 years her junior. My own feeling, under the circumstances, is that their decision must be respected. After all they are both adults; they appear to know each other well, and they must have taken everything into consideration including the age difference.

I don't want to go into a lengthy discussion on the question of religious or so-called "race" differences. You know very well what my views are on this. I would be very unhappy and disturbed if this has been a factor in your and the family's opposition to the marriage. You will agree that the most important thing in any marriage is the happiness and stability of the couple's married life. You know as well as I do that many marriages where the couple are of the same religion have failed, and there are many similar ones that have been successful. A few years ago exactly the same position as Shireen's arose with a niece of mine. The family members were opposed [to] it, and the grandparents chased her out of the house. But the young couple were determined and eventually her mother agreed. They are happily married and her mother and son-in-law are the best of friends.

I am aware, of course, that when the family opposed Shireen's marriage, it is because you all love her and you sincerely think that it will not be in her interest to marry Vincent. I have also told Shireen that she is still loved as always by all of you. And I can see in her letter that she loves you just as much. It makes her very sad to know that you are not with her to support her in the most important step of her life.

I want to make an earnest appeal to you and to Ebrahim, Zaheda and Yusuf. And to Daddy. I'm not fully aware of the attitude of each one of you, but now that Shireen and Vincent are already married, I appeal to you to accept the position and make her feel that she remains fully part of the family. Even if it is difficult, be big-hearted about the matter and try to conquer the prejudices that made some of you oppose the marriage. Try your best to accept Vincent also as part of the family. I'm sure that with the passage of time you will be able to overcome this tension and unpleasantness, and one day it will all sound like a bad dream. I hope to hear good news about this one of these days.

Recently I've been thinking a lot about the flat in Johannesburg. You know, it is now occupied by Mr. Ismail Ayob, the lawyer. He has been coming to see me about some legal matters, and when he told me that he stayed in that flat, a thousand thoughts went through my mind. I thought of the night of Shireen's birth and how we celebrated with Aggie and Ike. Then I thought of Solly Jooma[1] and how they were assaulted then and of his subsequent murder. I, of course, also thought of how you used to *skel*[2] us every now and then. And, of course, I thought of all the lovely food you cooked and the many pleasant times we had there. Mr. Ayob has also taken the flat next door and made the two flats into one.

Otherwise things are fine with us. You must have followed the reports about Nelson's health and the successful operation. He has been back at Pollsmoor for some time already, but unfortunately he has not been staying with us. But we have seen him twice and he looked fit.

This will be all for now. I am hoping to hear from Zaheda one of these days. I wrote to her some time last year and also sent her a birthday card. But she never replied. Could you do me a favour; please have a photostat made of this letter and send it to Zaheda. Perhaps that will also remind her to reply to me.

I hope you have been keeping well. Please pass my fondest regards to all members of the family and friends, especially Rookie and others.

Lots of love to you from

AMK

≈ ≈ ≈

Shehnaaz Meer—*23 February 1986*

Kathrada cannot understand why Shehnaaz, the daughter of Ismail and Fatima Meer, has not written and even believes he might have offended her somehow. He hopes she will write and also give more information about her baby, Nadia. The Meer family is well known to all Kathrada's colleagues and thus the keen interest for news. That Uncle Nelson caught a glimpse of Shenaaz and only relayed this to Kathrada much later, prompts Kathrada to reveal a side of Mandela, not well known—that he can be a tease. Kathrada writes about the surprise party, and how, after almost twenty-three years he feels nervous about holding a proper cup and saucer. Rumors of their release started as

---

[1] Solly Jooma was assaulted that evening by the police. He was later followed and murdered by a white policeman.

[2] *Skel*: an Afrikaans word meaning "to scold." Here it is used in a somewhat playful manner.

early as 1966 and have surfaced from time to time. Kathrada and his col-
leagues dismiss them as such and try to get on with their lives in prison.

~

A. M. Kathrada
Pollsmoor Maximum Prison
Tokai 7966
23rd February 1986

My Dearest Shehnaaz,

The ice had to be broken sometime, and I might as well be the one to
do it. This being Leap Year, I had thought the ladies would take the initiative, but obviously, what with women's lib and all, the roles seem to
have been reversed since I entered this institution.

First of all, let me check. I wrote to you on 24th August last year and
addressed the letter to Burnwood Drive. It was registered. I assume you
got it? Why then the sudden silence? I know, of course, that Nadia's
arrival must be keeping you very busy, but I doubt it if you would want
the young lady to be blamed for your silence. Could it be that I have
made myself guilty of some lapse or "crime" which has caused you
offence? I do not wish to exaggerate, but such thoughts have crossed my
mind. Although I could not think of anything that could have caused
resentment or annoyance, let me, nonetheless, apologise to you just in
case. For my peace of mind I shall expect a speedy response. If you still
have my last letter/s around somewhere, there are a number of things you
have to reply to. I should also like to know if you received the card I sent
just after Nadia was born.

Your silence has once again obliged me to rely entirely on the media
for news of part of the Meer family. Recently I read a report about your
ma's evidence in mitigation at a trial of a person who is in his 80s. From
the bit which appears, I got the impression that her evidence was beyond
the comprehension of the type of judicial officers who man the lower
courts. Unless, of course, the standard has radically improved in the last
couple of decades. I suppose I'm being too severe and subjective as a
result of close involvement in numerous cases as an accused, a witness,
or an interested party. But mine was one of a fairly general impression at
the time. Anyway, the article I refer to was accompanied by a photograph
of your ma. Am I right that she has put on a bit of weight? About Joel I
read 1 bit last week in connection with a labour matter. About you I last

heard a few months ago when Uncle Nelson had a "glimpse" of you after a visit. I remember the inordinate delay before he told us about it and the excruciating calm with which he related it. For this he was appropriately censured by both Uncle Walter and myself. But that's Uncle Nelson all over. No matter how affected or excited he may be about a particular incident or event, he still manages to display a calm which is unbelievable. We are convinced (and have told him so) that if he were to be called to the office and told that he was to be released tomorrow, he would return to the cell and tell us after an hour or two as, if it is simply one of those everyday things. He is a truly remarkable person. I must be careful not to give you the impression that he is a cold, unfeeling man lacking in emotions. On the contrary, he is a very warm, caring and friendly person. I must call myself to order and remember that I'm still supposed to be discussing the Meer family. I hope it will prick your conscience to be reminded that the last and only time we heard about Nadia was in your July letters! My enquiries have, of course, elicited the standard response. She is lovely, she is well. This is quite inadequate. We need something more substantial which only her mummy is going to be able to provide. And naturally we expect some photos of the young lady.

Let me return to Uncle Nelson. As you know, he has not been staying with us since his return from hospital. But we have been allowed a few "visits." The nicest was a surprise "party" on New Years Day when we spent a very pleasant hour together. Tasty snacks were prepared in the mess, and we even had tea in tea cups! When one is used to metal utensils for almost 23 years, it was not without nervousness that I handled a cup and saucer. The same thing happened on a few previous occasions. Anyway, Uncle Nelson looked extremely well and appears to have completely recovered. Nothing in his talk or demeanour gives one the slightest hint that he is the man about whom there is such an upsurge of feeling throughout the world.

I hope you are not among the gullible ones who are expecting his imminent release. I was surprised to learn that there have been crowds of people actually waiting outside the gates to receive him! Including persons like Eddie Daniels, Dullah, etc. Obviously the media and the "grapevine" have succeeded in persuading just about everyone that we are to be released. The only persons who remain unconvinced, and thankfully unperturbed by all the excitement, are ourselves. Surprised? You wouldn't be if you knew that the first stories about our "imminent release" started way back in 1966! We were actually made to fill in an official form containing details such as where we'd be staying after our release, etc. In 1971 friends actually sent clothes to Uncle Walter to wear on his release. In 1974 a story circulated outside that Uncle Nelson actually visited Lusaka. You know all about the State President's so-called "offer" of last year. And now the latest charade. I don't think I'm being unduly pessimistic or cynical. I think I'm just being realistic.

This being the position, all my visions and plans for the immediate future still relate to the prison situation. We are hoping to get moving very soon with the legal action about the refusal by the Prison authorities to allow me to do M.A. and also their refusal to allow my niece and nephew to visit me. The preliminary work is being done by Dullah, and I'm expecting to consult with Adv. Ismail Mohamed soon. Let's hope he can continue to add to his string of successes.

Oh I should tell you of the sad demise of the world-famous Mandela garden. Before he went to hospital, I had written instructions from Uncle Nelson about watering, weeding, etc., etc. Though my task was of a supervisory nature, I'm happy to say that we managed to carry out the instructions to the last leek and leaf of spinach. When we had harvested all the onions, mealies, (about 20 cobs), cucumbers (all 10 of them), tomatoes (a respectable amount), etc., we just started plans to plant beans and tomatoes when a surprise instruction was conveyed to us. In two days we (i.e., the 4 of us) were to be moved to another section of the jail! Away from the garden. On the Sunday we moved lock, stock and barrel. A new chapter of our stay at Pollsmoor has opened.

I should bring this letter to an end. We have settled at our new place and adapted ourselves to the new routine. Basically, of course, things are the same: the radio, newspapers, magazines, books, visits, letters, films, etc., etc. A couple of months ago we saw *Chariots of Fire* and thoroughly enjoyed it. I notice that Alice Krige and Vanessa Redgrave are together in a new film, *Second Serve*. Should be quite interesting.

I'm still following Uncle A.C.'s articles with interest. Every now and then in the series as well as in some editorials and other articles, I suspect I detect a familiar style which takes me back to a paper that was being published in the mid-forties. But I can't say for sure.

Keep well. Lots of love to you, Joel, Nadia, to all the folks in Durban, Cape Town, etc. I received a surprise Xmas card from Uncle Chota and Choti. It was nice.

All the best from

AMK

≈ ≈ ≈

Ameen Akhalwaya—*9 November 1986*

Ameen Akhalwaya is from an old and established family in Newtown, a suburb just south of downtown Johannesburg. He is on staff at the Indicator, *a newspaper catering mainly to the Indian community. After an inordinately long time Kathrada has finally become a subscriber. He now wants to ensure that he remains one and asks Ameen to help him.*

≈

A. M. Kathrada
Pollsmoor Maximum Prison
Tokai 7966
9th November 1986

My Dear Ameen,

Having been an old Newtonian and a neighbour of your grandfather and the rest of the Akhalwaya clan, I think I can safely dispense with the formal "Mr." when addressing you.

I have attempted to follow your work with keen interest ever since I first came across your name in the late seventies. (We were only allowed to read newspapers since September 1980.) I enquired from my sister-in-law who is an Akhalwaya, and she explained to me who you were.

Naturally there is a lot I'd like to discuss with you, but unfortunately our circumstances will not make it possible to do so. At this stage, therefore, I shall confine myself to the purpose of this letter; viz., the *Indicator.*

You are no doubt aware of the various attempts that have been made to get the *Indicator* to me; in fact you must be quite fed up with all the pestering in this regard. Although copies have been coming here, they have been withheld, ostensibly because they were not posted directly from the newspaper offices. Now I have received my first copy (October 1986) which came in the official wrapper. I'm told that I'd be allowed to get it as long as it comes in the wrapper. Could you ensure that it continues to be posted this way?

Secondly, about the subscription. I don't know who exactly has subscribed on my behalf, but I should like to ensure that it is not allowed to expire. Under the newest dispensation, subscriptions can be paid on our behalf. (Until two weeks ago, all subscriptions had to be paid directly by the prisoner.) I'll be pleased if you could either let me know who has made the arrangements or contact the person yourself.

While on the topic of the new dispensation, you'll be interested to know that we are now allowed to have T.V. and video. The first and only time I saw T.V. was when I was abroad in 1951–1952! As for video, I've only read about it. We're also allowed wrist watches and pets—cats, fish, birds. Being a prisoner, I can't see myself imprisoning another living thing, be it bird or fish. At least that's how I feel at present. We're also allowed to write poetry essays but not biographies or books. Also, all our visits are now to be contact visits. Hobbies such as painting, model planes, etc., are allowed.

For some years we've had our own F.M. radio; we've been seeing documentaries supplied by the Cape Provincial Library and also hiring commercial films. With all this and the papers, magazines and books, we keep ourselves well occupied. I have not been studying for the last two years as the regulations don't allow us to go beyond Honours—unless we have only 2 years of the sentence left. And I've got life which is indeterminate.

This will be all. You will, of course, appreciate that we are <u>not</u> allowed to write to the press so you will please treat the contents of this letter with discretion. Health and spiritwise we are fine.

Fond regards to you and the family from

AMK

~ ~ ~

Wilfred Kodesh—*14 November 1986*

Wolfie Kodesh, a longtime friend of Kathrada's, had been obliged to leave South Africa on an exit permit. This meant that he could never return and, unfortunately, he is not too keen on London, his home for more than twenty-four years. Kathrada recognized him in a photo taken at Dr. Dadoo's funeral. This photograph and Wolfie's letter brought back many happy memories of the old days. We learn that it was Wolfie who introduced Sylvia Neame to Kathrada and he speaks fondly of her "commitment, her support, her courage and willingness to perform onerous tasks." As a result she suffered much hardship, including police detention. Wolfie had a reputation for always finding himself sharing lodgings with a host of females, and Kathrada teases him about his "harem." He informs Wolfie of their concessions, radio and newspapers, and soon they will be able to get television.

⌀

Pollsmoor Maximum Prison
Tokai 7966
14th November 1986

My Dear Walied,

It is 14 months since your letter arrived! And at last I'm getting down to what I should have done ages ago; I'm sure you must have long given up all hope of hearing from me. However, since we're rapidly approaching the festive season and the year's end, I thought I should start 1987 with a clear conscience.

I noted in your letter that you were not exactly enthusiastic about living in London and, as you said, you had recovered from an operation and were raring to go. I hope our friends will be able to ensure that this letter reaches you wherever you are. I also hope that your health continues to be fine. Earlier this year I received some photos of Doc's funeral, and among those was one of yours together with Amien. You looked very well, and we recognized you without difficulty.

As you can imagine after so many years in jail, we thrive on nostalgia. And your letter, though very brief, brought back many memories of the old days. One point leads to another, and we almost invariably sink into a session of reminiscences.

Yes, I remember your bout of hiccups and also when you fell asleep at the steering wheel and many, many other memorable incidents, events, occasions . . . I'm smiling right now as I recall a Saturday morning when I visited your office and found you walking about with a potato chip pasted on your jacket shoulder by means of sellotape![1] Apparently you'd been having a bit of an argument and the lady accused you of having a chip on your shoulder. Even if the argument was serious, your demonstration with the potato chip had defused all tension and everyone—you and the lady included—was having a good laugh.

Tragically, that lady met a most horrendous death. It came as a terrible shock to all. I knew her since I was 12 years old and find it difficult to accept that she is no more.

---

[1] Cellophane tape.

Let's get back to the present. You mentioned the lady whom you introduced me to at the flat. In fact you brought 3 ladies along for lunch that day; it was with Sakina that I was to develop a close relationship. I understand she is happily married and settled on the Continent. We had met at the onset of a turbulent period which was to cause so much disruption in so many of our lives. I came to value her commitment, her support, her courage and willingness to perform onerous tasks and obligations. She endured much suffering and hardship as a result. I am, therefore, really glad that she is settled and happy.

I was hoping that you'd tell me a bit about ex-inmates of your "harem," people like Janap, Flazia, Amina, etc. If you see them, please convey my fond regards. I remember with embarrassment my performance at your place the night when Nel and Fawzia were there.

Things with us are fine. As you know, five of us were moved from Robben Island to Pollsmoor in 1982. Since November of 1985 Nelson has been separated from us. All of us, however, are well.

We've been given some new concessions, most important of which is the right to have T.V. and video. We hope to acquire ours soon. While it is not going to be like your ITV or Channel 4, at least technologically we're catching up with the 20th Century. You know, of course, that we've been allowed newspapers and radio for some years now.

This will be the lot for now. Keep well, and when you have some time, do write. Everything of the best to you and all our friends.

From

AMK

Since writing the above, we have acquired our T.V. It is Saturday afternoon, and there is only sports on the screen. Tonight we're looking forward to seeing *War and Peace*.

Helen Joseph—*30 November 1986*

Helen Joseph was a veteran in the struggle from the early days. Kathrada informs her of the various concessions the prisoners have won. He has acquired a television set and, in terms of prison life, that was "a giant leap into the 20th century." Other concessions were that he could wear a wristwatch, which he felt somehow made him feel less a prisoner. They may write poetry but not books or biographies. They may have hobbies and keep pets, but he does not feel inclined to cage any living creature.

∾

A. M. Kathrada
Pollsmoor Maximum Prison
Tokai 7966
30th November 1986

My Dear Helen,

By the time this reaches you, it will be a year since I received your letter. But I shall not attempt to make any excuses for the delay; I'm sure you are aware of the position regarding the quota for letters, etc.

Fortunately, through our visitors, correspondents and the media, we have been getting regular information about you. A few days ago we were able to share the disappointment of many people when you were not allowed to go abroad. Then as if by way of—albeit meagre—compensation we saw a lovely photo of yours with two of the Delmas youth.

I suppose it will be hoping for too much to expect to see you one of these days on the T.V. screen? As you've probably heard, we've recently been given a few concessions, at least one of which has already begun to radically influence the fairly established routine to which one almost invariably gets tied down. On 15th November we acquired our own T.V. set. In terms of prison life, this is a giant leap into the 20th century! A fortnight's experience is hardly sufficient for one to be able to give an assessment of the programs. I shall, nevertheless, venture a few opinions. From the entertainment point of view, I find Bill Cosby absolute tops. I've been enjoying him over the radio since our Robben Island days; it's a real treat now to view the Huxtable family. Little Rudy is delightful. Then I like *Cagney and Lacey*, of course. I haven't been excited by *Shaka Zulu*. Perhaps it is because I find myself in agreement with the view that the past has been tailored in order to suit present trends of thought in certain circles. You may be surprised to learn that I enjoyed the couple of sessions of *Boeremusiek*;[1] most probably because it takes me far back to my childhood days on the platteland. As for news, I still prefer the *Radio Today* morning sessions and the afternoon update, though it is nice to be

---

[1] *Boeremusiek*: Afrikaans music, which Kathrada would have grown up with in Schweizer Reneke, where that music was popular.

able to view some events live on T.V. For us the T.V. news is in some respects more interesting as it often deals with events and personalities in the townships. I have not yet experimented with the programs after 9 P.M.

That's enough for T.V. We are now allowed to have wristwatches. Personally, this hasn't made much difference to me as I've long possessed an alarm clock. It could, however, be said that wearing a watch does give one the feeling, or rather contribute towards making one feel less of a prisoner.

We may also write poems but not books and biographies. We can take up hobbies. And we may keep pets. My first reaction to the latter concession was that, being myself a prisoner, the last thing I would want to do is to imprison another living thing, be it bird or fish. Unfortunately my childhood love for cats appears to have waned a bit, hence I have not made any efforts acquire a kitten. I seem to remember that you acquired a cat of sorts in Pretoria, and if I remember correctly, you called him Horace?

One very valuable concession is that all our visits are now "contact visits." This, plus the T.V. concession, radio, newspapers, are only for "A group" prisoners which is a pity. They should be regarded as basic necessities and extended to all.

Otherwise we are all well. As you know, Nelson has not been staying with us ever since he returned from hospital at the end of 1985. But we have been allowed to see him a few times. He is very well and in high spirits as usual. Walter is doing well; he uses the exercise cycle for over an hour daily and runs in the courtyard. He is fit. Govan, Wilton and Elias are still on the Island.

You asked about my studies. They still refused to give me permission to do M.A. So I've not been studying during 1985 and 1986. This matter is going to be tested in court.

I'm celebrating my anniversary in December; I spent December of 1946 in Durban Central Prison! My 40th anniversary.

Good luck to you. Keep well.

Lots of love to you and all our friends from

AMK

≈ ≈ ≈

Enver Bharoochi—*14 December 1986*

Kathrada and his colleagues have recently been given special dispensation to have television sets. Through the efforts of Enver Bharoochi and his friends, each of the four Rivonia colleagues received one. Kathrada is "speechless" at this wonderful show of generosity and goodwill and he expresses their most sincere thanks.

∼

A. M. Kathrada
Pollsmoor Maximum Prison
Tokai 7966
14th December 1986
My Dear Enver,

As 1986 draws to a close, we can look back and say that in one very important respect it has been a memorable year. In the last month a dramatic change came about in our lives, and we are still in the process of making adjustments. I'm referring, of course, to the arrival of T.V. and our gigantic leap into the 20th century. In my last letter to you barely two months ago, I think I mentioned that we were not allowed to have T.V. At that time we had contemplated making a special application to the authorities to allow us to have a set for the festive month. Then, all of a sudden, we were informed of the new dispensation. And here am I sitting at my desk, unable to keep my eyes off the screen, trying to write a "thank you" letter to you and to ask you to convey special thanks to those wonderful people who have made it possible for us to have our sets. In particular, I refer to Ebrahim, "Poison" and N.K.R., whose magnificent gestures leave me speechless. I don't want to spoil things by reducing their generosity to material terms, although I can never minimise the extent of it. I would rather like to think of their gesture as supreme acts of friendship and brotherhood, something that can never ever be forgotten. It would have given me great satisfaction and pleasure to be able to thank each one of them personally or at least to write to them individually; but most unfortunately this is not to be, for reasons that I have to ask you to explain. I am confident that you will be able to convey our gratitude as well as, if not better than, we could ourselves. Please say that we are thoroughly enjoying some of the programs; indeed, a whole new world has suddenly been brought close to us and we are able to join with millions of people in laughter and joy—and also anger and frustration.

I would be guilty of a grave omission if I did not single you out for our very special thanks. You've been absolutely fantastic. Ever since you heard of the new dispensation, you spared no effort or time or energy to ensure that we got our sets as quickly as possible. My colleague, Walter Sisulu, criticised me for overburdening you. He just could not be convinced how impossible it was for me to persuade you not to overload yourself with the responsibility.

Our particular thanks must go out to Khayoum for so willingly lending us his own set while we were waiting for ours. I felt so guilty and ashamed for depriving him of it, especially while he was using it for his own exam preparations. We just don't know how we will ever be able to repay such kindness. Now that you have done so much already, I hope you will take things a bit easy and have a well-deserved rest from our problems and needs. These sets are certainly going to help us enjoy the festive season. At some future stage I shall elaborate on the various programs.

Things are fine with us. The T.V. has severely disrupted the usual routine, and I'm having to rearrange things a bit. If ever I'm given permission to resume my studies, I will have got quite used to the T.V. and it won't be so difficult to make more drastic adjustments. At present it seems as if we will be able to be ready for the court action early in the new year. Oh yes, this reminds me. Perhaps I'm wrong, but I get the impression that you were surprised and possibly disturbed that I undertook to advance the hiring fees. When they did not allow me to study for the M.A., I saved the study money and this remained in my account here. In addition the family and friends have been sending sums, hence I had the ready cash for this purpose.

This will be the lot for today. I'll most probably be only able to see you again after the wedding. Keep well. Lots of love to Maurieda, Khayoum, Nadia and all other family members and friends.

All the best to you from

AMK

Veena and Ramesh Vassen—*2 January 1987*

Kathrada remembers the day in 1983 when he held Priya, the child of Veena and Ramesh, in his arms—the first time since his imprisonment that he had held a baby. Of all the deprivations, none was so keenly felt as the absence of children in this male, uniformed world. He extols the virtues, innocence, and common sense of children, who do not complicate life but see it wholesomely.

∽

A. M. Kathrada
Pollsmoor Maximum Prison
Tokai 7966
2nd January 1987

My Dear Veena and Ramesh,

While the year is still young, I'm hastening to fulfill one of my oft-repeated resolutions to write to you. I've been wanting to do so ever since the day in 1983 when Ramesh brought Priya along to deliver an Eid parcel. I have recounted to various persons the impact of that experience which has been indelibly imprinted on my mind. I shall always remember how I returned to the cell that day with my mind in a whirl. It was the first time in 20 years that I had come in such close physical contact with a child; I actually held her and kissed her. You can imagine what that means when you consider that for 20 years ours had been a world of adult males—uniformed warders and uniformed prisoners. A world without children, an unreal world. Of course, since then, things have changed; all our visits are now contact visits and children are allowed to visit. A number of little boys and girls have come—babies, toddlers, creche—and school-going kids, making each visit a new and enjoyable experience. But they have in no way lessened the impact of Priya's pioneering visit.

I am not going to attempt a lengthy discussion on what it means to us to be able to have contact with children. A few words should give you some idea. Apart from one's freedom, in prison one suffers numerous other deprivations—family, friends, home comforts, social and cultural amenities, food . . . I could go on and on. In addition to the deprivations, there are restrictions and burdens galore. From day one prisoners seem to work towards lessening the burdens and generally improving the quality of life. While it is relatively less difficult to retain basic values, priorities and a general sense of balance, the temptation is ever present to lapse into bouts of selfishness, greed, acquisitiveness, and egoism. Fortunately, over the years, these have not developed into major problems, but the potential danger is always there.

In such a situation one needs a child's approach to things: openness, generosity, total absence of selfishness, no sense of property, no respect for adult red tape, a scorn for unrighteousness and injustice, a happy, carefree, loving attitude. Every visit from a child brings to us a breath of fresh air, a reminder of our responsibilities, a refreshing peep at the solid foundation upon which tomorrow's [world] will be built, a reassurance that we remain part of the world outside prison.

So I must thank you very much for having brought Priya along and also for the brief opportunity of being able to say "Hello" to Mukesh, Kemal and Salim. Thank you also for all the other acts of kindness that you have shown and continue to show. You folks and Dullah and family and all the other friends have truly made an immense contribution towards making our lives less burdensome. There is little that our own families can do which you have not already done.

It is because I truly value your friendship very much that I feel I should discuss with you a matter which is rather sensitive. I do so with great respect, knowing as I do your attitude and advice to me. I am referring to my friendship with J.N. and family. There have been occasions on Robben Island when uncomplimentary things about them have been heard and said. It caused hurt. I later discovered that some of these stories had been totally untrue while others had been exaggerated. About the only substantive criticism appeared to have been the link with the bank. And as far as I can gather, this still remains the main criticism in my view, and I admit I may be wrong. If this is the [gravity] of the case against them, it is not enough to render them beyond the pale. I must hasten to say that I am not attempting to persuade you to change your attitude. That would be presumptuous of me. But I thought I [should] tell you something about my long relationship with them. I met J.N. and Ismail (and Nelson) more or less at the same time in the forties while I was still at high school and they were doing law at Wits. At that time Blacks at Wits were few and they were held in awe by the community at large. But these 3 were outstanding personalities in their own right and not simply because they were Black. By 1945, when I was 16, I was no longer merely an admirer of these men but I could claim a degree of friendship with them. They did not treat me condescendingly but almost as an equal. In the same year I went to Durban for the first time; they had organised the trip and took me along. With the events of 1946 we became closer and worked in the same office. Then, of course, there was Flat 13 occupied by Ismail, but J.N. also virtually stayed there. In 1947 I moved in there and when they returned to Durban, the flat was left to me. (I stayed there till 1963 when I disappeared and was later arrested.) We maintained a close relationship while they were in Durban. I regarded them as my mentors, guardians, comrades and friends. Although our contact since my imprisonment has been cursory (almost solely confined to greeting cards), I have tried to keep abreast of information about them and their children. And I would like to believe that nothing has happened to diminish my regard for them and our friendship.

You could say my attitude stems from my personal philosophy which I try to apply both in my personal relationships as well as in public life. Simply stated, it amounts to this: "We must try to retain old friendships and constantly aspire to win new ones; we should avoid increasing the circle of enemies." I have found that, by pitching one's standards too high, more and more people are automatically excluded from one's circles until very few remain. In the process a lot of bitterness, anger, gossip, disappointment, strife and jealousy are engendered.

I'm not for a moment suggesting that my approach is applied regardless of principles. No, one's basic principles remain the guideline for one's behaviour. On the other hand, I do try to avoid elevating matters indiscriminately to the level of principles.

I think I have said enough for the moment. Obviously it is not possible to deal with the matter more fully. It is not something that can be satisfactorily discussed in letters or even at visits. Let us hope we will get an opportunity one day to meet under better circumstances and talk to our heart's content. In the meantime I hope I have not disappointed or angered you.

I wanted to write a lot more but I'll have to postpone it. I wanted to tell you a bit about the new dispensation which allows us to have T.V., videos, watches, pets, etc. And contact visits. I'm sure you've already heard about all this, but I wanted to make a few comments on the T.V. programs. Perhaps some other time.

You probably know that Farida and Fazlin visited me on Christmas Day and I also managed to shake hands with Rustum. It was lovely.

On Boxing Day for the first time in all these years, we were allowed to order full meals from outside. We really gave it a go in a big way. It was like eating at home. What made it even nicer was that Mr. Mandela was allowed to spend a few hours with us and enjoy the goodies together.

Ramesh, I must really thank you for your assistance with my letters from abroad. In fact I must apologise to you for giving you so much trouble. I received the last letter from your namesake, Bobby, in London together with the photos.

Thanks also for the Xmas card.

We are all keeping well. Lots of love to you, Mukesh, Trivesh and a special hug and kiss to Priya. Fond regards to all members of the family and friends.

From

AMK

~ ~ ~

Mukesh Vassen—6 December 1987

Kathrada wrote this long letter to the teenage son of his lawyer and friend, Ramesh Vassen, relating the importance of education and the continuing quest for knowledge. He writes how young people came to Robben Island and had initially scoffed at the idea of education. In the South African black townships at that time, the cry was "Liberation before education." While Kathrada and his colleagues were non-judgmental, they did try to impress upon these young freedom fighters the importance of getting a good education.

~

A. M. Kathrada
Pollsmoor Maximum Prison
Tokai 7966
6th December 1987

My Dear Mukesh,

You will no doubt be surprised to receive this letter from me. Unfortunately I've never had the opportunity to have a discussion and to exchange views with you. I am happy though that I've at least been able to see you and to say "Hello."

After being in jail for so long it is easy to lose touch with much of what is going on outside. It is true that newspapers, magazines, the radio and T.V. have made a huge difference; one can even say that the T.V. and video have thrust us into the mainstream of the 20th century. However, no amount of modern technology can satisfactorily bring us close enough to the people outside and especially to the young folk, to their ideas, ambitions—and their frustrations.

On Robben Island there was a huge influx of youth after 1976. I spent a lot of time talking to them and, more importantly, learning from them. It was a painful experience to witness so many highly intelligent and capable young men having to spend years and years shut away in prison when they should have been at school and university or in vocational training; or, in spite of adverse circumstances, they should have been trying to carve out the best possible future for themselves and their people. At the same time, I understood from them the reasons and the circumstances which influenced them to do the things which led to their imprisonment. I could not criticise or condemn them; I was too far away from the realities of their situation to pass judgement on them. But while they were going to be in prison, there was one thing we were certain they should be doing—and that was to study. You may be surprised to know that a number of the new arrivals came with the idea that to study was a waste of time, both outside and inside jail. They felt that the very first priority was to work for liberation; everything else was secondary. We prisoners are in no position to criticise or advise on strategies used by people outside. But my colleagues and I spent a lot of time persuading them on the necessity to study while inside. And we were happy that, by and large, we succeeded in this task. Many of the young men did extremely well and were grateful for our advice.

While discussing with the young men I continually had in mind my own personal experiences and I conveyed these to them. Let me share these with you as well. I became interested in politics at a very young age; at 11 I was already distributing leaflets, etc. In 1946 I was in my final year [of] matric. I was 17 then. In June of that year the passive resistance movement started in Durban when volunteers illegally occupied a piece of land which was for whites only, and they were imprisoned. Several university students gave up their studies to do full-time politics. Among them were I. C. Meer, J. N. Singh, Dr. Zainab Asvat, Dr. A. Patel. A school principal, Mr. Thandray, who was my teacher in Std. 3 also gave up his school. There was tremendous enthusiasm among the people. I too was carried away and left school before completing my finals. In December 1946 I too defied and was sentenced to a month's imprisonment which I spent in Durban jail.

Over 2000 volunteers went to jail. But in the course of time the enthusiasm waned; the students went back to university and numerous others returned to their jobs and professions. I did not go back and remained more or less a full-time activist until I was imprisoned in 1963. In jail there was a lot of time to reflect on the past and naturally I thought about my own experiences—my achievements, my failures, my joys, regrets; and that was my failure, [not] to go back and complete my studies when the opportunity was there and I was still young. Don't misunderstand me. I am not saying that I regret having gone into politics, but I am convinced that I could have completed my studies (and perhaps acquired a profession) and at the same time done my political work. I feel sure that, had I done so, I would have been able to make a better contribution. After a break of 19 years, I started studying again in 1968 on Robben Island. Do you know that one of the things I discovered with shock and shame was how really ignorant I was! Yes, I was even ignorant about some of the political matters with which I had grown up. I am dealing here with my own experiences only and not those of my fellow prisoners. Fortunately for me there were a number of outstanding intellectuals in jail with us. With their help I managed to resume my studies and, in the process, I think I was able to get a better grasp of our history, our, and of other aspects of our country.

On Robben Island I realised that I gave up studies outside mainly because of a youthful feeling of self-importance. In my immaturity I must have felt that things would not move properly without my contribution. How wrong and foolish I was!

I must once again stress that I do not for one moment regret having got involved in politics in spite of all the hardship it brought. But it was possible for me to continue with both studies and politics and in that way help me to understand things better at an earlier age. And I regret not having used that opportunity.

I have to end now. I am sorry that I've given you such a long lecture about myself and my experiences. I'll be happy if you can find some time one day to write and let me have your views. But I do not want [to] spoil your holidays by asking you to write immediately. I'm sure you have worked hard for your exams and deserve a good rest away from pen and paper.

I really enjoyed the last visit from Mummy, Daddy and Priya. We talked about all sorts of things and the 80 minutes just flew. I missed Trivesh but it's good that they did not bring him. It would have been a real punishment for the little chap having to sit and listen to all the adult talk. I felt sorry for Priya who must have been quite bored; but I enjoyed having her there.

Please tell Daddy that the original letter and 13 photos from Bobby Vassen were found and given to me. I also received the letter from Navi and the duplicates. When he sends the additional videos, the cost of hire, etc.

Keep well. Lots of love to Mummy, Daddy, Trivesh, Priya and other members of the family and friends.

All the best for the festive season and the New Year.

From

AMK

≈ ≈ ≈

Amien Cajee–*17 January 1988*

Amien Cajee, his wife Ayesha, and their son and daughter, Iqbal and Djamilla are now the occupants of Flat 13, Kathrada's home before his arrest in 1963. It had always been Amien's view that he was merely looking after the apartment until Kathrada was released, so he has now refurbished the place in readiness for his return. Kathrada is very moved by this magnanimous gesture and thanks his old and dear friend for doing this for him. However, he does not share the same optimism that he will soon be released.

≈

A. M. Kathrada
Pollsmoor Maximum Prison
Tokai 7966
17th January 1988

My Dear Amien,

It was a lovely surprise to receive your letter. It must have crossed with mine to Djamilla that she would respond to my entreaty to her to turn over a new leaf and write more promptly and regularly. Obviously I'll have to try harder to persuade her.

You and Ayesha looked very well in the photo. The books and the typewriter brought back many memories of the flat and its numerous inhabitants; of the friends, the countless visitors; of the wonderful neighbours and, of course of the incidents and events connected with the flat. It is truly a small slice out of our long and rich history. It remains my priority to ensure that it is written up.

I don't know how I can express my gratitude to you for your magnificent gesture to me regarding the flat. It is an act of friendship that can be equalled by few. When you say that you had especially kept it for me, I know that you sincerely mean every word of it. Through our long years of association, I came to admire your loyalty and devotion towards the family, towards friends and, most of all, towards the interests and general well-being of our people as a whole.

Visitors who have come to see me have remarked about your gesture with warmth and appreciation, and this I am sure reflects a more general attitude. I hate to pour cold water over the cheerful feeling that has been generated, but unfortunately we have to take account of the realities of the situation. I am not basing myself on any information that I have but as a result of past experiences, coupled with the negative track record of the powers that be and an assessment of the situation. I believe that you are being over optimistic. In my view there are no prospects of an early release. And I don't think that the activities or omissions of our colleague, Govan Mbeki, has in any way influenced matters. In all these years there was only one brief period when I thought that the approach of the authorities towards political prisoners had shifted, or rather was about to shift. That was in 1982 at the time of the legislation which purported to treat political prisoners on the same basis as the rest of the prison population. But the action, and more particularly, the inaction of the authorities soon disabused us of such ideas and once again placed the situation in its proper perspective. There has never been, nor is there at present, any intention to implement a policy of releases, remissions or parole (for political prisoners) to any meaningful extent. And I certainly don't think there is any reason to hold out hopes. However, thanks again for your gesture.

You mentioned the tremendous changes that have taken place around Jo'burg. We do have some idea about these, especially through the newspapers and T.V. Just the other night, we saw a bit about the Diagonal Street complex. We have seen how parts of Cape Town have changed. What is very confusing is the network of highways.

You also wrote of the increase in the number of professional people. When Zaheda visited me a few years ago, she said there were enough Black specialists in various fields to run a hospital. That's terrific. One of these days Iqbal will be joining the ranks as an engineer. I hope Djamilla will tell me more about his studies.

About Krish Naidoo; it will be a great pleasure to have a visit from him. Tell him to make an application to the Commanding Officer, enclosing his

I.D. number, etc. As you know, the applications are processed which takes a bit of time. Dr. Jassat applied to see me in December but was refused. They were, however, prepared to allow members of the House of Delegates to visit me! As you know, I refused that visit.

I was reading an article on the Hashim Brothers and the Lyric and was surprised to notice that Akbar had died. Please pass my condolences to the family. My greetings also to the Hashims. They really have a proud record in the running of the Lyric.

I was also sorry to learn of the death of Bubli's husband. My sympathies to her as well. The death of Goolambhai in Schweizer was a great loss. I learned with sadness of the death of my school principal, Mr. Nieman. There is one little error that Rafiq Khota made. Mr. Nieman was never principal of the Central Indian High School.

I have just learned with shock of the death of Percy Quboza. Please try to convey my condolences to his family and colleagues.

Both Nelson and Walter are well. Unfortunately they did not allow Nelson to join us for our Christmas lunch. But we did see him one by one. He is fine.

Good to hear about 1/4, Popeye, etc. I think one of these days I will have to summons them to appear at Pollsmoor to visit me.

My health is okay. Please remember me to all members of the family, the neighbours and friends. Fondest greetings, especially to old folks— Ouma, Mama, Helen, Jasmatbhai, Ismailbhai, Narsibhai, etc. Tell Helen I received her letter.

Lots of love to Ayesha, Djamilla and Iqbal. Tell Djamilla to write.

All the best to you from

AMK

≈ ≈ ≈

Oliver Tambo—*sometime in 1988*

Normally, any important political decision was discussed thoroughly by the Rivonia group before action was taken. In this letter to Oliver Tambo, however, Kathrada makes it clear that he is acting alone and without having consulted the others. In many letters to friends and family, he regularly bemoans the fact that there have been many inaccuracies in the history of the struggle and related historical events. He has always found these distortions and faulty assessments disturbing and is concerned about how future generations will be fed on these inaccuracies. He feels that, at least in his own case, he can remedy some of the misperceptions. He sets out reasons why he should not have the Isithwalandwe *Award bestowed upon him. This, he declares, is an award given by the African National Congress to honor only the most outstanding leaders in the struggle. He questions, too, the thinking behind honoring his sixtieth birthday, and finally, he sets out a list of adverse repercussions that could result if his letters were published while he is still imprisoned. Ultimately Kathrada agreed to accept the* Isithwalandwe *Award.*

~

[Sometime in 1988]

My Dear Brother,

First of all it is necessary to make it clear that this is a purely personal initiative. It is not done in consultation with my colleagues, and the contents, as well as opinions expressed, are mine alone.

My main purpose is to put right certain perceptions about myself. I am concerned that an image is being fostered both locally and abroad, which is not strictly in keeping with my real status and contribution in the political field. The recent conferment of the Isithwalandwe award upon me, and other proposed plans, have aggravated the position and induced me to write this.

Before proceeding further I wish to very clearly state that I feel most grateful and proud for the honour that the movement has seen fit to bestow upon me, and I sincerely hope that my action will not be taken amiss. I do, however, feel that I should state my feelings. I do so, not out of modesty, but because I believe that it is in the general interest of the movement to promote an accurate record of events and personalities in the struggle.

This view was strongly reinforced while I was studying History and African Politics with UNISA. The syllabus partially covered aspects of the history of our national liberation movement. Naturally I was more interested in the recent period, especially the 1940s onwards. In this I had the benefit of drawing on the vast knowledge, and memory, of Walter. In books, periodical and newspaper articles, and even in some theses, we noted numerous inaccuracies, distortions, exaggerations, faulty assessments, and careless scholarship. The obviously disturbing thing is that generations of students, and other interested readers do, and will continue to, imbibe this material in the belief that it reflects a true record of things.

Award

I believe that my role in the struggle, and my status in the organisations, did not warrant my inclusion among the recipients of Isithwalandwe. I do not for a moment minimise the significance of my 25 years in prison, but if it is felt that this achievement should be recognised, consideration should perhaps have been given to either a separate award for prisoners, or even Isithwalandwe—Class 1, 2, 3. . . .

Placing my name in the same league as Luthuli, Dadoo, Huddleston, Sisulu, Mandela, Kotane, etc., does not only not reflect the correct historical and political position, but carries the danger of reducing the prestige of the award.

It has been my understanding that Isithwalandwe is intended to honour outstanding national leaders for their exceptional qualities and leadership roles, for initiating innovative thought and direction, and for their pivotal contribution to the struggle.

I am not attempting to play down my long involvement in the movement, but I do not think that fact alone qualifies me for elevation to the "first team."

Let me give just a couple of examples of erroneous information about myself; this could have been a factor when comrades decided to bestow the award on me:

(a) I have never served on any organ of the Congress organisations at a national level.

(b) At the time of my banning in 1954:

(i) I was secretary of the Youth Action Committee, which was a joint action committee of the ANC Youth League and the SA Indian Youth Congress

(ii) I was a member of the Executive of the Transvaal Indian Congress. I was never the Secretary of the TIC as contained in at least one supposedly "authoritative" book.

(iii) I was never a member of the National High Command, as alleged in the Rivonia Trial Indictment. In fact I was not even a member of M K at the time of my arrest.

(iv) I was never a member of the S A Indian Congress Executive.

(v) If I were to describe my status in the movement at the time of my arrest, and during the years of my imprisonment, I would say that I have been among the group of "leading activists." I certainly would not describe myself as a "national leader."

Birthday

I understand that there are tentative plans outside to celebrate my 60th birthday in 1989. There is a suggestion of some sort of publication to coincide with the occasion.

The sentiments I have expressed above apply here as well. For basically the same reasons, I think that whatever is done should be commensurate with the information I have provided about myself, as well as my views.

But more important than that, I think the following should be borne in mind:

There had been plans to publish a biography of Walter on the occasion of his 70th birthday in 1982. This did not materialise. In 1987 he turned 75; for all intents and purposes the birthday passed virtually unobserved by the movement. No-one will dispute the fact that he is among the most senior leaders of the liberation movement, and if any birthday deserved to be widely observed it was his.

No doubt there must have been reasons for the omission, and I am not for a moment expressing any criticisms. At the same time it should be expected that at some stage the omission will invite questions. Any "high profile" celebration of my 60th birthday will serve to focus more strongly on the non-observance of Walter's.

Letters

There have been suggestions in the past about publishing my letters, and I have expressed my reluctance. I wish to assure our friends that my attitude is not because of "my modesty," as has been suggested. There are other—perhaps selfish—reasons.

While the reaction of the authorities cannot be predicted, it is unlike them not to react, even if it is out of sheer vindictiveness. They could prohibit me from continuing correspondence with certain individuals, or a category of persons. They have done this to me, and to others, in the past. I do not have to spell out how adversely this would affect us. Alternatively, or in addition, they may resort once more to the Robben Island type of censorship, when our letters were severely mutilated. And, in keeping with past behaviour, they may punish fellow prisoners as well.

I wish to conclude by stating that if, after having considered the above remarks, the folks outside still wish to proceed with their plans, I will submit to their judgement.

≈ ≈ ≈

Sonia Bunting—*13 March 1988*

Sonia Bunting was a co-accused with Kathrada in the 1956 Treason Trial, and like so many others, was obliged to go into exile. In 1988 she is still in London and as active in the struggle as ever. Earlier letters of theirs had gone "astray," but Kathrada does not dwell on this. Rather, he brings her up to date on the privileges he and his colleagues now have. Of the privileges, little has been done in the area of education and parole/remission for the "security prisoners." Kathrada writes about his missing Robben Island. At Pollsmoor there were only six Trialists and, now that Nelson Mandela has been moved, they are five. Kathrada then proceeds to write about the "geezers"—his term of endearment for his colleagues who are all senior to him. He reminds Sonia that Walter Sisulu was 52 when he began his life sentence.

≈

A. M. Kathrada
Pollsmoor Maximum Prison
Tokai 7966
13 March 1988

My Dear Sonia,

Hearing from you after 13 years was a real windfall. (I always maintained that No. 13 was my lucky number but more about that later.) After receiving your letter of 18th January, I made enquiries about the one of December 1986 which I had not received. However, my luck did not hold all the way as the Prison authorities would not let me have the poem. You did not get my reply to your letter of January 1975; neither did I receive anything from you—until the above mentioned. With such a huge gap between the letters, there's naturally a lot of ground to cover, but luckily you are not totally unacquainted with what has been happening to us.

There have been a number of significant additional privileges—newspapers, magazines, radio, T.V., video, hobbies, pets, contact visits. There has also been talk about allowing us to do M.A. and doctorates; just as there has been talk about treating "security prisoners" on the same basis as other prisoners on matters such as remissions, parole, etc. However, there has as yet been no evidence of any serious departure from previous policies regarding studies and sentences. For instance, after a four-month wait, I was informed that my application to do M.A. has been refused. The release of Govan and a few others can hardly be regarded as heralding a general shift of policy. But let us not concern ourselves with what is, or is not, likely to happen.

For me perhaps the biggest change has been the move from Robben Island to Pollsmoor. It was painful to be suddenly parted from colleagues with whom, for 18 years, we formed a large, happy family. It is true that at Pollsmoor I met up again with Walter and Nelson, whom I knew since my teen years, but including them we only formed a little community of 6. And that makes a big difference. The very fact of our being prisoners on Robben Island isolated us from the mainstream of humanity; at Pollsmoor our world was further narrowed down to by a situation which almost inevitably induces feelings such as boredom, irritability, loneliness. Luckily numerous factors have coalesced to keep these undesirables at bay. Apart from the obvious ones relating to our ideals, privileges such as newspapers, T.V., etc., have undoubtedly been contributory factors.

The move from the Island also meant being wrenched away from the relatively tranquil rural environment–from the birds, ostriches, buck, the flowers and all the greenery—to a veritable concrete existence. When we were staying with Nelson in another section of the prison, he had managed to get a sort of garden going which provided a tiny green spot in an otherwise grey and sombre atmosphere. For me personally, it proved to be an additional means of avoiding the monotony of routine. You see, I had to live up to my Indian stereotype and perform my duties as chief cook. Thank heavens my colleagues are not as expert in the culinary field as they are in the political; not only did they uncomplainingly consume my salads, etc., but they actually appeared to have enjoyed them! Alas, the garden was of a short duration. And, as you know, Nelson has been accommodated in another section of the prison since November 1985. That reduced us to 4.

I wish I could describe to you what it has been like to spend so many years with the old "geezers." They've been a constant source of inspiration and encouragement through difficult times; one could always turn to them for guidance and advice and lean on their ever-dependable shoulders when one is undergoing a low period. Walter remains his old lovable self; always calm, cool and smiling. And always deeply concerned about everybody's welfare, inside and outside jail.

Having said all this about them, I must hasten to add that staying with them should not be understood to be an unqualified blessing. By no means. True, not a single day passes without my teasing Walter about something or the other. And he unfailingly responds by laughing it away or he "counter attacks." But in all our exchanges there are certain strict parameters which may not be transcended. And there's the rub. You see, the "geezers" are generally mission-educated men, and as such, they have certain ingrained attitudes and aversions. They tend to be rather straitlaced which immediately restricts conversations to kosher subjects, absolutely prohibits the telling of "rude" jokes as well as the use of four letter expletives–even in anger! On very rare occasions have I seen any of them really angry. I always remember once on the Island when one of them, in a fit of rage and actually shivering, found himself frustrated by his inability to recall an appropriate expletive. This is how it more or less ended, "You . . . you . . . you . . . you fascist." An anti-climax if ever there was one.

Let me round off this bit of gossip with one last gripe. The geezers don't read *Andy Capp* or *Hagar, Blondie*. . . . and all my other favourite characters. Mercifully they do watch and enjoy the *Cosby Show* on T.V.

It is difficult for me to believe that Walter was 7 years younger than I am now when we were arrested in 1963! A lot of years have gone by. The geezers are aging gracefully. I have often said that prison life may not have altogether arrested the aging process, but it certainly seems to have slowed it down.

Your little quotation, "Time, you old grey man. . . ." was familiar, but I just couldn't place the author. While looking up my quotations book, I found the following lines by the same poet, Ralph Hodgson:

> The song of men divinely wise
> Who look and see in starry skies
> Not stars so much as robin's eyes
> And when these pale away
> Hear flocks of shiny pleides
> Among the plum and apple trees
> Sing in the summer day.

My remarks about not wanting to imprison birds and beasts were perhaps a spontaneous and emotional gut reaction. I have since been reminded of the therapeutic value of fauna and flora, especially for prisoners. And I have never forgotten *The Birdman of Alcatraz* which I read many years ago. A couple of months ago I saw media photos of a South African prison showing a prisoner with his caged bird and commentary extolling the positive value of pets. However, I have not yet persuaded myself to follow the example. And I doubt it if I will.

I try to visualize how things were on Robben Island in 1975 when I received your first letter and what I said in reply. We had a largish garden and there was the daily inspection by the mainly Indian gardeners who would gather around and have animated discussions on the prospects of the chili plants! Then there were the daily music programs over the red-iffusion system. Harry Belafonte's present visit to Southern Africa reminds me of the L.P. record we had containing songs by him and Miriam Makeba. In his song, "Silvia" he sang about her bringing him a little coffee and a little tea, and he complained that she brought him just about every damned thing but she didn't bring him the jailhouse key!

Let me move on to something else before I start becoming nostalgic about Robben Island. Just now I'll give the impression that I'm actually hankering after another jail instead of setting my sights on the outside. After all [is] said and done, basically one jail is the same as another.

Forgive me, but I've just realised that thus far I have written only about myself and the happenings here. And worse still, I must have simply repeated what you in all probability already know. I must confess I had forgotten about the wooden bowl, but it's good to know that, apart from its utility value, it continues to serve as a link between us. I do remember, of course, that Brian fetched me from the docks the day I arrived back from overseas. Looking back at my numerous visits to Cape Town makes me want to make another confession but for which I feel rather ashamed. You see, apart from a courtesy call at Barrack Street, it is almost as if I consciously avoided meeting political colleagues. Except, of course, for Jack, with whom I often stayed, and others whom I'd meet in Walmer Estate. I was to realise the consequences of this years later when it dawned on me how few political colleagues I personally knew in the Cape. I am ashamed to say that I don't think I even met a person like Blanche! To think that Alex stayed with me at my flat during the Treason Trial, and I did not meet his wife and kids!

This reminds me of No. 13; I said I'd say something about it later. During one of the recesses, Alex wrote about Flat 13 in *Up My Alley*. The seed must have been planted in my mind ever since, and I had harboured the wish that Alex would one day help me write a book about the flat. Unfortunately he is no more, but I feel as strongly as ever that the project must be fulfilled. So much has happened there and so many interesting personalities have stayed there or visited, it will be a pity if it is unrecorded.

I have to end this letter now. Unfortunately, for reasons which you will appreciate, I will not be able to correspond with you as regularly and frequently as I would like to. Don't be surprised, therefore, if you don't hear from me again for many months. Rest assured that you folks are always in our thoughts. It is wonderful to hear of the achievements of your children and the children of other friends in the academic field.

Keep well. Lots of love to you, Brian, Peter, Stephen, Margie and their spouses and kids. Love also to all the other folks you mentioned, especially to the lady you refer to as "one of your girlfriends"!! Incidentally, did you know that I met her for the first time in Middleburg?

We are all well. I last saw Nelson at Xmastime. He was fit and, as usual, in high spirits. Walter reciprocates his love and kisses. And so do I.

All the best from
AMK

≈ ≈ ≈

Zohra Kathrada—*12 June 1988*

Kathrada remembers fondly Zohra's visit. "The fact that they have kept you away for fourteen years was enough to embitter one," he writes. This is one of the remarkable qualities that he and the other "Robben Islanders" possess, to this day—the total lack of bitterness toward their captors, no matter how harsh the treatment meted out was to them. Looking back over the twenty-four years, Kathrada writes of his "family"—of Walter Sisulu, his father, and Nelson Mandela, his elder brother. Their relationship goes back a long way, Kathrada writes, and cites an example. Equally important, Kathrada stresses, is that the relationship "is not confined to politics."

≈

A. M. Kathrada
Pollsmoor Maximum Prison
12th June 1988

My Dear Zohra,

Your letter of 2nd June arrived yesterday. Many thanks. Thanks also for the R100. Some Kathrada females have suddenly decided to surprise me with an "avalanche" of letters. In the last couple of weeks I got letters from Nallie, Fathima, Aziza and Zohrabibi. Nazir also wrote, and Yasmin's Mohamed who writes regularly. So I am fairly well informed at present. I suppose they must have been inspired by Eid, and I'm sure I won't be hearing again from the ladies for a long time. So you will have to continue with your "news service" as usual.

Your visits have been the most memorable event for me in many years. The fact that they have kept you away for 14 years was enough to embitter one. But fortunately I have been able to avoid succumbing to a feeling of bitterness, otherwise life can be very unpleasant. If indeed there ever were valid reasons for the persistent refusals, I would like to hear them one day. But I don't believe there were.

Anyway, let's, for the present, not think of what has happened. Let us rather look to the future. All things being equal, I shall in all probability be seeing you again at the end of the year. You will try to send me your tentative plans beforehand. As you know, Cape Town is extremely crowded at that time so you will have to make your hotel bookings well in advance. I know that some friends have suggested that you stay with them, but I don't think it is advisable to bank on that because they themselves may be planning to go away.

Some of the folks you met here, such as the Vassens, Omars, etc., do occasionally go to Jo'burg. I told them to contact you when they do. I'm sure you won't mind entertaining them. I don't know if Veena (i.e., Mrs. Vassen) told you that her sister stays in Lenasia.

Thanks for conveying my greetings to Ouma, Uncle Isu, Aunty Ayesha, Shireen, etc. It's a relief to learn that Sayed Nathie's illness is not what was originally suspected. I received a letter from Vincent with photos of Shireen and Amelia.[1] The baby is so big already. Please thank Tania for her Eid card and explain to her that because of the quota, I am unable to send her a card. For this reason, I always send one to Mammie to cover the family.

I am always happy to hear about my former neighbours at Kholvad House. All those good folk have a special place in my heart. I must have

---

[1] Vincent Francis and Kathrada's godchild, Shireen later divorced. Vincent was a television journalist and was killed in Angola while on assignment.

often mentioned how those lovely children looked after me when I was under house arrest. I can still vividly recall the day when the newspaper photograph of the kids was taken; an American T.V. network (I think it was CBS) made the kids T.V. stars over a decade before T.V. came to South Africa. I remember the old lady, Cajee Goribai, well. I'm sorry to hear of the death of Apa's brother, Ahmed Jassat, whom I knew. You will be surprised to know that, although I and my neighbours were on the friendliest terms, there was no direct communication between me and the womenfolk. Whenever we had anything to convey to each other, we used to do it through my friend, "Quarter." It was a very satisfactory and happy arrangement. Once I start on this topic I may just go on and on so I better move on to something else. We'll return to Kholvad House in another letter.

Today we have completed 24 years of our sentence. Yes, staying with the same people for so long is, in many ways, like a family situation. In general (especially when we were many on Robben Island) we became like a sort of extended family. But within that large family one develops special bonds—like between father and son, brother and brother, etc. I came to know Uncles Walter and Nelson since about the mid-1940s and have ever since then enjoyed a close relationship with them and with their families. Outside and inside, but more especially in jail, Uncle Walter became a sort of father to the whole community. He is such a gentle, caring person and he takes a great deal of interest, not only in us, but also in our folks outside. At Pollsmoor, where we are so few, the bonds between him and myself were very much strengthened, and we have a very relaxed and comfortable relationship where we are able to discuss all sorts of things. Of course, I do tease him quite a bit; otherwise my day would not be complete. Uncle Nelson I regard as an elder brother, although he is turning 70 on 18th July.

Let me give you an example of how close our friendship was outside. At the beginning of 1962 my banning orders had expired; they were only re-imposed in October when I was house arrested. During the 9 months of "freedom" I was able to move about all over the country. Both Uncles W. and N. were still restricted. Some of their children were schooling in Swaziland and they wanted to come home for their holidays. Somebody had to fetch them so I went. But at their school in Mbabane I met up with a problem. The Mother Superior (who was principal of the school) would not release the children to this here "stranger." You see, at the time there were rumours that some unfriendly people were planning to kidnap these kids. Try as I did, I just couldn't persuade her that I was genuine; in fact they didn't even want me to see the girls. Then, just as I was about to give up, Uncle Walter's little Lindi happened to see me and she came running up to me calling out my name. Then they brought Uncle Nelson's Markie and she also knew me. The third child was the late Advocate Nokwe's relative who did not know me too well. But on the strength of Lindi and Markie's responses to me, the Mother Superior released all 3 girls in my care and I brought them home. This was 26 years ago. Today Lindi has 2 children and she is doing a doctorate in England. Markie has 3 kids and she is doing post-graduate studies in America.

I could say much more, but this is just one small example to show that our relationship is not confined to politics. Oh, incidentally, after Uncle Nelson and Oliver Tambo closed their law offices in 1960, Uncle Nelson carried on his practice from Flat 13. From what I have said above, you will see that when you meet Mr. Sisulu you will be meeting someone from my extended family.

I wanted to comment on a number of other points mentioned in your letter, but this is already getting too long and I'll have to leave them over for another time. Uncle Enver informed me of Thakur's death. It was really tragic. I remember him well; he was a very nice person. I sent a sympathy card. I did not know Oom Ben but heard of him at visits and in letters. It seems he had really become part of the family. I'm sorry I never met him.

As you probably know, Eid fell on the same day as Uncle Walter's 76th birthday (18 May) so we celebrated the occasion with a huge feast. I can imagine how you looked on Eid Day as I still have a picture in my mind of your first visit in the pink dress. It was very nice.

I must end now. I hope your mother is feeling better. What a disgrace about the racialism in the clinic. I remembered the birthdays of Shamim and Kaylash yesterday; please wish them for me when you see them.

Thanks for the info about your Sputnik; what I am not clear about is whether it works by electricity or is it hand-operated? I am still going to comment one day about judging the unseen. Have you read through the affidavit yet?

Keep well, and lots of love from
AMK

~ ~ ~

Zuleikha Mayat—*2 July 1988*

A very interesting letter that gives us insight into Kathrada's beliefs, his long-time association with Messrs. Sisulu and Mandela, and his abhorrence for any-thing that smacked of racial prejudice. The letter opens with him thanking Zuleikha for the Eid gift and how in earlier days he would celebrate all the reli-gious festivals with his friends, including a visit to Helen Joseph on Christmas Day. He recalls the day in 1950 when he had the audacity to challenge Nelson Mandela to a public debate and how Nelson Mandela exposed him in a pub-lic meeting a short time later. Even today, he and Kathrada joke about this incident.

~

A. M. Kathrada
Pollsmoor Maximum Prison
Tokai 7966
2nd July 1988

Dear Zuleikhabehn,

Many thanks for your letter of 2nd May which reached me on 17th May. Thanks a lot also for the "Eidy." Happily we are not affected by the Eid Day controversy; we celebrate on the day the goodies are delivered. I suppose we should be hanging our heads in shame for putting our emphasis on the culinary aspect of Eid! But I do assure you that we are never unmindful of the manner in which Eid Day unites us in spirit with all you good people who constantly have our welfare at heart as shown by the cards, letters, Eidy visits, prayers and so many other things.

Our Eid fell on the 18th May which is also Walter's birthday. So we had a double celebration. Outside we hardly ever celebrated our birth-days, but Eid Days often saw us getting together at the late Aminabai's place; Diwalis we'd be together at Jasmatbhai or Narsibhai's places while at Christmas time we'd go [to] Nelson or Walter's places in Soweto. So to some small extent we are carrying on an established tradition. Oh yes, on Christmas Day we'd also be popping in at Mrs. Helen Joseph's place. It was wonderful; throughout the day friends would call at her house, convey wishes, have some refreshments and depart. What a grand old lady! I'm happy that the practice still continues. The numerous visitors cannot fail to be inspired by that indomitable lady. We are saddened by her recent illness and hope that she will once again conquer the setback.

Helen is now 83. In one of my letters I teased her about an incident during the Treason Trial. There was a brief period during that marathon trial when we dismissed our lawyers and conducted the defence ourselves. We called Helen as our first defence witness and we had to help prepare her evidence. Nelson and Advocate Nokwe were, fortunately for us, the two lawyers among the accused which was an advantage. In taking down her statement, Nelson asked what her age was! And, typical woman that she is, her reply was curt and final. Nelson simply moved on to the next question.

Walter turned 76 and Nelson will be 70 on 18th July. I knew them from my teen years and have come a long way together. The three of us were co-accused in 3 major trials—the Defiance Trial, 1952; the Treason Trial, 1956–1961; and Rivonia. Apart from the legal aspects, there were literally scores of incidents that we recall and, of course, a lot that we can tease one another about. I like to rag them about their Youth League days, particularly about an incident when we found ourselves on opposite sides of a dispute. I wonder if Abu Hurera will still remember it? Nelson and I happened to meet in Commissioner Street (in 1950), and what began as a friendly exchange, developed into an argument during which I, with the "wisdom" of my 21 years behind me, made certain utterances to which Nelson took umbrage. This I was to discover later when at a formal get-together of senior men from all over the country, Nelson complained about me. (I was a doorman cum messenger-driver at the gathering.) I was shocked and shamed by the accusation. As if this was not enough, Ismail [Meer] got up and asked Nelson and the gathering to dismiss my behaviour as an intemperate outburst of a "youngster." My humiliation was complete. Today we are able to joke about [it].

I think it is appropriate for me at this stage to say something concerning the UDW[1] "adjustment problem" to which you made reference recently. It is always painful to read reports of ethnic tension and friction; it is much worse when the reports relate to problems in a supposedly enlightened environment such as a university campus—and a campus of underprivileged students at that! However, in the background of the socio-economic-political situation such problems are virtually inevitable

---

[1] UDW: the University of Durban–Westville, originally the university established by the apartheid government for Indians only.

and understandable. The surprise should be that they are not worse. When ideologues and lawmakers have ordained that, from the cradle to the grave, human beings be nurtured to accentuate so-called differences among them, what else can one expect? Your positive approach is most encouraging and one hopes that it reflects the attitude of the students. The University of Western Cape is systematically educating students and staff alike about the oneness of human beings; in the process, they are resisting and eradicating dangerous concepts such as "minority groups," "minority rights," etc. This is not to say that they deny the existence of a plurality of languages, religions and other cultural traits. When I reflect on the fashionable practice of certain people to harp on "fears of Black majority" and the need to "protect minority rights," I always wonder if these persons are simply not repeating, parrot-like, some unfounded and certainly unsubstantiated assertions made in times gone by. Please forgive me for trying to refute the arguments by invoking my own experiences. I know it is not scientific, but I believe that experiences such as ours should be taken into account. Apart from my social and political association since childhood (which I have referred to above), for the past 25 years I have been part of so-called "minority groups" among an overwhelming "African majority"; for the past 6 years I have been in a "minority" of one. A prison environment is, by definition, tailor-made for all sorts of frustration, jealousies, suspicions, envy and tension. An aggravating factor was the differentiation in the diets, clothing, etc., of the "Coloureds" and Indians on the one hand and Africans on the other; the Africans, of course, receiving the less favourable treatment. (Happily this differentiation has since been done away with.) I would not be truthful if I claim that "racial" tension was completely absent; it must be remembered that the Island had inmates from a number of political groups, at least one of which was known for its extreme narrow "nationalism," and a generally "anti" outlook. In spite of this, and especially considering the time period and numbers of inmates, these periods of tension were so brief and far between that, at most, they can be included as footnotes in the story of our imprisonment. And they came nowhere near physical confrontations between groups. Never did we feel threatened or insecure. In fact, with the passage of time, these aberrations virtually disappeared. The important thing to bear in mind is that there is no secret or complex formula for the maintenance of harmony and good fellowship. It is basically a question of having mutual respect for one another; the relinquishing of misconceptions about cultural traits, customs and practices that are different from one's own and the willingness to learn about them; the absolute avoidance of any suggestion that one particular culture is superior—or inferior—to others. I could add a few other do's and don'ts, but they are superfluous. To put it simply, all that is needed is for one to behave naturally; it will be found that the basic values and behaviour patterns learned in the course of upbringing are universal and are sufficient to transcend all barriers in the path of friendship and understanding.

Let me turn to a couple of other matters. Sometime last year I mentioned the wedding of my nephew in Cape Town, but I left out the bride's name, thinking that it would make no sense to you. Imagine my surprise when, in the course of a conversation, Kader Amien asks me if I knew "Mrs. Zuleikha Mayat" of Durban! He then told me of his friendship with Aslam and how he was in and out of your place while he was at university there. My nephew is married to Kader's sister, Rabia, who, incidentally, is in Cape Town at present for her confinement.

We have avoided going to court on the question of allowing my niece to visit me; the Prisons Department allowed her to come after refusing permission for 14 years! The question of my studies is not yet settled. I have submitted another topic and am waiting for an answer.

I'll have to leave other matters for a future letter.

Fond regards to you and the family from

AMK

≈ ≈ ≈

J. N. and Radhie Singh—*16 September 1988*

There were two people who made a deep and lasting impression on Kathrada when he was a teenager: J. N. Singh and Ismail Meer, who were both studying law at the University of Witwatersrand, Johannesburg, in the mid-forties. They were for Kathrada "role models" in every sense. In this letter when he recalls his first trip to Natal, he writes about them in their "Wits" blazers and the "general impact that university students made on our young minds." During this period, education was highly valued and seeing a young black in a university blazer symbolized success. In this letter to J. N. and his wife, Radhie, also a lawyer, Kathrada thanks them for their card and the update on their family and their travels. Nelson Mandela and Walter Sisulu were good friends of the Singhs and also political colleagues. However nice it was to see Mandela, Kathrada is concerned about his health and hopes that after his

hospitalization, he will be allowed to go home. But Kathrada is not that hope-
ful and surmises that if Mandela stays in so will they. Kathrada had last seen
J. N. Singh and Radhie in 1962. As one does with old friends, Kathrada rem-
inisces about the places they had frequented in Johannesburg and in Natal,
places, including their own homes that were later "declared white areas." Even
now as he thinks about this, it pains and grieves him. He recalls how memo-
rable and historically important those times were, and hopes fervently they will
be recorded for posterity.

~

A. M. Kathrada
Pollsmoor Maximum Prison
Tokai 7966
16th September 1988

My Dear J.N. and Radhie,

Thanks a lot for your birthday card and the sentiments expressed
therein. Thanks also for the update on the various family members and
on your travels. Walter also wishes to thank you for his birthday card. We
met Nelson on 4th August; as always you and other friends featured in
our discussions, and I think he said he had received your card but I'm
not too sure.

When no reply came to our application to spend Nelson's birthday
with him, we assumed that it had been refused and we started focussing
on Christmas in the hope that we'd be allowed to be together then. We
were pleasantly surprised, therefore, when, on the morning of the 4th
August, we were told we'd be spending a few hours with him later in the
day. It was wonderful to be with him; and, following established practice,
he systematically informed us about things—in jail and outside. And we
did likewise, albeit not as neatly and systematically as he did. The lawyer
in him is as keen, wise and dynamic as ever. We got a full picture of the
"Brown episode"; we could not but admire Nelson's firmness and great
presence of mind. I don't think his standpoint has been adequately
reflected in the media. He also told us of the visit of Amina and Yusuf[1]
and the tidbits he got from them. Walter and I were as thrilled as he was
when he told us of your trip to Jo'burg together with Ismail, Chota, etc.

---

[1] Yusuf and Amina Cachalia, a couple who had been at the forefront of the struggle.
Now that Nelson Mandela is at the Victor Verster Prison, he can have unlimited visits and
the fact that the Cachalia's were able to visit suggests a great relaxation of who could visit.

(Helen's card, which you wrote for her, only reached me the day after; i.e., on 5th August.)

As nice as our visit was, we were quite disturbed about his health. He coughed quite a bit and his voice was just a bit above a whisper. Ordinarily this shouldn't have caused concern, but in all the years in jail this was the first time that we saw him in this condition. (In 1974 when virtually the entire prison population was literally down with flu, Nelson was unaffected; he was up and about helping us and attending to our needs.) We became even more anxious when, a week after our get-together, we learned that he had been admitted to hospital. We have no further information about him apart from the media reports. Like everybody else, we hope that he will not return to Pollsmoor or to any other prison but [be] allowed to go home. However, based on past experience, there is no reason for optimism.

If Nelson remains in jail, it means that we will remain inside. Which, in turn, means that we will be unable to visit you in Durban and reminisce about the old days. However, if it is convenient for you, it will be lovely if you can pay a visit to Pollsmoor. The best thing is to send your application to the Commanding Officer together with your I.D. numbers. Once it is granted, the permission remains valid for any time; a suitable date for the visit can then be arranged—even by phoning the local Censor Office. There has been some relaxation about visits, and I think there is a good chance that you'll get permission. Earlier this year, they allowed a niece and nephew of mine to visit me—after refusing them for 14 years! They only conceded on the eve of a Supreme Court application. Yet, last year the authorities were prepared to allow members of the House of Delegates to visit me! Fortunately the prison official asked me beforehand if I would accept that visit and I indicated that I would not. After receiving your card last month, I asked a friend to convey to you that your visit would be most welcome; any time would be suitable except December. The position has since changed; the folks who had booked for December are now coming in October. I thought I should just inform you of this. But, of course, your visit doesn't have to be this year; any time that suits you is okay by me.

Your mention of Ishana, Avanthi, Hamid, Bis, Benny brought back many memories. I last saw the girls in August 1962 when I spent the evening at your place. And I last saw you, Ismail, etc., at Ahmed's place in October of the same year. I must have had a feeling that those months were going to be my last in "freedom." From Durban I came to Cape

Town. On 22nd October 1962 I was placed under house arrest. Then Rivonia . . . Robben Island . . . and now Pollsmoor. When I think of you folks, I remember that my first trip to Durban was with you and Ismail. I also remember the evening trip on George's boat. I still picture you and Ismail in your Wits blazers and the general impact that university students made on our young minds. Then there's Flat 13, Chancellor House, Progress Buildings, End Street . . . so many, many things. On my first trip to Durban, we spent a night or so in Pinetown and the rest at Mansfield Road. It is painful to think that these places, as also the home in Schweizer Reneke where I was born, were all declared white group areas.

Those were interesting times which are tragically being forgotten. At the beginning of our stay on Robben Island, there were many young people who believed that our political history began with Sharpville 1960! Then came the post-Soweto youth who maintained that history started in 1976! Almost every month we still come across articles (and serious textbooks) which perpetuate such views. Most of the authors are invariably young people who write out of ignorance; there is a great dearth of material on our history, especially from the 1960s onwards.

What makes me even more conscious of this is the T.V. series *Roots*, the last episode of which we have just seen. Our recent past offers enough scope, not only for serious historical works but also for novels, short stories, etc. I just hope that our young people are doing something about it. It is encouraging to know that, in the Cape, especially at the University of Western Cape, progress is being made in this direction. I've heard of the "Leader History Foundation." Perhaps this will partly answer the wish I am expressing?

When you mentioned Benny Sishy, I could not help but have a quiet chuckle because it brought to mind how Ismail used to relate how Benny's mother responded when a message was left with her that Benny was to "take the chair at the City Hall steps."[2] It's good to hear about him again; I last met him in London in 1951. Hamid and Zabie tried to visit me a few years ago, but there were some technical problems. I hear about Bis now and then from his sister in Durban. I've recently managed to reestablish contact with a Canadian friend with whom I was in Budapest. He is in the Department of French Literature at the University of Toronto and knows a number of mutual friends from South Africa. He may even know Avanthi and Terry. His name is Ben Shek.

---

[2] Protest meetings at the City Hall steps in Johannesburg were frequent.

I have to end now. The two of you are sure making good use of your retirement years. When next you fly off to see the girls, please convey my love to them and their spouses and, of course, to Shamishka. Lots of love to you, to Suni and to all members of the family and friends.

We are keeping well. I'm still waiting for permission from the Prisons Dept. to do M.A. They refused my first application because they found my topic undesirable.

Walter joins me in sending best wishes. If we have another surprise get-together with Nelson, I'll certainly pass your greetings.

All the best from

AMK

≈ ≈ ≈

Zohrabibi Kathrada—*19 September 1988*

Kathrada congratulates his niece on the birth of her second son. On the subject of babies, Kathrada gives a touching and humorous account of his elaborate practice on how to hold a little baby, including detailed study of photographs from magazines of people holding their babies. On the day of his niece's visit with the new baby, Kathrada loses courage and freezes. All he can do is look at this new little human being in awe and wonder. On returning to his cell he promises himself that when his godchild, Shireen, comes with little Amelia, he will be ready and prepared. When mother and child do come, Kathrada is once again terror-struck, but moves to make the effort, whereupon Amelia lets out a yell. Secretly, Kathrada probably welcomed this and was quite content to see Amelia on her mother's lap. Now more determined than ever, he is definitely going to be ready when Shehnaaz and her little daughter, Nadia, come along.

≈

A. M. Kathrada
Pollsmoor Maximum Prison
Tokai 7966
19th September 1988

My Dear Zohrabibi,

Thanks for your note and the birthday card. We had the usual little "celebration" with lots of food. Congratulations on the arrival of Zakaria.

Nazir did mention it to me, but he had not yet heard what the name was. How is Yusuf reacting to his brother?

Rabia came along to introduce me to little Khadija. I knew beforehand that she was coming so for many days I started to practice how to hold such a small baby. I took careful note of how Prince Andrew held Fergie's little Beatrice, and I studied photos in magazines and newspapers and I was well prepared. Or at least that's what I thought. But when Kadija finally pitched up, all my newfound knowledge and courage simply vanished. All I could do is to stare at her in awe and admiration. But I just couldn't hold her. She is lovely. I went back to my cell and decided that this won't happen again. I had two weeks to prepare for the next occasion when my godchild, Shireen, brings her 6-month-old, Amelia, to visit me. But, once again, success eluded me—this time, fortunately, with Amelia's cooperation. I made one bold effort to hold her, but she let out such a yell that I promptly abandoned all further efforts. Thereafter she just sat in her mother's lap and stared at this strange creature—and occasionally smiled. Now I am preparing for my third encounter which hopefully will be in a month or two when Shehnaaz brings her Nadia and Khiyara.

I suppose you know that Nazir's wedding date has been fixed for 15th January. Will you be going up to Jo'burg for the occasion? He is doing very well in his law studies and should be completing next year. He told me that Aziz and Ahmed are also doing well at university.

A couple of months ago I had a surprise letter from Aziza. She writes very well. She tells me she hasn't decided yet what she is going to do after matric. She seems to be quite bright and it will be a pity if she abandons her studies. I will be replying to her soon. I also owe Yasmin's Mohamed a letter; I hope to write to him today.

I assume you have already been to Schweizer as planned. I hope you will be telling me about the trip.

I am expecting to see Cassim one of these days when he comes to fetch Rabia and Khadija. Zohra and Enver are coming in October. I'm sure you know that they have been overseas again. I had a card from Zohra from Portugal.

It was sad to hear of the death of Fatoo's mother. She was a grand old lady. Did I tell you of her visit to me at the time of Cassim's wedding? It was a very nice visit. I have written to Fatoo.

I'm getting a bit worried about Shamim's silence. In one of my letters I made some light-hearted remarks, and I am now wondering if she did not get annoyed by them. Next time you are in contact with her, please try to find out. I'd like to know if Leila has started schooling and also about Rubina and Alia.

Are you intending to enroll Yusuf at a creche? I think I mentioned something about it on his birthday card.

This is all for now. When will you be starting work again?

I am keeping well. I haven't got permission yet to do M.A. My first application was refused by the Prisons Department. I applied again in June.

Keep well. Lots of love to you, Ali, Yusuf, Zakaria and all the family members.

Love and best wishes to you.

From

AMK

        ~ ~ ~

Ben Shek—*29 October 1988*

White attitudes toward race and color are painfully slow to change in South Africa, Kathrada notes as he receives photos from Ben Shek of himself and his family. A few years earlier, these photos would not have been allowed, just as the photographs of Kathrada's nephew and Irish wife were not permitted. Kathrada recalls that he had "committed the ultimate crime" of having a lady friend who was white. He muses that in some quarters, this situation would have been considered more serious than crimes of high treason or sabotage. Now that laws prohibiting relationships across the color line have been discarded, such photos are permissible, as are visits from white friends. He comments on the one-sidedness of history in depicting and celebrating the arrival of the white settlers as "civilizers," while ignoring the civilization of indigenous people. Kathrada also provides a keen insight into how, through holding on tenaciously to their goals and beliefs, he and his compatriots have not fallen prey to "unbecoming behavior." What boosted their morale were visits, correspondence, reading, sports etc. He asks about friends from the Budapest days and admits that his idealism then prevented him from seeing everything. Now, he can observe shortcomings in the way they carried on their own struggle without diluting his "fundamental beliefs and goals." Rumors of release still abound but he dismisses them. The film Judgment at Nuremberg *reminds him of the situation in South Africa and he hopes the message penetrates the minds of the "herrenvolk."*

~

A. M. Kathrada
Pollsmoor Maximum Prison
Tokai 7966
29th October 1988

Dear Ben,

Thanks for your letter and the photos; knowing the family, albeit through impersonal means such as letters and photos, helps to narrow the great distance that separates us. You look almost the same as you did when we last met except your somewhat sparser plumage! A warm hello to Jean and Ghitta. We, of course, spell it Gita which means songs. At least I think that's the meaning.

It is interesting how values and perceptions differ from country to country. Here, although morsels of enlightened thought do penetrate the antediluvian outlook of the privileged, the process is painfully slow and, by and large, they remain obsessed with race and pigmentation. A few years ago I would not have been allowed to receive these photos just as I was not given the photos of my Irish niece and their children. But before my imprisonment I had committed the ultimate crime by having a lady friend who was white! I read a book on Robben Island (written by a turncoat) which described her as "a blue-eyed blond with a peaches and cream complexion," the consummate attributes of a member of the *herrenvolk*. Naturally direct communication between us became impossible from Robben Island; by that time our relationship had been revealed in her own trial in the media and in books. With the atmosphere, the attitudes and laws of those years in mind, I have often tried to picture the situation had we been arrested for transgressing the law which prohibited male-female relationships across the colour line. I wouldn't have been surprised if many of my captors were to regard high treason and sabotage as lesser offences! Anyway, in our so-called "reform" era the Immorality Act and Mixed Marriages Act have been discarded so that letters, photos and even visits from whites are no longer taboo. Though the abolition comes nowhere near to meeting our fundamental aspirations, I suppose one can be thankful for small mercies!

Your remarks about the Bicentenary of white settlement in Australia and the 40,000th year of the Aborigines bring to mind several similar events that were celebrated in South Africa this year. There was the 500th anniversary of the rounding of the Cape by Bartholomew Diaz; the 300th of the arrival of the French Huguenots who were escaping from religious persecution; the 40th year of Nationalist Party rule. These were all essentially white events, celebrated almost exclusively by whites and virtually ignored by Blacks. The settler events are portrayed as the arrival of "civilizers" from Europe to a virtually uninhabited country! The existence of indigenous iron-age civilisations hundreds of years before the whites is all but ignored by historians; a relatively small group of archaeologists is conscientiously engaged in discovering, preserving and recording the rich heritage of the indigenous people.

I have mentioned to some friends that reminiscing about the past is one of the favourite pastimes of prisoners. It can be amusing, informative, educational and recreational. It can also be morale-boosting and therapeutic. After being together for so many years, we must have related to one another just about every anecdote, every event, every joke and every experience that we have undergone. We must have exhausted our memory books, and every now and then we find ourselves repeating some or other story. Once a colleague begins to narrate something, it is often possible to guess what is coming and to complete the story. It is a situation tailor-made for boredom, frustration, tension and a host of negative forms of behaviour. The tenacious reminder of our goals and ideals and our attachments and obligations have, by and large, prevented our falling prey to unbecoming conduct. I would be making an incomplete assessment if I did not include the positive contribution of various other factors towards our general well-being—the regular visits and correspondence, studies, sports facilities, newspapers and other reading matter, the radio, T.V. and video. Incidentally, among the library films which we see, there is a fair number of Canadian films which are generally of a high standard, educational and informative. A little while ago we saw one on Dr. Norman Bethune. There is one Canadian who is not exactly our favourite—a chap called John Phillips who regularly broadcasts reports to South African radio. The man [is] vicious, malicious and venomous. He and the reporter in Lisbon are prime examples of what media persons should not be.

With our situation as I have tried to portray above, you shouldn't be surprised that I manage to remember many people and things. It's not so much my good memory but the constant repetition that helps to imprint names, events and experiences in one's mind. Let me name some colleagues from our Budapest days; any information about them will be welcome: Jacques; Djallati; Re Ki Jun; Sergei. I am sorry to learn that our friend Paul Gillet is no more. When I think of him, I remember the night we spent a few hours at the pub across the Danube. It was a very cold wintry night. On our way back Suzanne either fell or rolled in the snow and, as a result, caught a terrible cold which kept her in bed for quite a while. There is one aspect which made a strong impression on my mind. It was well past midnight when we were returning home, and on the bridge we saw men in civilian clothes doing some sort of work while they were being guarded by armed, uniformed men. Somehow we gathered that these were political prisoners. Because of my youth, immaturity, enthusiasm and refusal to accept that there could be anything wrong in the socialist countries, I must have dismissed this at the time. But after the 1956 events, this and numerous other things started coming back to me with some force. Were these not signals that were to eventually lead to October 1956?

Anyway, I am not expecting that we should enter into a discussion on this; for one thing, my circumstances do not allow me to do so. But I am happy that, with the passage of time and hopefully with greater maturity and broader outlook, I am able to identify and talk about shortcomings even in our own situation in South Africa without in any way diluting our fundamental beliefs and goals.

I'm afraid I have to once again end this letter rather abruptly. You must have heard that in August our colleague, Nelson Mandela, was admitted to hospital for T.B. He is presently in a clinic where he is reported to be doing well. This has once again given rise to a wave of speculation about his "early" release which, theoretically at least, would have bearing on the position of the rest of us, especially my cellmate, Walter Sisulu, who is 76. My own view, however, is that there will be no releases—our adversaries still want their pound of flesh.

Last week we saw *Judgment at Nuremberg* on T.V. It is very relevant to our country and one can only hope that its message has penetrated the minds of the establishment and its supporters. It reminded me of my own visit to Auschwitz from where I brought back a handful of human bones as a constant reminder of the evils of racism.

Love and fondest wishes to Jean, Ghitta, Elliot and yourself. Greetings also to all mutual friends. Unfortunately it is not possible for me to send a photo of myself. Though a bit early, let me wish all of you everything of the best for 1989.

From

AMK

∿ ∿ ∿

Yasmin and Nazir Kathrada—*18 December 1988*

After a quarter-century of being imprisoned, Kathrada looks back and says that when he went in "there was no magic or secret formula to meet the challenge that lay ahead. What was needed was determination, a positive approach and above all to doggedly maintain the basic values with which we have grown up." This has worked for the prisoners and he tells Yasmin and Nazir to follow these values as they go through married life together.

∿

A. M. Kathrada
Pollsmoor Maximum Prison
Tokai 7966
18th December 1988

My Dear Yasmin and Nazir,

The most common form of measuring one's time in prison is by calculating the number of years; in our case in terms of cold statistics this amounts to 25 years, 5 months and some days. Looked at from such a restricted angle, one simply gets a picture of fragmented units of time—monotonous, drab, unchanging, unexciting and tedious. It does not cover the essentially vibrant community that inhabits the world within a world—its spectrum of experiences, its collective and individual emotions, thrills and responses, its fears, its joys and sorrows, its hopes, its confidence, its loves and hates, the unbreakable spirit, the fellowship, the hardships, the morale. These and much more make up the prison community. Naturally these generalised feelings find expression in a myriad specific forms in every hour of every day of every year.

One may choose any one (or more) of the specific forms and use them to measure his period of incarceration. Some will select their academic achievements. (I know of a former inmate who did his J. C.,[1] matric, B. A. in jail and completed his LLB outside.), others may select visits and/or letters from special persons, some may use important political

---

[1] J. C.: the Junior Certificate, an examination that a student could take in the tenth year of schooling.

events as measuring instruments while there may be a few who would calculate their periods in terms of the different types of prison labour he performed—there are many approaches to the matter.

In this letter I propose to employ births and marriages (of my nieces and nephews) to measure my time. At the time of my arrest there were 16 nephews and nieces—all unmarried. Two joined the clan later. Fourteen of them got married while I've been in jail, thus adding to the number of nieces and nephews. Then followed their offspring—21 of them. In addition are my "godchildren," Shireen, Djamilla, Amelia, etc.

Each one of the marriages meant a lot to me, and I celebrated them in my own way. And the arrival of each baby provided its own special kind of thrill. (You know, of course, that until a few years ago, we had not seen or touched a child.)

Your coming marriage marks another milestone in my incarceration, and I want to join with all the family members and friends in extending my heartiest congratulations to you. Though I will not be with you physically, my thoughts and good wishes will be with you on the big day and always.

As on previous occasions, I should like to point to some similarities between marriage and the prison situation! Difficult to believe when the institution of marriage represents beauty, grace, nobility, elegance, love while the general picture of the prison institution is one replete with vulgarity, harshness, violence, filth, corruption, inhumanity and much else. Admittedly, these elements are not absent in prisons, but they are not relevant to the aspect which I am dealing with today. I want to talk about aspects such as a break from past lifestyles and the entry into new environments, about new friends and new relationships, about the need to curb one's individualistic streaks in order to fit into the greater whole, about new responsibilities and new priorities, about a situation where the pronoun "I" will be used less and less while "we" will come into more general usage. Yes, they are both situations which call for sacrifices and compromises—and radical adjustments.

One enters into marriage voluntarily while one has no control over one's imprisonment. By its nature, a marriage is virtually synonymous with happiness and the fulfillment of dreams. A prison situation, on the other hand, is tailor-made for everything that is negative; it can be an ordeal and a period of unmitigated hardship and unhappiness and the destruction of dreams. But it does not have to be this way—and, indeed, I would like to think that our quarter of a century in jail has been anything but negative or wasted. At the very outset we realised that there was no magic or secret formula to meet the challenge that lay ahead. What was needed was determination, a positive approach and above all to doggedly maintain the basic values with which we have grown up. I believe that these requirements are equally valid for a successful marriage.

I am confident that both of you are well endowed with all necessary ingredients for a happy and enduring marriage. My heartiest congratulations to you. May your future be filled with sunshine and blue skies and laughter; may your every wish be fulfilled and may your every endeavour be crowned with success.

Lots of love to you.

From

AMK

Uncle Walter asked me to convey his best wishes and love.

∾ ∾ ∾

Fati and Kader—*14 January 1989*

Kathrada sends his congratulations and best wishes to a couple about to get married. This letter, while offering sound advice to two young people about to become husband and wife, provides another window to prison life and the value system and philosophy that kept the Rivonia prisoners together. He writes that it is easy to indulge in self-pity and to feel sorry for oneself and to see prison in a very negative way. What he found was "great warmth, fellowship, friendship, humor, and laughter, of strong convictions; of a generosity of spirit and compassion, solidarity and care." This letter and the one to Nazir and Yasmin, written on 18 December 1988, helped to build an understanding and appreciation of how Nelson Mandela, Walter Sisulu, Ahmed Kathrada, and the others were able to walk out of prison after twenty-six years without bitterness, remorse, or a sense of feeling cheated, in short, devoid of any negative feelings.

∾

A. M. Kathrada
Pollsmoor Maximum Prison
Tokai 7966
14th January 1989

My Dear Fati and Kader,

How wonderful to start the New Year by joining with the two of you and all the other family members and friends in celebrating your marriage. Although the prison walls will prevent me being with you in person, rest assured that I will be with you in spirit to share your happiness and be part of your dreams and aspirations for a bright and rosy future.

It is possible that, to many, a message from prison may conjure up a picture that is incongruous with a festive occasion. The stereotype image of a prison is one of forbidding high walls; a grim, cold atmosphere, prosaic, harsh, vulgar, violent; an atmosphere of desperate, unsmiling faces; angry, bitter and frustrated beings.

Admittedly a prison situation is tailor-made for the projection of such an image. Every inmate, to a lesser or greater degree, is vulnerable to unwholesome influences. However, as in every situation which occasions a radical change of environment, the basic challenge that faces a person is one of adjustment. You have to approach the new environment in a positive state of mind. It is easy to succumb when faced with prospects of a lengthy and nightmarish existence and consequently dwell on one's miseries, hardships, the manifold deprivations and negative experiences. Someone has written about two prisoners looking out of their cell window—the one saw iron bars while the other saw stars. How true!

Naturally one does not uncomplainingly accept all the wrongs and hope for the best. No, but one has to accept that their are certain realities over which one has no control. For example, the very fact of being in prison means that one has to endure certain deprivations, the chief of which is the loss of one's freedom. Secondly, one is thrust into a community in which you have no say as to who your fellow inmates should be. Having come to terms with these and similar unchangeables, you immediately set about the task of adapting yourself to the new environment and where necessary and possible you immerse yourself in the intolerable. In the process, brick by brick, you are building up the other—and certainly in the case of security prisoners—the real picture of prison life. It is a picture of great warmth, fellowship, friendship, humour and laughter; of strong convictions; of a generosity of spirit of compassion, solidarity and care. It is a picture of continuous learning of getting to know and live with your fellow beings, their strengths as well as their idiosyncrasies; but more important, where one comes to know oneself, one's weaknesses, inadequacies and one's potentials. Unbelievably, it is a very positive, confident, determined—yes, even a happy community.

Looked at from this perspective, the prison situation offers some comparisons with marriage. Both involve a radical break with the past and adjustment to new environments; both bring new responsibilities and require self-examination; both claim wider loyalties; both face new challenges, which necessitate sacrifices and compromise while retaining basic values; both situations require one to temper but not obliterate one's individualism in the interest of the greater whole.

To move away from a self-centered lifestyle to one where the individual personality is largely submerged in a wide, social unit is a profoundly humbling but enormously rewarding experience. How is this experience to be measured? The years of marriage are reckoned by means of gemstones—diamonds, gold, sapphires, etc. This, to my mind, is unfortunate as they have become closely associated with wealth and materialism. It somehow robs a noble institution of its grandeur and beauty. As measuring instruments, I would prefer to borrow from nature's beautiful gifts, especially if one can still find some which are uncommercialised and not debased by man. I would use the tulip, rose, carnation, azalea, maple, cedar, violet and a host of other beauteous creations as symbols.

The general tendency is to measure imprisonment in terms of the number of years served. To my mind this [is] an inadequate and hopelessly unbalanced method. By reducing prison life to cold, impersonal statistics one is blotting out the deep, multidimensional experiences, feelings and interests of a vibrant community. There is a variety of means to portray one's imprisonment without having to resort to years, months, days . . . which are almost meaningless, fragmented units of time. One can use significant political occurrences as milestones; or social, sporting, cultural events; or one's personal experiences such as studies, visits, letters; the arrival and departure of fellow inmates and many more. One of my favourite methods is to describe my incarceration in terms of the joyful events in the lives of family members and friends. How much nicer and thrilling it is to be able to look back at each new birth, growth, the childhood years and the attempts of the little ones to communicate to me by means of a drawing or a few pencil marks on a sheet of paper, the schooling, adulthood, marriages and the arrival of new babies!

Thus I would like to think of 1989, not at marking my 26 years in jail, but as yet another family milestone, represented by your union and that of Yasmin and Nazir. In this way time assumes a personal significance and becomes more meaningful.

My thoughts will be with you on your big days and I shall talk about you with love, admiration and pride. On the threshold of your new life you carry my good wishes. May good luck, happiness and success be your constant companions in the long, healthy and cheerful journey that lies ahead.

Lots of love.

From

AMK

P.S. Don't forget the wedding photos and video.

Zuleikha Mayat—*25 March 1989*

After many years of corresponding, Kathrada and Zuleikha finally meet each other and Kathrada thanks her for the visit, short though it was. From her last letter Kathrada had learned something about the Salman Rushdie "imbroglio." He laments that certain colleagues are no longer there to provide background information on such events and confesses that his knowledge of the controversy surrounding Satanic Verses *is weak. He regrets not having kept up with his languages generally. His letter moves on to a discussion of prisoners and their plight and their secret agonies and sufferings. Somehow, he writes, he and his colleagues have been able to escape the gloom and sulks and bitterness. Once again, rumors have surfaced of their release, "a charade that started in 1966" and one that leaves him and his colleagues unimpressed.*

A. M. Kathrada
Pollsmoor Maximum Prison
Tokai 7966
25th March 1989

Dear Zuleikhabehn,

Your letter of 1st March (unregistered), much to my surprise, reached me on 7th March!! Record time! This, plus your American letter, makes me want to suggest that we revert to unregistered letters; but I'm hesitant. Having in mind the long history of "lost" letters, I think the old saying is still valid; namely, two successful unregistered letters don't make a Pollsmoor summer.

I must thank you for taking time off to visit me. After all the years of contact by letter, it was a real pleasure to meet you in person. Luckily the authorities processed your application in record time, and some Transvaal folks who had booked to come decided to postpone their visits thus leaving space in my quota for February. Pity the 40 minutes passed so quickly. One cannot even contemplate discussing any particular topic at length; one is obliged to jump—often incoherently—from one thing to another and try to absorb a mass of information. Fortunately in our case this problem is somewhat mitigated by the letters we have been writing. Partly as a result of a habit since childhood, but mainly because of the prison situation, there is a greed for all sorts of information and I have to impose on you and other friends to be my constant sources.

Under the circumstances your "onslaught" on the Rushdie affair is more than welcome. I am not exactly enthusiastic about reading lengthy articles and books on complex issues that require mental effort, hence my knowledge of the Rushdie imbroglio has been peripheral. I doubt it very much if I would go out of my way to read his *Satanic Verses* even if it was not banned. Your observations have greatly helped my understanding of the issues. You know, in the sixties and seventies we had on Robben Island several very outstanding intellectuals, and I could always turn to one or other of them to enlighten me on just about anything. People like Dr. Neville Alexander, Mac Maharaj, Dennis Brutus, Andrew Masondo, Leslie van der Heyden, Kader Hassim, Fikile Bam, Nelson, . . . There is Walter who to my mind is <u>the</u> expert on the history of the liberation movement. I have just named a handful; there were many more. With the influx of the youth after the Soweto uprising, there came a huge crop of bright and knowledgeable young men who had so much to impart and to teach. Here at Pollsmoor we are only 4 and the range of expertise has consequently dwindled. I often find myself frustrated by the absence of persons I could turn to and I have to rely on visitors and correspondents.

Your mention of Iqbal took me back to my childhood years. It was in 1940 or so when I was in Std. 4 and befriended a classmate, Cachalia. Through him I met his uncles, Moulvi and Yusuf, and I soon became a regular at their home. Soon Yusuf decided to take me in hand and gave me lessons from the Hadis. He also felt it was necessary for me to learn some Urdu poetry, and one of the poems/songs he taught me early on was Iqbal's *Sarè jahan sè a—Hindustani hamara*. Planned indoctrination?

Perhaps. But not one bit to be regretted. The temptation is great to write more about those years but I have to move on.

Your reference to Iqbal's poem about the bird in the cage lamenting over freedom reminded me of the well-known song *Pingra kè panchi rê tera dard re janê koor*. Let me try out my Gujarati: [What follows are these words written in Gujarati script]. (For Censors: No one knows the agony of the bird in the cage.)

I suppose there is some merit in the poet's observations that, behind the smiles lurks many a sorrow. When I last heard of him (many years ago) Faiz Ahmed was himself in jail in Pakistan. From what I've gathered the prison conditions there were such as to cause [a] great deal of suffering and sorrow. In addition to the generally known universal complaints of prisoners, it would be most surprising if every prisoner did not have his own private agony and suffering. Some have much to agonise about, others less; some manage to disguise or hide their problems, others are less successful at concealing. Like all prisoners, security prisoners are not immune from personal problems. If anything, because of their generally longer sentences, they should be more vulnerable. However, our experience on the whole (especially on Robben Island) has been that affected individuals have not allowed themselves to be plunged into prolonged periods of gloom, sulkiness or rejection. In my view this is because in time of trouble there is always someone to turn to, some older inmate to boost up the spirits and provide guidance and comfort. You see, the great advantage we have over common-law prisoners is that all of us share certain basic ideals and we are all sentenced for similar offences. There is a harmony and sense of oneness among security prisoners which transcends superficial parochial differences, a relationship which is unfortunately absent outside.

I think I have previously written about my regret at not being able to speak Urdu. At Madressa we spoke only Urdu and got along well. Then I went and forgot it. It's inexcusable. Now, after 26 years of not speaking it, I'm also in difficulties with Gujarati. I don't think I could satisfactorily go through a 40-minute prison visit in Gujarati. One would have thought that, after all these years of opportunity, I would have been fluent in one of the African languages. But I failed. I was doing quite well when I was doing special Xhosa for B.A. After getting through (21 years ago), I neglected it and made little progress.

I'll stop now with my catalogue of failures and proceed with something else. I notice that Mrs. Thatcher has once again spoken about

Nelson's release; I just hope we don't have a repetition of 1985 and 15 November 1988 when waves of expectation and excitement swept through the country—followed by the inevitable disappointment. The powers that be remain as determined as ever to derive maximum benefit for themselves by continuing to hold out the carrot of release while having no intention to release us. It's a charade that started way back in 1966 already and, therefore, we remain unimpressed by the goings on. Oh yes, after every few years they will let out an individual or two—on grounds of illness or old age; e.g., Mbeki, Mthopeng, Gwala. Walter will be 77 in May and we won't be surprised if he is next. On the other hand, there is Oscar Mphetha; he is older, has had a leg amputated and is bedridden in hospital–he has finished over 3 years of his 5-year sentence but they won't let him go. Yet they continue to proclaim that "security prisoners" are treated the same as common law prisoners!

I hope I don't give you the impression that I'm being embittered by these things. I think I have learned quite a bit about the workings of the system and am able to take a realistic approach to things.

A few weeks ago the Prison authorities informed me that I could proceed with my M.A. but on condition that I do not quote banned literature or quote the words of listed persons! This sounds like no permission at all; my lawyers are looking into the matter.

This is all for now. Yes, it is difficult to explain the concept of imprisonment to a child, yet their reactions can be most interesting. A few years ago 2-year-old Shameez came along with her mother and during the visit informed me that she did not like police! I was quite encouraged by her remark. But alas–a few minutes later she looked at me and said, "I don't like you"!!

Good to hear about your mother, about Sikosi and all other friends. Oh yes, I had a nice letter from Jesse and Vallabh. I will be replying.

Fond regards to all family members and friends.

From

AMK

∾ ∾ ∾

Mohamed—16 April 1989

When Kathrada went to Robben Island in 1964, there were no grandnephews and grandnieces. It is all the more remarkable that he can establish a warm and loving relationship with children, many of whom he has not yet seen. He is pleased that all the young family members have passed their examinations at school and at university. Kathrada offers encouragement where improvements can be made and congratulations where Mohamed has excelled. On the question of languages, Kathrada encourages him to read good literature in English and Afrikaans and hopes sincerely that he is still speaking Tswana. He relates the visit of little Khatija and confides to Mohamed that he does not think she likes jail or her Uncle for that matter.

∼

A. M. Kathrada
Pollsmoor Maximum Prison
Tokai 7966
16th April 1989

My Dear Mohamed,

Thank you for your very nice letter which I received in February. I was very happy to see that all of you who are at school and university have passed. Your results were quite good on the whole, but you will have to work harder to improve on the 44% that you got for Maths. Although your 58% for Science is a good pass, you should try to get over 60% as you have done in all the other subjects. Your 75% in English is excellent. I can now see the reason why you write such nice letters. I hope you are interested in reading books, magazines and newspapers. There are also some T.V. and radio programs which you may find interesting. You see, it is necessary to perfect the use of the language, but it is no good to be able to speak and write perfectly if you are not able to speak and write about <u>interesting things</u>. That is why it is so important to read good books; they will help to give you new and interesting ideas and increase your knowledge. What I am saying about English also applies to Afrikaans. When you were younger, you could also speak Tswana. I hope you have not forgotten it.

Do you know what Aziza and Nazira are planning to do? When Uncle Mohamedy was here, there was talk about them attending a Technikon. I hope they are not wasting the year.

I was very happy to see your Mummy, Ferhad and Riaz. I didn't know that Ferhad talked so much. He told me he can speak Tswana. He also told me about all his animal pets. Aunty Rabia and Uncle Cassim also came but Khatija did not come with. I think she does not like jail. I think she does not like me either; whenever I tried to hold her she cried and just wanted to go back to her mummy. When she sat comfortably on her mummy's lap, she stared at me and gave me a toothless smile. I hope she is well. It was also nice to see Aziz, Zohrabibi, Uncle Ali, Yusuf and Zakaria. Yusuf is very talkative; he even went to ask the warder why I cannot come home.

I hope that you have received the autographed photo of Brian Stein who used to play for Luton. I don't know for which team he is playing now. He is originally from Cape Town, and all of us are very proud of him. Ask Aunty Rabia to tell you more about him. And don't forget to write and thank our friends in England who sent you the photo. Which game do you prefer, cricket or soccer? It was a privilege for you to be allowed to play a game in the senior cricket side. Pity you did not have a chance to bat.

I got a letter from Uncle Nazir and Aunt Yasmin together with lots of photos. It was a very nice affair. I heard that Uncle Yusuf also got married. Did you attend?

It was sad to hear of the death of Miriambai Cajee. Please pass my sympathy to Dr. Cajee and all other family members.

This is all for today. Lots of love to you and to all at home.

From

AMK

≈ ≈ ≈

Patricia Long—*13 May 1989*

This is an eloquent testimony to people like Patricia Long, who had never met Kathrada but stood firmly with the ANC in its struggle for freedom and the dawn of a new South Africa. Pat was a staunch member of the Anti-Apartheid Movement of Great Britain and a dedicated and tireless worker. She had sent Kathrada money, which he saw as an "act of friendship and solidarity towards the movement and its ideals." He tells her of the day Walter Sisulu was moved and he hopes this will be the precursor to the 76-year-old's freedom. Two days after Walter Sisulu's departure, another colleague, Wilton Mkwayi was transferred from Robben Island to join Kathrada. They both thank Pat for her generous gift and act of friendship. Wilton Mkwayi will write.

≈

A. M. Kathrada
Pollsmoor Maximum Prison
Tokai 7966
13th May 1989

Dear Pat,

I believe you won't mind my dispensing with the formal salutation and addressing you as Pat. I must hasten to assure you that this discourtesy on my part is not due to the unwholesome influences of prison culture. You see, I found myself in a quandary when I had to choose between "Ms. Long," "Patricia," "Patsie" or "Pat." I had to bear in mind factors such as familiarity, feminism, presumptuousness and chivalry. . . and finally decided that Pat may be the most suitable. If I have made myself guilty of doing wrong, I think that you and other mutual friends should bear part of the blame. I'll tell you why, and hopefully my explanation will also clarify the reason for the very long delay in writing to you.

Sometime towards the end of last year, a Prison official asked me to endorse a cheque of £100–00. I asked him who the sender was, the country of origin, etc., but he was unable to provide any information. He also said that there was no accompanying letter. Some time later I was told of a "technical" problem which apparently necessitated the cheque having to be returned, at least once, possibly twice. To cut a long story short, it was not until the 25th April this year that I eventually came to know the name and address of your good self! Even then there was no accompanying letter.

With this scanty knowledge and suspicion that you are a friend of mutual friends, I am writing to express my thanks for your very kind gesture. Although, by all standards, it is a considerable sum of money, I would not like to measure its value in purely monetary terms. To regard it in its material context would, to my mind, reduce the largeness and real meaning of the gesture. I prefer to view it as an inestimable act of friendship and solidarity towards the movement and its ideals, in quest of which I and many others have been imprisoned. I am merely the vehicle through which this friendship is being conveyed. Solidarity and friendship are feelings that cannot be quantified and measured by material means. I'm sure you will agree.

When one day the experiences of our prison years are recorded, it will be possible to place in proper perspective the enormous significance of

us by our families and friends, both old and new, South African and for-
eign and from all walks of life. Ranging from the simple greeting card or
the solitary placard to the unprecedented Wembly concert, these magnificent demonstrations contributed tremendously as constant sources of
encouragement and morale. They gave the lie to our adversaries who,
right from the time of our arrest, went to great lengths to drum into our
heads the prognosis that within a short few years we would be forgotten
by our families and our people.

I'm writing this letter on the assumption that you are in regular contact with mutual friends and thus well-informed about aspects of life
here. I'll, therefore, spare you the agony of having to share our unchanging and boring routine.

There has been one interesting development in the last couple of
months which the folks at your end may not be aware of. When my cell
mate, Walter, was on his exercise cycle on the morning of 15th March, I,
as usual, reminded him that it was the Ides of March and, while we did-
n't expect a tragedy analogous to that of Julius Caesar, the day was nevertheless pregnant with possibilities. At 10 a.m. Walter was called by the
prison officials and when he didn't return after 4 or 5 hours, we promptly
resorted to the favourite prisoners' pastime; viz., speculation. After being
taken for a visit to Nelson, Walter was rehoused in the cells previously
occupied by Nelson. We were allowed to be with him for a few hours a
couple of weeks ago. He is in good health but lonely. I wouldn't like to
hazard a guess as to what they have in store for him; we can only hope
that the move is a prelude to good news. Two days later on 17th March
we were given a pleasant surprise when Wilton joined us from Robben
Island. He has taken Walter's place in the cell which he and I occupy.
Wilton also thanks you for the gift and sends regards. He will be writing.

Keep well, and fond regards to you and other friends.

From

AMK

P.S. If you do write one day, I suggest that you register the letter.
Otherwise send it via Mr. Vassen's offices.

Marie Kola—*19 July 1989*

Kathrada thanks Marie Kola for the photos, and as he is always interested in the education of the young, he inquires about her daughter's studies. Through the photos he feels he really knows them and when asked to send a photo of himself he informs Marie this is not possible. He describes their visit to Nelson Mandela in his "luxury prison," which he discusses but adds that "stripped of all these fineries . . . he is still a prisoner." The newest concession is that Kathrada and his colleagues can wear civilian clothing. For Kathrada the right to choose is wonderful. From the time a prisoner enters prison the right to choose is taken away. Now he has it back and it means a great deal to him.

∿

A. M. Kathrada
Pollsmoor Maximum Prison
Tokai 7966
19th July 1989

My Dear Marie,

I am sorry that I have taken so long to reply to your letter which arrived at Christmas time. But as I have previously said, very little happens here to break the monotony of our day-to-day lives, and I have to try to avoid repeating the same old things.

Before I go on to tell you of a few developments since my last letter, let me thank you for the photographs. All of you look very nice, especially Enver and Cliadna who is lovely. Photographs, as the cliché goes, help to narrow the distance between us; I can almost claim that I "know" you all. I assume Enver is still keeping busy as a salesperson? I would like to know a bit more about Cliadna's university studies. What are the 3 subjects that she is doing? What are her majors?, etc. I hope she is enjoying university life. You must be quite an expert golf player by now? Does Peps still play?

You mentioned that Enver turned 21 in August last year and that Cliadna was 19. I wish you had mentioned the dates. You see, I'm also an August "baby"—21st August. Am I right that Cliadna's birthday is in October?

Talking of birthdays, yesterday Nelson Mandela turned 71. According to the press, 16 of his family members—his wife, children and grandchildren—spent 5 hours with him at his luxury prison house. This is the first time in 27 years that he has been able to see so many of his families together. Until last year, he (like us) was allowed only two visitors at a time for a 40-minute visit. On Friday 14th July we [i.e., his fellow accused] were taken to his place which is about 30 miles from Cape Town. We celebrated his birthday 4 days in advance. We spent over 4 hours together and we were happy to see him fully recovered. This was our second visit to him, the first one was on 23rd December. The house is large and luxurious; thick wall-to-wall carpeting, guest rooms with bathrooms en suite, expensive furniture, kitchen with all the modern gadgets, swimming pool, gym, T.V. room. . . . However, stripped of all these fineries, one fact remains inescapable: he is still a prisoner, obliged to while away his days and months and years alone. In this respect we are better off; at least we are four at Pollsmoor; we can talk to each other, exchange information, discuss any problems that may arise, etc.

Coinciding with our Friday visit to Mr. Mandela was a new privilege which has been extended to us; we are now allowed to wear civilian clothes. It was a very nice and different feeling to be dressed up in a suit. But, apart from the relief resulting from the ability to shed the green prison uniform, perhaps of greater significance is the fact that, after 26 years, the right to choose has been extended to us. Now the ability to choose a tie or the type of shoes or colour of the suit may seem very unimportant to the general public. But it means a lot to prisoners. You know, from the moment that one enters a prison, one loses the right to choose. Everything is laid down according to fixed rules and the prisoner has to accept them; he has no choice. The opening and closing of doors, the food, the bedding, the clothing, the hours outside the cells—every single aspect of our lives is strictly governed by rules. This relatively small concession regarding clothing is actually a major departure from established practice and very welcome.

This will be all for today. I heard yesterday that Shamim [Dos's daughter] was involved in a serious car accident and broke her leg in 3 places. Her mother and children were not hurt. Please thank Roisin for her St. Patrick's Day card. It is very much appreciated. You asked if I could send you my photo; unfortunately not. Perhaps they may allow us later.

Keep well. Lots of love to you, Peps, Enver, Cliadna and other family members and friends. All the best from

AMK

≈　≈　≈

Navi Joseph—*3 October 1989*

Kathrada thanks Navi and through him all the hundreds of well-wishers who sent greetings on his sixtieth birthday. In addition to all his South African friends, there were greetings from the anti-apartheid branches from Nottinghill, Barnett, the Irish in London, from the MP, Paul Boateng, and from people in other parts of the UK, Scotland, Ireland, Wales, and as far away as Germany. He wishes he could find a way of thanking all of them, but the quota system is still enforced. The photos Navi had sent brought back a flood of memories, as did his description of the foods prepared for the party. Kathrada remarks that the food then was almost identical to the food sent to him while he was detained under the Ninety-Day Detention Laws.

～

A. M. Kathrada
Pollsmoor Maximum Prison
3rd October 1989

My Dear Navi,
Thank you for your letter which arrived on 28th September together with the photos. Your beautiful birthday card did come, but it was after I had registered my strong protest—in fact it arrived on the very day that my letter was posted.

You did well to tell us a bit about the celebrations; apart from brief mention by Zainab, Sadie and Ms. Long (to Wilton), we had heard absolutely nothing. Through you I want to say a big "thank you" to all the folks who have done and said such nice things about me. Much as I would love to, it is not possible for me to write to each one of them personally. Unless the authorities make some major concessions regarding our quota of visits and letters, this will most probably be my last letter to you this year. The same applies to other friends with whom I communicate; please explain my position to them. Special thanks to Sadie, Mary, Brian & Sonia, Sally, Dasoo and family; Nottinghill, Irish and Barnett AAMs, especially Mr. Paul Boateng; Shanti, Ramnie and family; Ms. P. Long; Tom, Bob, Aunty Kissie and all the people who signed the cards. There are numerous messages from friends I do not know—from UK, Ireland, Scotland, Wales, Germany, etc. I wish I could find a way of thanking them.

Tell Zainab[1] I was happy to receive her card, letter and photos and to be introduced to Zenobia, Anand, Dilnaaz and Ebrahim. The achievements of these young people and their visions must do her proud. Yes, I am aware of the death of her brothers. Satch, whom I knew since my childhood, was a good friend. The news of his death was quite a blow.

There was a nice little message from Udesh, the son of the late Dr. B. T. Chetty. He recalled meeting us at their home in Overport. I have often wondered what happened to his sister; she was in Std. 7 when I last saw her sometime in the fifties, and what impressed me very much was the way she discussed the Shakespeare play they were studying. Tell Udesh (who, by the way, is a surgeon in Edinburgh) that Dr. Motala has been keeping me informed about his Uncle Vasu and family.

The photos you sent are lovely, and I am tempted to say something about each one. I must, however, single out the 3 stalwarts for special mention; namely, Mary, Betty and Cassim. Because of reports about their ill health, I had formed certain images in my mind. What a pleasant surprise to find that my impressions were completely wrong. Not only do the ladies look well but they are attractive. Walter also made very complimentary remarks about them. (I can't wait to see the old chap again as he has given me fresh ammunition to tease him.) Looking at our friend, Cassim, I'm trying to imagine the words of wisdom that he is in the process of uttering. Although he had not remained visibly active, he kept in touch with developments, and I always valued his observations and comments. Incidentally, one of the things that surprised me about the late "B.T." was his knowledge of theoretical works and the extent to which he kept in touch with contemporary happenings.

You must have heard that Mary's book on Nelson has recently been partially unbanned—it can be used in university libraries. I will certainly try to get it if and when I am given permission to do M.A. (There was a slight error in the M . . . Star[2] write-up. The position is: I completed Hons. in History and also an Hons. in African Politics. But I have not yet been able to proceed with M.A. because of restrictions imposed by the Prisons Dept. My proposed topic is "Black Politics in S.A.—A Historiographical Analysis." The Prison authorities say I can go ahead provided I do not quote banned books and listed persons. Both UNISA

---

[1] Dr. Zainab Asvat, one of the stalwarts of the struggle.

[2] *The Morning Star*: the Communist Party daily of Great Britain.

and other academics agree with me that the conditions laid down by the Prisons make my task impossible.)

To come back to the stalwarts. You must have heard that Helen[3] was one of the speakers of the Selborne Hall birthday gathering. She is really tremendous and a great inspiration. Last month she tried to visit Nelson, Walter and myself but was not allowed. It was heartening to be remembered by other grand old ladies such as Ouma Bhyat, Mama, Mrs. Thandray, Ma Sisulu, Mrs. Saloojee, etc.

When I look at the names of persons who were present at the two London functions, a whole lot of thoughts go through my mind and many memories are rekindled. I found myself experiencing the gamut of emotions—happiness, pride, regret, nostalgia, disappointment. Some thoughts made me become sentimental, while with others I had to hang my head in shame. I shan't expand on these for fear of giving you more skeletons out of an already full cupboard. You see, I'm hoping that with the passage of time your memory for skeletons will have dimmed somewhat, and I don't exactly feel like coaxing you into remembering.

The biryani, the cake, the South Indian food, the salads and continental dishes—all brought back different memories of various people and different places. I could never forget my 34th birthday while under 90 days when the aunties from Fordsburg, Ayesha [Mrs. Amien] and Sylvia combined to give me a treat. And do you know what? They brought biryani and South Indian dishes, birthday cake, salads! Coincidence!

Of course, we did not have special birthday songs nor Whitney Houston's music. (By the way, she was 11 days old that day!) nor did we have the honour of Ngugi's kind words. But we were allowed to share the food and we stealthily managed to exchange a few words; above all we felt a closeness with our dear folks outside. It was a memorable celebration. (I also received a beautifully knitted red jersey.)

I have got Ngugi's *Petals of Blood* and am waiting for it to be returned; I hope to get stuck into it then.

You mentioned Sylvia; I had a lovely letter and card from her and have replied to the address which was on her letter. I told her to let you know if she receives my letter. Pass my love to her when she visits London.

I assume John Matshikiza is the son of the late Todd? Todd and I were good friends; he was a regular visitor to Flat 13. Yes, I do remember

---

[3] Helen Joseph: indefatigable freedom fighter and old friend of Kathrada's.

Bessie from the days of Progress Buildings. Nice to hear about Lindi, Patsy, Abe & Poppy, Errol, Peggy, Enver, Winnie, Arthur & Jenny, the Legums, Sam Ramsamy, Helga, Rika, Dennis, Edith, Joel, Freni and all the other folks you mentioned.

Regarding Afrikaans, I think you were being a bit generous in putting me in the same category as Nelson. Like other Transvaal *plattelanders* of our generation, I grew up with Afrikaans and from an early age picked up the words of songs and poems. I still retain a love for these and for the language, but much to my regret I have not developed. The little that I have learned since my youth has been haphazard. I do, nevertheless, try to follow interesting happenings on the Afrikaans Front. Nelson, on the other hand, studied Afrikaans systematically on the Island; he wrote the *Taalbond* exams and reads books. He speaks it well (though his pronunciation is atrocious).

I'm reminded of a heated argument on the Island between a BCM chap and an APDUSA[4] guy. The BCM fellow advocated the total banning of Afrikaans in the new S.A. which was, of course, opposed by the APDUSA chap. I won't expand on this save to say that the latter thought he had delivered the coupe de grace by bringing yours truly into the argument as a person who grew up with Afrikaans being virtually his first language.

Incidentally, after the then Minister of Justice, Jimmy Kruger (he who was left cold by Biko's death),[5] had a discussion with Nelson (on the Island) he sent Nelson a gift of Afrikaans books. I notice in the press that the present Minister of Justice is also quite taken up by Nelson's interest in Afrikaans and Afrikaners. Only problem is he seems to think that this is a sudden development which was influenced by the treatment that Nelson had received from Afrikaner medical personnel!! How ignorant they are. And how presumptuous.

I'd like to say a lot more on the question of Afrikaans and related matters but it will have to wait till next year.

I'm continuing this letter on 5th October, and I'm reminded that it is exactly 27 years since the death of our friend, Oosie.[6] I can still clearly

---

[4] The Black Consciousness Movement (BCM) was founded by Steve Biko.

[5] The Minister of Justice, Jimmy Kruger, when asked about the killing of Steve Biko in detention made one of the most distasteful and callous responses when he said it (the death) "left him cold."

[6] "Oosie" Oosthuizen: a friend of Kathrada's who committed suicide.

remember the day of that tragedy and events surrounding it. Much has to be said about that.

Do you know what? On 5th October 1962 I lost a friend and, as if to compensate, I gained another. Saliema, a lovely young lady was born in Cape Town on that day. Our families have been friends for some time but I only came to know her after I was transferred to Pollsmoor.

I better end now. You should have heard from Zohra by now. She wore the T-shirt at the rally. I also saw it when Mrs. Vassen and the kids visited me. (Did I ever tell you that she is J.N.'s brother's daughter? J.N. and Radhie[7] have applied to visit me. I hope it will be granted. They refused Fatima and Ismail.)[8]

I last saw Nelson on 5th September and Walter on 20th. They are very well and send greetings. For some reason, unlike previous visits, this time they took me alone to see Nelson.

Good to hear that O.R.[9] is improving. Best wishes to him. Ramesh sent a message about the death of someone in U.K. Unfortunately I didn't get it clearly but I got the impression that it was "H." If so, please pass my condolences to Iris and family and friends. Unfortunately Ramesh was not allowed to see me that day.

Have you ever given thought to the specific role of the TIYC[10] in directly or indirectly influencing the leftward trend in Black politics? It would be an interesting study.

A last thought before signing off. I heard it on the radio, "Better than to count the years, make the years count."

Love to all the family and friends.

From

AMK

P.S. Don't give up the search for the two manuscripts. Greetings and thanks to Father Huddleston, Mr. E. S. Reddy and others who sent good wishes.

---

[7] J. N. Singh: one of Kathrada's early role models and senior in the Congress movement.

[8] Ismail and Fatima Meer: two staunch, dedicated, and lifelong Congressites, who played an influential role in Kathrada's political development.

[9] O. R. Tambo: president of the ANC in exile.

[10] TIYC: The Transvaal Indian Youth Congress.

Ahmed Kathrada was released from prison on 15 October 1989.